Travellers in the Golden Realm

Travellers in the Golden Realm

How Mughal India
Connected England to the World

LUBAABA AL-AZAMI

JOHN MURRAY

First published in Great Britain in 2024 by John Murray (Publishers)

1

Copyright © Lubaaba Al-Azami 2024

The right of Lubaaba Al-Azami to be identified as the Author of the Work has been asserted by her in accordance with the Copyright, Designs and Patents Act 1988.

Maps drawn by Barking Dog Art

A CIP catalogue record for this title is available from the British Library

Hardback ISBN 9781529371321
Trade Paperback ISBN 9781529371338
ebook ISBN 9781529371352

Typeset in Bembo by Hewer Text UK Ltd, Edinburgh
Printed and bound in Great Britain by Clays Ltd, Elcograf S.p.A.

John Murray policy is to use papers that are natural, renewable and recyclable products and made from wood grown in sustainable forests. The logging and manufacturing processes are expected to conform to the environmental regulations of the country of origin.

Carmelite House
50 Victoria Embankment
London EC4Y 0DZ

www.johnmurraypress.co.uk

John Murray Press, part of Hodder & Stoughton Limited
An Hachette UK company

For Gaza. Colonial violence continues to burn,
but the human spirit burns brighter.

Contents

CONTENTS

Afterword: Accidental Empire   249

Mughal Family Tree

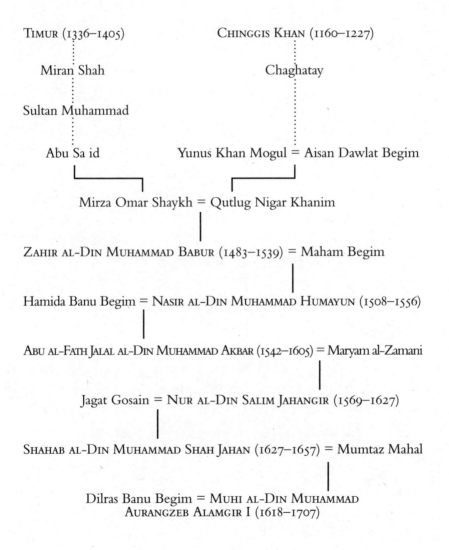

TIMUR (1336–1405)   CHINGGIS KHAN (1160–1227)

Miran Shah   Chaghatay

Sultan Muhammad

Abu Sa id   Yunus Khan Mogul = Aisan Dawlat Begim

Mirza Omar Shaykh = Qutlug Nigar Khanim

ZAHIR AL-DIN MUHAMMAD BABUR (1483–1539) = Maham Begim

Hamida Banu Begim = NASIR AL-DIN MUHAMMAD HUMAYUN (1508–1556)

ABU AL-FATH JALAL AL-DIN MUHAMMAD AKBAR (1542–1605) = Maryam al-Zamani

Jagat Gosain = NUR AL-DIN SALIM JAHANGIR (1569–1627)

SHAHAB AL-DIN MUHAMMAD SHAH JAHAN (1627–1657) = Mumtaz Mahal

Dilras Banu Begim = MUHI AL-DIN MUHAMMAD
AURANGZEB ALAMGIR I (1618–1707)

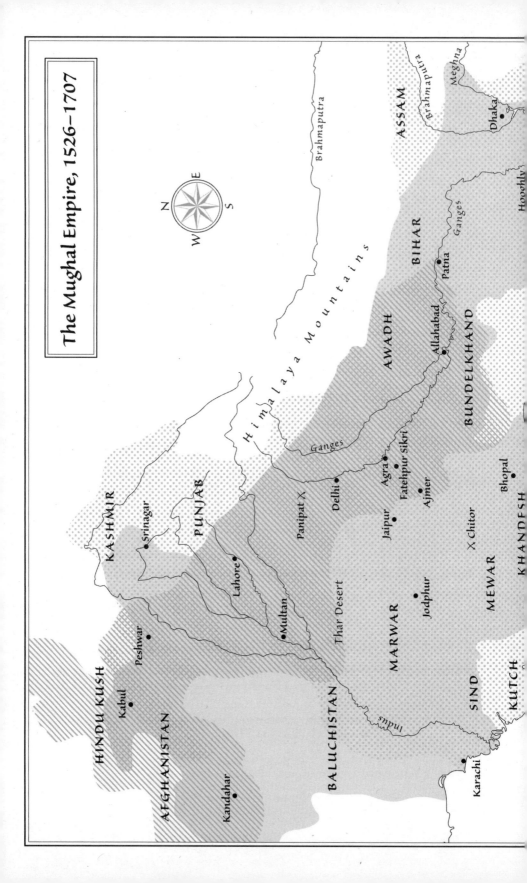

The Mughal Empire, 1526–1707

N
E
W
S

Brahmaputra
Brahmaputra
Meghna
ASSAM
Dhaka
Hooghly
Ganges
BIHAR
Patna
Himalaya Mountains
AWADH
Allahabad
BUNDELKHAND
Ganges
Panipat X
Delhi
Agra
Fatehpur Sikri
Ajmer
Bhopal
Jaipur
X Chitor
KHANDESH
KASHMIR
Srinagar
PUNJAB
Lahore
Thar Desert
MARWAR
Jodhpur
MEWAR
HINDU KUSH
Peshwar
Multan
Kabul
AFGHANISTAN
BALUCHISTAN
SIND
KUTCH
Indus
Kandahar
Karachi

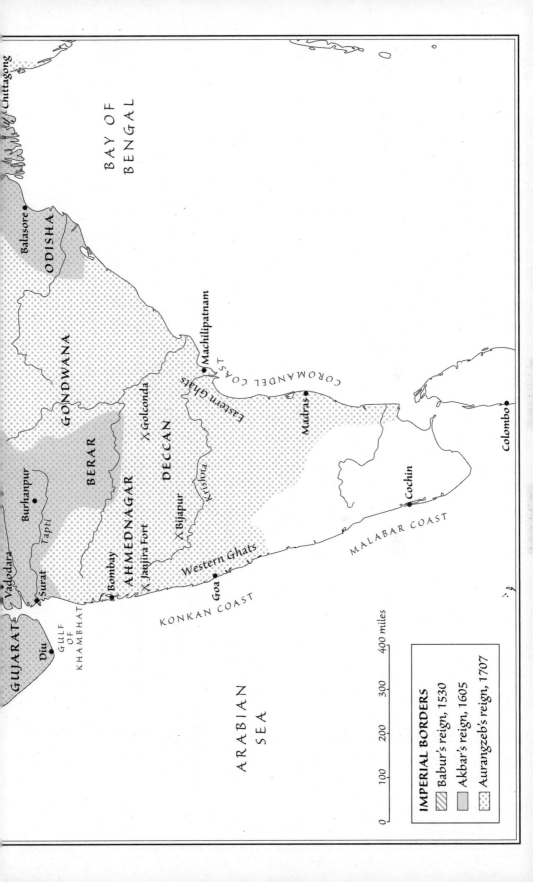

Chittagong

BAY OF
BENGAL

Balasore

ODISHA

GONDWANA

BERAR

Machilipatnam

X Golconda

Eastern Ghats

COROMANDEL COAST

DECCAN

AHMEDNAGAR

Madras

Krishna

Burhanpur

Tapti

X Bijapur

Vadodara

Surat

Bombay

X Janjira Fort

Cochin

Western Ghats

Goa

GUJARAT

Diu

GULF
OF
KHAMBHAT

KONKAN COAST

MALABAR COAST

Colombo

ARABIAN
SEA

0   100   200   300   400 miles

IMPERIAL BORDERS

Babur's reign, 1530

Akbar's reign, 1605

Aurangzeb's reign, 1707

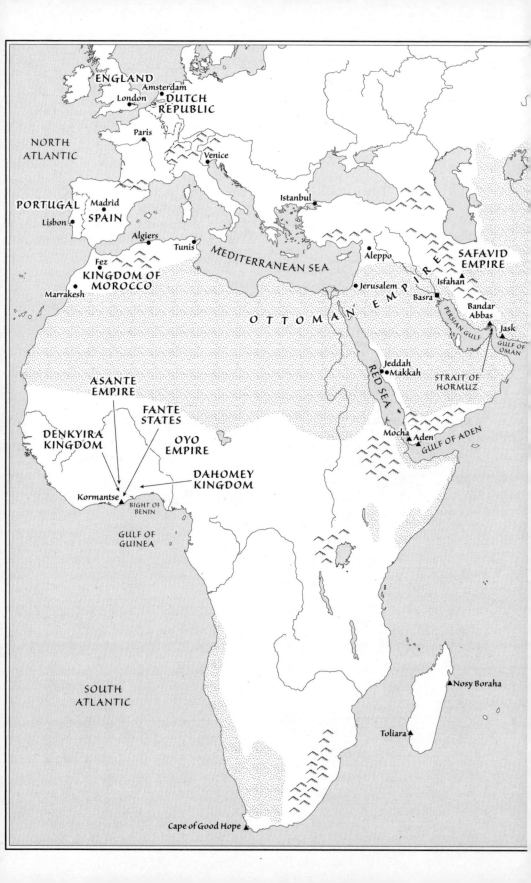

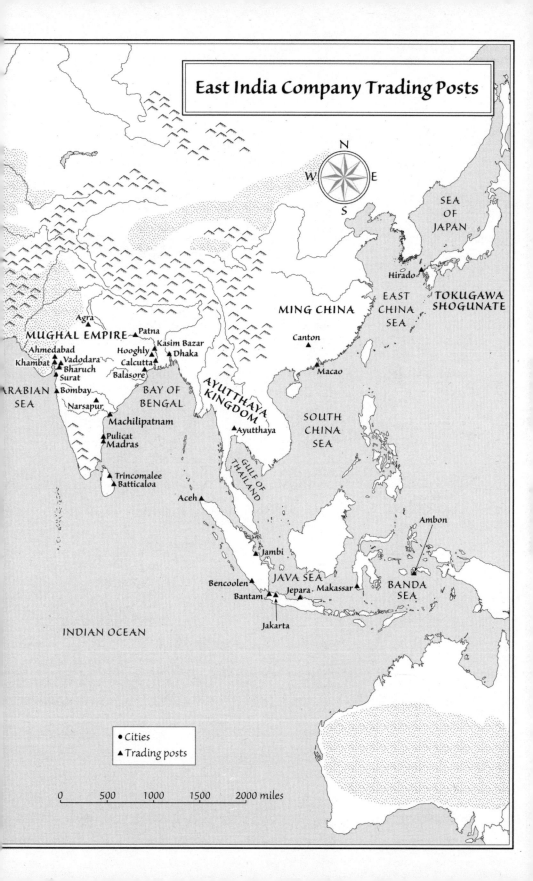

And now land was close at hand, the land so many others had longed to reach, that lay between the Ganges, sprung from the earthly paradise, and the Indus. Take courage, my brave men, who have set your hearts on the victor's palm. You have arrived: the land of wealth abounding lies before you.

Luís Vaz de Camões, The Lusiads (1572)

Introduction: Forgotten History

O N A COOL morning in early January 2020, in the bustling Bangladeshi port city of Chittagong, my husband and I flagged down an auto-rickshaw. We were intent on a historical adventure. Conveying our destination to the driver, we huddled back in the seat of the vibrant green three-wheeler as it sped off. Auto-rickshaw rides were always enjoyable, but this time the trip was coloured by an additional dash of anticipation. The engine revved and spluttered as the driver expertly wove his way through the winding roads of Chawkbazar, one of the busiest districts of the city. Eventually he brought the diminutive taxi to a shuddering halt before a simple red-brick gate topped with a sign in elegant Bangla script. This was the entrance of Hazi Muhammad Mohsin College, one of the oldest educational institutions in the city. Over the past few months I had been attempting to trace the location of a seventeenth-century European monument in Chittagong. My investigations had finally led me here, to this respected state college.

Making our way through the leafy campus, we sought directions from students milling about the grounds and were pointed towards a hill with a steep flight of steps. At the top there were a number of nondescript buildings serving as student dormitories. Yet, nestled behind them, shadowed by the canopy of surrounding trees, was a ruin comprised of tightly packed bricks with watchtowers rising at its corners. Nothing about the dilapidated building indicated what it once had been. The only sign, posted on an outer wall, warned in Bangla that the building was unsafe and not to be entered. Asking around, however, its name among locals confirmed my suspicions: the structure was known as *Portugal bhobon* (Portugal building). This, then, was the ruin of the seventeenth-century Portuguese building I'd been tracing. Its architectural design mirrored almost exactly another far better preserved seventeenth-century Portuguese structure in the capital, Dhaka; a Catholic church set in the spacious grounds of the Holy Rosary Church that traces its history back to late seventeenth-century Portuguese missionaries. The Chittagong ruin was, however, no church. By its location, built atop a hill, and complete with watch-towers, it was likely once a fort. Similar hilltop forts can be found in India, particularly Goa, once the capital of the Portuguese settlements in Asia. Here in Chittagong, however, the fort was more likely to have been a hideout of the many Iberian pirates who, in the seventeenth century, made a base of the region and terrorised Bengal's waterways. Notably, many English pirates too plied their violent trade from this coastal port during that period, and may well have availed themselves of this very fort.

The legacies of England's and Europe's early history are laced through the city of Chittagong, not just in the hilltop ruin at Mohsin College but in the very geography and etymology of the metropolis. In the historic old town, by the banks of the Karnaphuli River whose waterways were once haunted by European pirates, is an area named Firingi Bazaar. *Firingi* was the term used by the Mughals and their Indian subjects from at least the sixteenth century, specifically for the European foreigners who first arrived at those shores centuries previously. *Bazaar* speaks to the primary impetus of those first arrivals: trade. Further living legacies of this early history are to be found in the local Catholic diocese, headquartered at the Cathedral of Our Lady of the Holy Rosary. The diocese traces its roots to early seventeenth-century Portuguese arrivals, as testified by a memorial to this early community within the cathedral's spotless grounds. Scattered across the city are also Anglican churches, with signs highlighting their foundation by early English arrivals who, centuries gone by, had travelled to and resided in these lands.

The history of early Anglo-European travellers to the Indian subcontinent is hidden in plain sight, not just in Chittagong but throughout the region. Forts, churches and tombs, tangible monuments of a dynamic past surviving in bricks and mortar, are dotted across the landscape, many preserved as sites of heritage and tourism. More potently, the histories remain alive among the descendants of those who lived it; like the Chittagong locals whose name *Portugal bhoban* harks back to the hilltop fort's earliest roots, and the local Catholic communities whose surnames – Gomes, D'Cruz, Costa – speak to a European heritage. The very land recalls the *firingis* – English, Portuguese, Dutch, Italian, French – who once travelled there intent on trading in these rich realms.

Yet, back in England today, these thriving histories are barely whispered, less spoken of. Instead, the historic relationship between England and India is predominantly viewed through a lens of the British Empire. With colonial rule still in living memory, looted artefacts still in British possession, and the consequences of empire continuing to impact lives to this day, Britain's colonial control over India dominates understandings of the history between these two lands. In Britain, the story has centred on the nation's dominance over its Indian colony and subjects. For many years libraries have been filled with books about British rule in India, the 'Jewel in the Crown' of the empire over which the sun never set. Cultural productions have been no less prolific: films, dramas, documentaries, art and beyond tracing this relatively recent past. More recently a renewed attention to the violent realities and legacies of colonialism has meant freshly critical writings are re-examining Britain's imperial heritage and casting light on the brutality and pillage that established and sustained it. In these discussions, too, the light is shone brightest on the British colonial period in India. You'd be forgiven for thinking that the British Empire in India was the sum total of the historic relationship between these two lands. In fact, for much of my life I too believed this to be the case.

My parents, who were born and raised in Bangladesh, told us stories of Britain's rule and looting of the Indian subcontinent; they recounted how figures such as Tipu Sultan, an eighteenth-century ruler of the southern Indian Kingdom of Mysore, resisted. The Raj remained fresh and raw for them, given their parents were British subjects who had spent their youth experiencing the oppressive indignities of colonial domination and who had campaigned for independence. In 1947 when Britain finally departed, having carved up the land into Pakistan and present-day India, my grandparents' generation experienced the elation of self-determination devastatingly mingled

3

with communal bloodshed triggered by Partition. In due course my parents' generation became the first born into independence, but they too were not spared the violence of empire. The newly created Pakistan, indifferently doodled into being by an English lawyer as a two-part nation separated by a vast stretch of hostile Indian territory, did not last. In 1971 a bloody war of independence founded Bangladesh from the erstwhile East Pakistan while West Pakistan became what is modern-day Pakistan. By this my grandparents' generation endured the staggering experience of their national identity being shredded and stitched no less than four times: British colonial subjects to Indian, Pakistani and, finally, Bangladeshi citizens.

For my elders, empire was both a searing lived reality and enduringly painful memory. For me, heir to this bruised heritage and born and raised English, Britain's complex history with the Indian subcontinent has always been tightly woven into my being; a sonorous presence in my lived reality and identity. With the violence of empire still tangible, its discourses burgeoning in literature and the arts, along with the mass of extant writings, cultural accounts and stories of my forebears, it seemed that the formative relationship between the two countries was crystallised during this period. Yet, as I researched further, I found a treasure trove of previously unexamined historical sources that evidenced a relationship dating much further back, to at least the reign of Elizabeth I. Amongst these sources, were a footnote on the travels of an English sea captain who undertook the lengthy voyage to India in the early seventeenth century; an observation on the Indian preference for tobacco recorded in a 1661 English treatise on coffee; even mention of an English diplomat who served at the Mughal court. I was astounded. Here was evidence, backed by primary sources, of a relationship reaching as far back as the days of Shakespeare.

What followed was a deep – and deeply personal – dive into Britain's earliest history with India, a process that would ultimately lead to both a doctorate and the book that is now in your hands. It was a project both to unearth a hidden history and search for my own pasts. What I found was near two centuries of decisive and dramatic encounters between these two lands that had been neglected by the majority of writings and cultural productions on the history of Britain and India. It was and continues to be a staggering gap in the story of one of the most recognised and recounted relationships in history. This book is a contribution towards filling it in, which also offers up a larger, more complex and infinitely more interesting account of the history we thought we knew.

And, as my travels in Chittagong revealed, in the countless tangible historical markers and living legacies across the Indian subcontinent, the foundations of this far earlier yet lesser spoken of encounter were always there, waiting to be unearthed.

In 1526 the Mughal founding father Zahir al-Din Muhammad Babur (d. 1530) captured northern India from the Lodhi sultanate of Delhi. Of his triumph, Babur's daughter, Gulbadan Banu Begim (d. 1603), proudly wrote that 'the treasures of five kings fell into his hands'.[1] With this foundational wealth, Babur settled into his new Indian home and set about establishing his kingdom. The Mughal realm he founded went on to become one of the largest and most prosperous centralised states in pre-modern history. Its immense wealth was such that in 1600 Mughal India's gross domestic product (GDP) was beaten only by that of Ming China, and by the end of the century India had surpassed China too. As Babur and his descendants governed, they absorbed their surroundings, becoming committedly Indian and remaining so. Then, as now, this was a land of many cultures and traditions, and the Mughals wove themselves indistinguishably into the rich tapestry of Hindustan. Both administration and households came to reflect the nation in all its variety. Excepting the turbulent reign of Babur's son and heir, Humayun (d. 1556), the Mughal monarchs went on to consolidate and expand their Indian dominions, particularly through the seventeenth century. Humayun's son Akbar (d. 1605) completed the process of administrative consolidation such that his successors, Jahangir (d. 1627), Shah Jahan (d. 1666) and Alamgir I (d. 1707), could focus on expansion. By the time of Alamgir I's death, in 1707, the empire was at its zenith, having absorbed most of the Indian subcontinent.

Mughal governance over this immense and expanding kingdom was characterised by a centralised bureaucracy with the emperor as ultimate authority in a system formalised under Akbar. In central government, the emperor functioned as chief executive beneath whom were four ministers of state who answered directly to him. The empire was further split into regional *subah* (provinces) where the same structure of authority was duplicated. Each *subah* was overseen by a *subahdar* (governor), appointed by and accountable to the emperor and his ministers. Each *subah* had further regional divisions with administrators and officials at local level. The ministers, governors and senior administrators of the empire were drawn from a Mughal nobility whose status was awarded based on a numerical military system of ranking. In this *mansabdari* system the numerical rank or *mansab* corresponded to status, salary and the number of cavalry under an individual's command – this could number from the hundreds to the thousands: for example, the highest ranks of usually up to twelve thousand cavalry were reserved for royalty.

Beyond the formalised administration was a further powerful arm of imperial authority: the *zenana*. Similar to the *haram* of the Ottomans, the *zenana* was the royal residence where the emperor along with the women and children of his household resided. This included the immensely influential Mughal queens and princesses, who often held sway over the emperor. The Mughals traced their bloodline from the central Asian conqueror Timur (d. 1405), in whose realms the political and material authority of royal women was marked. Timur's chief consort, Saray Mulk Khanim, not only held a leading position at the Timurid court but held a lavish court of her own, hosting foreign dignitaries. Timur's sister Qutlug Tarkhan Aga was a close confidante who actively roused her brother to military action. Gohar Shad, chief consort of Timur's successor Shah Rukh, was similarly politically influential, not only throughout her husband's reign but in the succession struggles following his death. A patron of architecture, among her commissions is the grand Goharshad Mosque in Mashhad, Iran. Born of this imperial bloodline, Mughal royal women wielded immense political influence and material clout. From Aisan Dawlat Begim, grandmother and chief political adviser to Babur, to Nur Jahan Begim, chief consort and joint sovereign with Jahangir, Mughal queens and princesses were often the power behind the throne of this commanding empire. Newcomers to Mughal lands, including English traders, thus often found that the gatekeepers in

India were not the emperor or his administrators but the queens and princesses who, in the words of England's first ambassador to India, Sir Thomas Roe, were 'more inaccessible than any Goddess'.[2]

It was precisely at this time of Mughal ascendancy that English arrivals first landed on India's shores. The earliest itinerant travellers, singular individuals adventurous enough to brave the perilous journey alone, later made way for the more concerted arrival of the East India Company (EIC), whose legacy in India would prove most enduring and notorious. Yet, crucially, the EIC's arrival was far from intentional. India had never been the primary target of the Company. The aim of the merchants who braved the voyage around the Cape had been the great spices of the East, to be found primarily in the Indonesian archipelago. This they marked as their target, battling deadly months at sea amid storm and disease to make landfall at the cluster of diminutive Moluccan islands from which cloves, nutmeg and mace were exclusively sourced. However, their failure to successfully barter in English goods and the greater regional currency of Indian textiles was the impetus that first turned these Company traders towards Mughal shores. Whereas England's primary export of woollen broadcloth, thickly woven and dyed in deep colours, could not be sold in the sweltering Moluccan heat, the great lengths of delicately woven airy cotton imported by India's traders to the archipelago's spice markets enjoyed a roaring trade. In the pursuit of spice, these same textiles were in turn sought by the EIC, heralding the decision to send the first English ship, captained by William Hawkins, to Mughal shores in 1607. The earliest EIC contact with India was thus an afterthought; a detour in pursuit of an altogether different mercantile prize.

This little-known fact is at the heart of the untold story within these pages. For the first century and a half at least of English travel to India, the English presence in Mughal lands was as struggling merchant petitioners plying an abortive trade whose impact in the thriving state and society hosting them was negligible. While the first trickle of early individual English travellers made way for larger collective voyages and exchanges, the English and their activities remained largely insignificant to the broader concerns of India and its rulers.

In considering this forgotten history a striking fact emerges: the British Empire in India was never intentional. Furthermore, it was singularly unpredictable. The greatest hindrance to the English advance was arguably its timing. The first travellers and traders arrived during the Mughal golden age, a period covering the reign of the founder Babur (1526–30) to that of Alamgir I (1658–1707). The Mughal Empire in this period constituted one of the most expansive, wealthy and powerful states in the world, and throughout the seventeenth century it only advanced its position further. The India these first English pilgrims encountered was thus a vast and thriving realm. It was abundant in natural resources and possessed advanced manufacturing industries that produced some of the world's most demanded and profitable commodities. It retained sweeping, well-equipped armies that expanded an immense territory overseen by a complex state bureaucracy. Its Mughal rulers, both male and female, governed with formidable authority, and access to the region's mercantile treasures was hard-won. For the English merchant arrivals, hailing from an impoverished and distant northern island still reeling from the aftermath of the Reformation and the associated isolation from Europe, inroads into a burgeoning Indian marketplace was the sole aspiration – and a sufficient challenge. For over a century their experiences in Mughal India are the stories of travellers and traders arriving as humble entrants desperately seeking access to the splendour and mercantile wealth of a vast – and singularly indifferent – superpower.

That England would one day come to govern this territory was beyond imagining, less premeditation or expectation. As English travellers and traders stumbled through seventeenth-century Mughal lands, this fact only became clearer. While the Mughals enjoyed their greatest era, the English were barely a blip on the Indian horizon. For the imperial authorities, the English relevance – when eventually acknowledged – was confined to the role of the modest East India Company fleets in the Indian Ocean, as the Mughals played off maritime Europeans against each other to protect Indian interests at sea. Meanwhile, the EIC itself faced hurdle after hurdle, and battled relentlessly against an ever-present threat of dissolution. In its London headquarters, political intrigue combined with financial strains, maintaining the Company at the precipice of ruin for much of the century. In far-flung India, trials at home threatened to cripple an already struggling English trade as it battled to maintain its efforts while simultaneously facing violent and often far superior European competition.

Amid their struggles, the English marvelled at the resplendence of the Mughal realms. They saw riches beyond imagining – from the magnificent gold thrones of the Mughal court and the countless pearls and jewels adorning the emperors to the abundant diamonds sourced in the mines of the Deccan Plateau. In a land of power and blinding abundance, the English arrivals were enthralled and desperate to scrape a share, not only by penetrating the Mughal market but also by absorbing cultures and customs. On India's assimilative shores countless English arrivals actively sought to become Indian; absorbing language, culture and cuisine in an effort to identify with and advance in the golden realm of the so-called Great Mughal. They conversed in local tongues, adopted local attire, maintained households that followed Indian customs and acquired Indian spouses. By this, England's first arrivals increasingly embraced a new Anglo-Indian identity. Far from any notion of capturing India for England, India captured the English, who were most willingly caught.

The English traders primarily sought India's dazzling array of fragrant spices, vibrant dyes and luxuriant textiles ranging from lush woven cottons to richly brocaded silks, returning to England to trade in these treasures. In the process England itself was also enrichingly transformed; Indian flavours, goods and cultures became tightly knitted into English culture. The marvellous stories brought home by the early travellers to India found their way into the great cultural productions of the day. From the glittering Indian stones in the crown described by Shakespeare in *Henry VI* and Marlowe's wildly popular dramatic portrayal of the Mughal ancestor Timur in *Tamburlaine* to the voyage to Bengala (Bengal) mentioned in Milton's *Paradise Lost*, India attained an unprecedented cultural currency in seventeenth-century England.

On the other hand, like the Moluccans, the Indians were far from keen on English goods, not least the great bolts of coarse woollen broadcloth imported from Cornwall. Where items did succeed in piquing interest, the advanced industries and crafters of India replicated them with an expertise that rendered England's imports all but redundant. Yet, this disadvantage compelled an internationalist creativity among traders that helped forge pivotal and lasting global connections for the English. EIC trade in Mughal realms not only extended to profitable commerce in the Moluccas but birthed inroads in global markets from China and Japan to West Africa and the Americas. By this, the period reveals itself as a tempestuous era of England's mercantile and global birth, centred in India against the backdrop of a rising Mughal power.

These critical early connections are the historical foundations of today's Britain. The delectable, spiced inflections of British cuisine and vibrant multicultural make-up of Britain's communities all draw threads from these first travellers and their voyages to India over four centuries ago. Yet, while these early histories remain alive and visible in South Asia and among its diaspora, echoes have weakened before the historical proximity and overwhelming discourses of Britain's empire, which has come to define the history of the Indian subcontinent and England. In Britain itself the history is near forgotten; relegated to the dusty corners of centuries-old archives in favour of a more concerted engagement with the British Empire. Nonetheless, the heritage of this momentous yet forgotten past remains alive in the nuances of Britain's melded cultures and still tangible treasures scattered across the nation. Whether a surreptitious grind of pepper to season a dish in a rural Yorkshire kitchen or a vast mural in the UK Parliament, here too these earliest relationships are hidden in plain sight, waiting to be recalled, revived and acknowledged. In these pages this long-forgotten history is finally brought back to life. It is a tale of a grand realm of monarchs, an island nation of merchants and a British Empire that almost never was.

PART I
Seeking Paradise

I

Good Hope

O N 25 MAY 1570 a figure clutching a scroll of paper was lurking
outside the Bishop of London's palace at the north-west corner
of St Paul's cathedral precinct. The residence before him was a grand
affair, described by the chronicler John Stow as 'a large thing for
receipt; therein divers kings have been lodged and great households
have been kept'.[1] But this figure was no guest of this great house.
Casting a glance to check he had not been followed, he approached
the front door, swiftly unrolled the sheet of paper and with firm and
decisive strikes nailed it to the ageing wood. Each pound echoed
across the deserted churchyard and deep within the palace. Conscious
that he had likely alerted the residents, the man swiftly fled down the
cobbled streets. While the Bishop's Palace no longer stands, the document nailed to its door would leave a permanent legacy.

The man was John Felton, a wealthy resident of Bermondsey and
well-known Catholic sympathiser. The document he risked life and
limb to affix to the bishop's door was the *Regnans in Excelsis* (He
who reigns on high), the bull of excommunication issued against
England's Protestant queen by Pope Pius V. In it the Pope declared
Queen Elizabeth I a 'heretic and favourer of heretics' who along
with her followers 'have incurred the sentence of excommunication
and to be cut off from the unity of the body of Christ'. With
European rulers increasingly receptive to Protestant teachings that
challenged papal authority, the Holy See deployed excommunication as a weapon against continental monarchs succumbing to what
were seen as heresies against the Church. Among the most famous
recipients of this bull were England's Henry VIII, following his
marriage to Anne Boleyn in 1533, and thirty-seven years later their
daughter, Elizabeth.

The excommunication probably meant little personally to the queen. As a staunch Protestant, she did not bow to the Holy See to begin with, so was in all likelihood unconcerned with what the Pope thought of her or her faith. However, the excommunication had significant implications for the nation she ruled, and that was something the queen most certainly did care about. Declaring Elizabeth I a heretic was not simply a matter of evicting her from the Catholic Church; it was also an inflicted severance of England's relations with Catholic Europe. The bull *Regnans in Excelsis* created a formalised schism between England and her Catholic cousins, opening Elizabeth's realms to potential invasion by any of the Continent's Catholic monarchs on the pretext of reclaiming England from heresy.

The queen responded harshly and decisively, and John Felton would be the first to feel the force of this. Within days he was arrested and imprisoned at Newgate. There he is alleged to have declared 'by writing, signed by his own hand' that 'the queen . . . ought not to be the queen of England'.[2] Soon after he was imprisoned in the Tower of London where he was tortured upon the rack. He was subsequently found guilty of treason and sentenced to the peculiarly brutal punishment of being hung, drawn and quartered. On the day of his execution before a baying crowd at St Paul's churchyard, the scene of his crime, Felton refused to seek pardon for his actions, zealously rejected the services of attendant Protestant clergy and insisted that he had done nothing more than promote a proper papal statement. Thereafter the hapless man was unceremoniously hung to the raucous sound of jeers. While still conscious, Felton was cut down, whereupon the hangman proceeded to disembowel him. As his heart throbbed before his own fading eyes, Felton called upon Jesus before finally breathing his last. Elizabeth I had set an example, soaked in blood, for the papists in her realm. England's Catholic subjects had their first martyr.

The queen's suppression of English Catholics was an aggressive reaction to the threat posed by the papal bull, both within England from her Catholic subjects and also from the Continent. Isolated as she and her realms now were, Elizabeth I made a pragmatic decision: to sustain her nation she would seek fresh trade and diplomatic partnerships beyond Christian Europe. The profitable inroads in trade that were being made by English merchants with the powerful and wealthy empires of the East, including the Ottomans, Moroccans and Persians, were encouraging. So the queen shifted her attention from the West to the East. And among the lands upon which her gaze fixed was India.

Elizabeth I may have been the first English monarch to seek direct trade with India. However, she was far from the first in her nation to show an interest in that distant part of the world. England has enjoyed a long-standing love affair with India that can be traced to medieval times. For evidence of this, one need go no further than Hereford, the historic English county town of Herefordshire, a few miles shy of the Welsh border on the River Wye. The town's greatest attraction is the magnificent medieval cathedral that rises majestically by the riverbank. Hereford Cathedral is of remarkable architectural beauty, but beyond its built facade lies an even greater treasure: a vast medieval map, the Hereford *Mappa Mundi*. Dated to around 1300, the map was the creation of one Richard of Haldingham or Lafford. In this remarkable early cartographical creation, India's place in the early English imagination is immortalised with stunning late medieval artistry.

The Hereford *Mappa Mundi* is of little use as a practical navigational guide. It presents the world as a seemingly continuous mass of land, interrupted at its heart by a sizeable forked body of water feeding an arterial network of rivers. There are also notable absences: created at a time preceding Christopher Columbus's famed voyage west across the Atlantic, the *Mappa Mundi* only features the three continents then known to Europe: Asia, Europe and Africa. It draws on the form of the popular medieval T and O map wherein the world is depicted as a flat disk oriented with the east at the top. The three known continents are accordingly structured with the largest landmass of Asia at the top, Europe on the lower left and Africa on the lower right. In doing so it creates a spiritual and material vision of the world and its creation. At its easternmost pinnacle, positioned above the material world, is depicted the Heavenly Paradise with a seated Christ looking down upon the world and his peoples. Below him, at the easternmost point of the material world, is the Earthly Paradise, illustrated as a circular island ringed with fire. Within this, standing between the celestial rivers that flow through it and beyond its borders, are humanity's parents, Adam and Eve. And just beneath these twin paradises is none other than India, a swathe of land bordered in the north by a flowing Ganges that is nourished by the waters of the Earthly Paradise. In the south it is rimmed by the Indus, where a stately elephant ambles near the famed river's mouth. Encircled and enriched by boundlessly fertile heavenly waters, in this medieval and biblically inspired map India is a site of almost spiritual and divine aspiration. It is a place of enrichment and the pathway to the Earthly Paradise itself.

For today's observer, the orientation of the map is perhaps a particular curiosity. In medieval times, as often now, cartography was as much about navigation as it was an ideological view of the world. Modern maps, most often based on the Mercator projection (1569) created by Flemish cartographer Gerardus Mercator (d. 1594), are north oriented, with Europe and North America positioned at the top and southern continents such as Africa and Asia positioned at the bottom. Inaccurate scaling also renders Europe and North America erroneously large relative to Africa and Asia. The result is a north-oriented and Western-centric representation of the world in which non-Western lands and peoples are rendered diminutive before the larger and ascendant nations of the West. By contrast, medieval European maps were usually east oriented, with Asia – rendered twice the size of Europe and Africa – in the ascendant position at the top. This reflected the dynamics of the period, where the nations and empires of Asia were far more advanced materially, politically, technologically and militarily in comparison to the struggling states of Europe. It is no wonder, then, that India featured so prominently and aspirationally in the English imagination.

Through classical and medieval European writings, India was particularly celebrated for its legendary riches. As early as Pliny's *Natural History* in the first century CE, India is imagined as a land of fantastical creatures and immense wealth ready for acquisition. Chief among these riches was the costliest commodity of the era: spices. Fiery peppercorn, heady nutmeg and fragrant clove, delicate yet intensely aromatic culinary staples to be found in every kitchen spice cabinet today, were then a rarity exclusive to the Indian region yet the most in demand globally. European clamour for spices was such that it pushed the commodity to the heights of lore. In the most widely circulated work of travel writing in fourteenth-century Europe, Sir John Mandeville's *Book of Marvels and Travels* (c. 1356–66), India 'sweet with the flavours and fragrances of all sorts of spices' is home to the fabled Fountain of Youth whose spiced waters not only 'changes its flavour every hour of the day' but heals all sickness.[3]

Added to this was the abundance of glinting gold and precious gemstones in India's bountiful mines. For centuries the mines of Golconda in southern India's Deccan Plateau were the global centre for diamonds. It was here the famed Koh-i-Noor, among the world's largest diamonds, was sourced, eventually and controversially finding its way into the crown jewels of the British monarchy. Here too Mandeville illustrates the desire for India's burgeoning diamonds by an exceptional elevation; watered by the rivers of the Earthly Paradise as India is, the gemstones are imagined to procreate 'and bring forth small children, that multiply and grow all the year'.[4] These ideas would persist through the centuries, to be echoed in the theatres of seventeenth-century London, where India's 'bowels of the earth' would be imagined to 'swell with the births / Of thousand unknown gems and thousand riches'.[5] From medieval times, then, India was held as sacred and aspirational not only for its proximity to the Earthly Paradise but for its marvellous wealth and commodities. These ideas continued to inform and inspire throughout the sixteenth and seventeenth centuries, when the Virgin Queen determined a new global direction for her nation. As England contemplated its future bereft of its traditional allies in Europe, 'gold-fingred *India*' remained a promising frontier of great wealth.[6]

Although medieval Europe spent abundant time fantasising about India, it had yet to achieve a direct seaward route of travel to those parts. This left European traders largely dependent on Arab inter-mediaries, particularly from North Africa, to access the lucrative merchandise that was emerging from Asia. These middlemen traders made good on their monopoly to inflate prices and profit generously from their European customers. The zeal to circumvent the interme-diaries and access the world's most profitable goods at source was such that it launched some of the most significant European voyages of discovery of the fifteenth century.

Between 1410 and 1414 the *Imago Mundi* by the Chancellor of the University of Paris, Pierre d'Ailly, appeared. The work, a series of astronomical treatises, included a series of maps representing various views of the world that included mapping India at the highest point of Asia below the Earthly Paradise. Significantly, d'Ailly claimed that India was located in the furthermost region of Asia while Spain was located in the westernmost region of Europe, such that Spain and India were proximate via a westward route. In 1492 Christopher Columbus, inspired by his own heavily annotated copy of the *Imago Mundi* and generously funded by Queen Isabella I and King Ferdinand II of Spain, embarked on this very route. His mission was to identify a westward path to India, a project he enthusiastically defended to his sovereigns with reference to d'Ailly. Instead, famously, Columbus encountered the American continents he and much of Europe did not know existed. The 'West Indies' and the idea of the 'American Indian' drew directly on Columbus's historic navigational errors.

Soon after Columbus, in a similar albeit more accurately conceived project to seek out India, the Portuguese explorer Vasco da Gama became the first European to reach India by sea, in 1498. The navigator established an ocean route around the Cape of Good Hope on the southern tip of the African continent. This passage opened up a route that Europeans would follow thereafter, linking India with Europe for the first time. Da Gama's feat fundamentally transformed Europe's experience of the world; maps were redrawn, trade was reshaped and the Portuguese navigator's achievement was immortalised in verse by Luís Vaz de Camões as Portugal's national epic, *Os Lusíadas* (*The Lusiads*). Whereas until this point India had remained a potent space in the European imagination, both da Gama and, in his own befuddled way, Columbus made India a tangible reality for Europe.

The Portuguese soon established a settlement in India, expanding to create the Estado da Índia (Portuguese State of India) headquartered in Goa on India's western coast. With violent jealousy they defended the newly opened trade route they had founded; from 1505 armoured Portuguese carracks patrolled the vast waters of the Indian Ocean, running an immense protection racket. This required all non-Portuguese vessels engaged in Indian Ocean trade to purchase a *cartaz* from the Portuguese Viceroy of Goa to avoid the seizure and confiscation of ships and merchandise. Eventually, the Mughals too would be subject to the *cartaz*, their vast vessels often setting the going rate for passes.

While the Portuguese controlled the East Indies trade for much of the sixteenth century, other Europeans inevitably followed, hungry for a share of the region's rich commodities. This included French, Italian and Dutch traders. The generously funded Dutch East India Company, or Vereenigde Oostindische Compagnie (VOC), formed in 1602 only a few years after the founding of the Dutch Republic, was especially noted for its naval and military strength, which posed a challenge to the Portuguese monopoly. Bulky and dated Portuguese carracks were no match for the swift armoured vessels in which the Dutch voyaged. The VOC first directed their efforts towards the Spice Islands in the East Indies (now part of the Indonesian archipelago) with a view to controlling the trade in pepper, cloves, nutmeg and mace that originated there. By 1605 they had captured the island of Amboyna, dispossessing the Portuguese. By contrast, England was slower and considerably more modest in its efforts in the Indies, trailing behind fellow its Europeans. It took a papal bull issued against its queen over a century after the route to India had first opened to change that.

The newly excommunicated Elizabeth I had initially busied herself nurturing relations with the far more proximate and regionally powerful Ottoman Empire and Kingdom of Morocco. In 1578 she sent William Harborne as her ambassador to the Ottoman court to establish an understanding between their two nations. The trade agreement Harborne negotiated would become the foundation for Anglo-Ottoman relations for the next three centuries. The queen's priorities were not without reason. The Ottomans were not only the most powerful and wealthy state in Europe but held sway over the crossroads of the lucrative Mediterranean trade. In this space the Moroccans too were similarly useful allies for England.

Both the Ottomans and the Moroccans had a further advantage to recommend them: like Elizabeth I, they detested the Spanish and their king. Catholic Spain was a constant reminder of the fall in 1492 of Muslim Spain, al-Andalus to the Catholic invaders from the north.

The brutality inflicted on Muslim Spaniards and Moriscoes during this period led vast numbers to seek refuge in Morocco, where the desire to reclaim al-Andalus remained high. For England, the zealous Philip II and his machinations were a thorn in the side of the queen, whose successful defeat of the Spanish Armada in 1588 would be a defining victory. Indeed, such was the shared animosity that Elizabeth I sought assistance from Moroccan king Ahmad al-Mansur to resist the Spanish Armada. Some years later, in the late summer of 1600, al-Mansur appointed an ambassador to the court of the English queen with a similarly conceived mission to negotiate a military partnership against Spain.

Tall, turbaned and distinguished, Abd al-Wahid ibn Mas'ud al-Annuri swept into London with a stately sixteen-man entourage of Moroccan diplomats. This first embassy from an Islamic nation to arrive in England took up residence on the Strand, near the Royal Exchange. The group, gracefully robed in floor-length linen, bearing gold-hilted scimitars and noted for diets so distinct that their hosts left them to manage all their own provisions rather than attempt to cater in ignorance, attracted more than a little curiosity. During the six-month embassy, al-Annuri was hosted multiple times by the queen. At these audiences he proposed that it would 'be an act of compassion and humanity for the benefit of all mankind if her serene majesty should embrace the perpetual friendship between her and the serene emperor his master [al-Mansur] and join forces against the King of Spain'.[7]

More intriguingly, the ambassador suggested a particularly notable benefit to such a partnership; that the two monarchs thus allied 'could also wrest the East and West Indies from the Spanish'. A combination of Spanish coffers filled with masses of plundered New World gold and Portuguese merchants' iron grip on the spice trade in the East Indies had rendered the Iberian Union under the Spanish Hapsburgs the wealthiest and most influential kingdom in western Europe. A strategic alliance between Morocco and England could undo this, as al-Annuri reasoned, given the king of Spain's power 'comes solely from his control of the Indies'.[8] Such a partnership could enrich and empower both the North Africans and the English in one fell swoop. The ambassador's proposition was a bold one and England did not ultimately see it through, despite the very real temptation. However, it coincided with another fierce debate then taking place in Elizabeth's I court as to England's possible engagement with India. Al-Annuri's proposal is likely to have had some influence on the latter's outcome.

Less than a year earlier, on 24 September 1599, a bustling group of men had gathered at London's Founders' Hall, a stone's throw from Smithfield. A cross-section of the capital's social strata was in attendance, from the Lord Mayor, Sir Stephen Soame, proudly bearing his glinting gold chain of office, to merchants, mariners and the odd battle-scarred military veteran. Most prominent among the crowd was Sir Thomas Smythe, auditor of the City of London and a wealthy merchant who had achieved prosperity through overseas trade. The purpose of the gathering was a singular one: to set up a joint stock company 'for the advancement of trade of merchandise within this realm of England to set forth a voyage this present year to the East Indies and other the islands and countries thereabouts'.⁹ Smythe had already raised the sum of £30,133 6s. 8d. (over £3 million today) from 101 city merchants to invest in the company. The task before them now was to petition the queen to establish the company by royal charter. As such the meeting was the inception of what would become the East India Company. A petition was duly submitted, with expectations of a swift approval for the new company intent on 'the honour of our native country'.¹⁰ Yet the opposite proved to be the case. Since the 1598 passing of Philip II, England had begun peace negotiations with Spain, an effort that English trade in the East Indies could complicate by creating unwelcome competition for Iberian interests there. The Privy Council therefore immediately put a halt to the formation of the company while negotiations with Spain progressed.

By the summer of 1600, however, peace talks had collapsed. Soon after, al-Annuri's Moroccan embassy arrived, encouraging the queen to seize control of the Indies from Spain by military force. Although war was not a prospect Elizabeth I sought, she must have been reminded of the lucrative trade in the Indies for which a group of merchants had petitioned only a year earlier. With evaporating desire for appeasement with the Spanish, a far cheaper path to the prosperous Indies for England had already presented itself, waiting patiently in the wings for her word. Militarism gave way to mercantilism, and on 23 September 1600 the 'General Meeting of the Adventurers for the East India voyage' was informed of 'Her Majesty's pleasure having been signified that the adventurers should proceed in their purpose and accept of her certificate as an earnest of a further warrant to be afterwards granted to them'.[11] A few months later, on 31 December 1600, the company received their royal charter from the queen: 'A privilege for fifteen years granted by Her Majesty to certain adventurers for the discovery of the trade for the East Indies'.[12] The East India Company was formed, and Sir Thomas Smythe became its first governor. Over a century after the Portuguese had opened a direct sea route to India, England was finally ready to voyage east.

As sixteenth-century England battled through the seismic shifts of the Reformation that brought on Elizabeth I's excommunication, many leagues away, in India, an altogether different transformation was under way. The wellspring of this was a young central Asian prince, heir to the Kingdom of Fergana on the northern Silk Road in what is today eastern Uzbekistan. Zahir al-Din Muhammad Babur claimed imperial ancestry on both sides. By his mother, Qutlug Nigar Khanim, he hailed from the dynasty of the famed Mongolian conqueror Chinggis (Genghis) Khan. By his father, Umar Shaykh Mirza, king of Fergana, he was descended from the successor to the Mongols, the central Asian conqueror Timur. The prince was thrust into the field at a tender age; when he was just eleven his father died, leaving him the task of retaining control of a kingdom for which many rivals vied. In this precarious moment, Babur owed all to the determination of two women: his mother and his maternal grandmother, Aisan Dawlat Begim. The firm hand of his mother, who, in his own words, bore 'all the severity of a quartermaster', raised him to the discipline of a king,[13] while the political guidance of his grandmother was what ensured his fortitude as a conqueror.

It is no exaggeration to say that Aisan Dawlat Begim prevented Babur from meeting an early grave. As challengers targeted Ferghana, assassination attempts were a regular occurrence for much of Babur's early years. The careful mentorship and deft manoeuvrings of this remarkable grandmother protected the young prince and nurtured him in the craft of princes. As Babur reverentially wrote, 'For tactics and strategy, there were few women like my grandmother, Aisan Dawlat Begim. She was intelligent and a good planner. Most affairs were settled with her counsel.'[14] The formidable lady was certainly not one to trifle with. She had proven her mettle early in her marital life when she was kidnapped by one Sheikh Jamal al-Din Khan and given as a 'gift' to an officer. When the officer arrived in her room, she had him seized, stabbed to death and flung out of a window, declaring 'I am the wife of Yunus Khan; Sheikh Jamal gave me to someone else; this is not allowed by Islamic law, so I killed the man, and Sheikh Jamal may kill me also if he likes!'[15] This fearless confidence she instilled in her grandson, and he made good use of it when the prospect of claiming India arose.

In addition to defending his birthright in Fergana, Babur attempted to seize the prestigious city of Samarqand, capital of the erstwhile Timurid Empire and home of Timur's mausoleum. However, he eventually lost both and, possessed of a strong entitlement to rule, spent years in anguished exile as a king without a kingdom. In frustration he complained of how 'My mother and I – not to speak of lands – were unable to possess a single village or a few pair of oxen'.[16] Here too, the role of Qutlug Nigar Khanim is revealed in Babur's alignment of his rule with that of his mother.

Things took a positive turn in 1504 when, with his mother by his side, he successfully claimed Kabul, in Afghanistan. Set against a mesmerising backdrop of mountains, the rectangular city was a thriving multicultural metropolis and centre of trade, and its new ruler marvelled at its richness. The valleys around the city abounded in fruits and nuts that varied through the seasons; from winter offerings of bejewelled pomegranates, succulent grapes, apricots, plums, crisp apples and almonds to summer citrus fruits of every kind. The city's markets enjoyed a booming trade, attracting vast caravans hailing from central Asia and India, with Kabul's merchants claiming profits of some 400 per cent by Babur's reckoning. The caravans of India alone consisted of some twenty thousand carrier animals piled high with great bales of plush textiles, sacks of aromatic spices and varieties of sugars.

Witness to the arrival of such wealth, it is perhaps unsurprising that it was here in Kabul that Babur's mind turned to a far greater prize, that of India. Babur spent several years leading incursions into India, beginning in 1505 when he targeted what is today north-west Pakistan. Through years of raids he celebrated the birth of his first children; 1508 saw the arrival of his heir, Humayun, after which the proud father intent on a ruling dynasty took on the elevated title of *padshah* (master king). In 1519 another son was born, whom Babur pointedly named Hindal, meaning 'Take India!' In 1526 that aspiration was at last realised, at the Battle of Panipat against the then ruling dynasty of Delhi, the Lodhi sultanate headed by Sultan Ibrahim Lodhi.

Babur's conquest of India was a remarkable feat. Faced with a Lodhi army of a hundred and eighty thousand cavalry and fifteen hundred elephants, Babur's forces numbered a mere twelve thousand. However, his superior weaponry, including field cannon, proved decisive in securing the battlefield. Within half a day of the battle's commencement, his army overcame the Lodhi forces and victory was claimed. The newly crowned conqueror was elated, paying tribute to 'God's grace and generosity [that] such a difficult action was made easy for us, and such a numerous army was ground into the dust in half a day'.[17] In the wake of his conquest, Babur summoned the entirety of his Timurid and Chinggisid family to join him in India, announcing: 'The Most High has given us sovereignty in Hindustan; let them come that we may see prosperity together.'[18] The Mughals had arrived, ushering in a new era for India. The newly founded Mughal Empire rose to become among the largest and wealthiest states in the world. By 1600 it governed up to 150 million people and ruled an area of around 3.2 million square kilometres.

In the sixteenth and seventeenth centuries there were three leading Islamic empires: the Turkish Ottoman Empire that stretched from Europe to the Middle East and North Africa, the Persian Safavid Empire in the Middle East, and the Indian Mughal Empire in Asia. Of these the Mughal Empire was by far the most demographically diverse, with its rulers governing as a religious minority. The Mughals thus prioritised pragmatic diplomacy over religious purpose and identity in their governance. They combined imperial expansion with cultural assimilation and synthesis; as they conquered and settled, they adopted local traditions. Mughal founder, Babur, although originating in central Asia, arrived and settled to become indisputably

Indian, establishing one of India's most powerful and venerated empires. His descendants continued in this tradition, marrying and raising families in the land they made home, adopting regional languages, customs and cultures while their courts, state offices and households reflected the rich variety of their empire.

When the first Europeans arrived in India, throughout the sixteenth and seventeenth centuries, the immense diversity of the land was not lost on them as they encountered and engaged with the Mughals and their remarkable realm. Among the many faith groups that populated the region were Hindus, Jains, Buddhists, Muslims, Christians, Jews and Zoroastrians. Early European travellers often recorded their observations of the various communities, albeit not without the biases of an outsider encountering a tradition to which they are alien. The Venetian traveller Cesare Fedici (d. *c.*1603) commented on the practice of *sati* in Vijaynagar, observing, 'if a married man die, his wife must burn herself alone, for the love of her husband', while the Spanish Jesuit Father Antonio Monserrate (d. 1600) reported on the festival of Holi.[19] Among Muslim communities in India were Sunnis and Shias; while the Mughal rulers were Sunni, Monserrate recorded the observance of Muharram 'held in honour of Asson [Hasan] and Hossen [Hussain], grandsons of Muhammad by his daughter Fatima' by Indian Shias.[20] The varied Indian traditions were further diversified by the Mughals, who brought with them Turkish and Persianate traditions to create an Indic and Perso-Islamic composite culture in an assimilative process that formed the Mughal state and its citizenry.

For Europeans seeking trade, Mughal India was especially attractive as the world's largest economy, matched only by that of China. Throughout the seventeenth century India's GDP surpassed the combined GDP of western Europe. Against India's 22.6 per cent share of world GDP, that of England was a paltry 1.8 per cent.[21] India was the source of some of the world's most desired and lucrative commodities, from an expansive array of aromatic spices and vibrant dyes to rich woven textiles and stunning gemstones. The Indian economy was agrarian, with Mughal coffers funded by land taxation. In the vast and ever-expanding empire, this made Mughal India self-financing. This was in notable contrast to many western European states who were crippled by debt and dependent on trade. The

Mughal state was singularly not dependent on commerce, and its regional commercial partners were prioritised over European newcomers to boot. For the first English arrivals and England itself, India offered a great deal, and a potential trade partnership was entirely in the former's favour. India, however, was in no need of English trade, and had scant interest in English goods, chief of which was thick woollen cloth unsuited to Indian climes. This fact inevitably played out in the struggling and stumbling efforts of the English throughout their first century of forays in India.

Trade efforts in India led by the English East India Company would chiefly define England's historic relationship with India from its inception. However, English traders were not the first to set off for nor reach India from England. That distinction was the preserve of a solitary English traveller who had reached India's shores in 1579, two decades earlier than the Company's formation. Elizabeth I approved trade in India to help remedy the economic fallout caused by England's isolation from Catholic Europe. It is certainly ironic, then, that the first English person to set foot in India was not an agent of the queen seeking a mercantile and diplomatic partnership after her nation's severance by Rome. Rather, it was an English Catholic refugee, Father Thomas Stephens, who fled persecution by his Protestant queen to travel to India.

2

As Musk Among Perfumes

EARLY ENGLISH TRAVEL to India has long been associated with two things: trade and empire. This largely held true for much of the English presence in India – trade from the seventeenth century and empire from the mid eighteenth century. But the very first English arrivals to India were inspired by neither commerce nor conquest, but by Christ. Father Thomas Stephens was the first English traveller to India to voyage there by sea. His objective was to join fellow Jesuits in Goa on their missionary cause among the Hindu communities. Stephens made the journey in 1579 aboard a Portuguese ship. However, he was not the first Englishman believed to have reached those Asian shores. That distinction can be traced back seven centuries earlier to one Sighelm, Bishop of Sherborne, and the court of King Alfred the Great (d. 899 CE).

Little is known of this early medieval English travel to India apart from the fact that it seems to have happened. The *Anglo-Saxon Chronicle*, originally compiled during the reign of Alfred, records that the king dispatched Sighelm in 883 bearing gifts of alms for Christian communities in India. William of Malmesbury (d. 1143), an Anglo-Norman monk and historian famed for his chronicle of early English history, *Gesta Regum Anglorum* (*Deeds of the Kings of the English*), also records Sighelm's pilgrimage, with the additional details that the bishop completed the journey to India and returned to England bringing with him 'brilliant exotic gems and aromatic juices in which that country abounds'.[1] Even in God's service, then, India's treasures and fragrant commodities took centre stage.

Sighelm's apparent travel to India took place long before the Portuguese had opened a direct path by sea around the Cape of Good Hope, in 1498. His journey would therefore have taken him overland;

a long, laborious and expensive route. Perhaps that is in part why there doesn't seem to be a record of any English traveller having journeyed to India for the next several centuries. It was Father Thomas Stephens who finally followed in his medieval predecessor's footsteps. However, this time the journey would be by the somewhat swifter Portuguese route by sea, and there would be no return.

Thomas Stephens was born in 1549 in the tiny hamlet of Bushton, Wiltshire, an hour from the monument of Stonehenge. His merchant father's prosperity enabled a privileged schooling, following which he likely spent time at New College, Oxford. This early academic training would serve him well in India, marking him for scholarly distinction: not only was Stephens the first Englishman to voyage to and settle in India, he is the first English linguist and poet in any of the Indian languages.

It would, however, be some years before Stephens undertook the voyage east. Between 1572 and 1574 he was to be found wandering around England disguised as a servant and proselytising for Roman Catholicism alongside Thomas Pounde. The wealthy gentleman Pounde was a fallen favourite of Elizabeth I, and it is he who seems to have developed a zeal for travelling to India, inspired by the letters of Francis Xavier (d. 1552), founder of the Jesuit mission there. This zeal he instilled in his companion, and together they planned to commit themselves to the Society of Jesus, or Jesuits, at Rome, and thereafter make the journey to the Portuguese settlement at Goa, on India's western coast. On the eve of their departure in 1574, however, Pounde was betrayed to the queen's officers, arrested and imprisoned as a religious dissident.

At this, Stephens seems to have determined life in England was far too dangerous to endure and promptly fled to Rome. Now a religious refugee, he was never to return and certainly never to forget the oppressions he and his co-religionists had faced in England. Years later, in a letter to his brother, he would recall how he 'fled from England', adding the grim caution, '"Be on your guard against the snares of your enemies," is a maxim that you should highly treasure.'[2] On arrival in Rome, Stephens enrolled as a novice in the Society of Jesus at San Andrea on 20 October 1575. Never losing sight of the prize, in 1579, following ardent requests, he managed to obtain the permission of the Society to voyage to Goa to join the Jesuit mission there. The dream he and his friend had nurtured was finally becoming a reality, albeit the incarcerated Pounde was never to participate in it.

Stephens could barely wait. He immediately travelled to Lisbon, arriving at the end of March. A few days later he joined a group of twelve Jesuits aboard a five-vessel Portuguese fleet destined for Goa. On 4 April the fleet, carrying England's first seafaring traveller to India, solemnly set forth to a fanfare of trumpets. The journey proved long and difficult, marred by disease, piracy and the ravages of an inhospitable sea. Of the perilous voyage and eventual arrival, Stephens wrote to his father in a letter dated 10 November 1579. Most of this letter is spent detailing the voyage, but the final section briefly describes India and its peoples. Having fled religious persecution in his English homeland, the traveller writes grimly of his fleet's attack near Madeira and the Canary Islands by an 'ill-occupied' English pirate vessel. Meanwhile, contrary winds – or indeed none at all – combined with mercurial elements 'thick and cloudy, full of thunder and lightning and rain, so unwholesome' such that in the face of 'such evil weather' the struggling fleet began to despair of rounding the Cape at all.[3] Amid dwindling endurance and desperate prayers, India was eventually sighted and the fleet made landfall on 24 October. Seven months after setting sail from Lisbon, an exhausted Thomas Stephens staggered on to the bustling shores of Goa, a weary and relieved refugee and migrant to India.

It was nearing the end of the monsoon season. Sweltering humidity mingled with the drenching showers that poured in short but intense bursts. Goan inhabitants knew the season well and dressed sparingly, many of the men bare-chested and wrapped in 'an apron of a span long'.[4] This was quite a contrast to the Portuguese arrivals, who were oppressively bundled in long-sleeved shrunken doublets, starched and broad linen ruffs fitted close at the neck and wrists and voluminous breeches complete with stockings. Having spent the first three decades of his life in Europe, this new land several thousand miles from the tiny hamlet of his birth must have been quite the sensory experience for Stephens, and a stark contrast to the English weather he was used to.

In his letter to his father, Stephens marvels at his new surroundings: 'Of the fruits and trees that be here, I cannot now speake, for I
should make another letter as long as this. For hitherto I have not
seene tree here, whose like I have seene in Europe.' The Indian people
he encountered proved hospitable and welcoming, treating the new
arrivals 'with passing great charity'. He particularly admired palm
trees that bear 'a fruit called cocoa [coconut]', the water of which he
terms 'wine of the palm tree'. Writing to his brother four years later,
Stephens goes into exacting detail on the many uses of this versatile
Indian tree and its refreshing fruit. From the 'oil, liquor, toddy, syrup,
sugar and vinegar' extracted from its fruit to the seaworthy rope spun
from its husk and the use of its branches in building huts, the traveller
can barely contain his astonishment at the abundant resources offered
by this single tree.[5]

While Stephens observed his surroundings with fascination, and
recorded it for his family back in England, it would not be long
before he himself assimilated into his new home. The next four
decades that remained of his life would be spent in India, dedicated in
its entirety to the Jesuit mission.

Since their arrival, the Portuguese in India had evolved to a two-part
yet interdependent presence: the one centred on trade and conquest
led by the Portuguese Viceroy of Goa, the other on proselytising
and conversion led by the Society of Jesus. The founder of the Jesuit
mission in India, Father Francis Xavier, was also an original founder of
the society itself. Born in 1506 in Navarre, the fifth son of a minor
nobleman, Xavier was educated and later taught at the University of
Paris. Missionary ideals coloured his aspirations early on, as he and a
group of friends initially harboured hopes of travelling to Jerusalem
to spread the message of Christ. When this plan did not ultimately
materialise, they turned their zeal to formally establishing themselves as
a religious institution. In 1534 they founded the Society of Jesus as a
Roman Catholic order of priests committed to missionary work,
securing formal approval from the Pope in 1540. When King John III
of Portugal (d. 1557) sought priests to serve his settlements in India,
Xavier's dream of evangelising in distant lands was finally realised. In
1542 he sailed from Lisbon as Jesuit superior and papal representative to
India, arriving at Goa on 6 May. His time spent in India and its

surrounding areas was marked by personal asceticism and an indefatigable missionary zeal that often translated into an aggressive and violent
religious expansionism, as he campaigned to save what he saw as idolatrous Hindu souls. By the time Stephens arrived, the Jesuit presence
in India was well established: the Catholic community numbered
thousands and there was a range of Jesuit-run institutions, including
churches, colleges and hospitals. In fact, so settled was the mission that
it had begun setting its sights on the highest halls of the land, the
Mughal *darbar* (imperial court) and its celebrated reigning emperor,
Abu al-Fath Jalal al-Din Muhammad Akbar.

With the conquest of India at the Battle of Panipat, Babur had not
only established his dynastic rule in Hindustan but proven his imperial mettle. Following the battle he dispatched his son and heir, Nasir
al-Din Muhammad Humayun, to Agra to seize the Lodhi royal
palaces and treasury and have Babur's rule announced at Friday
prayers. Agra would later be established as the new capital of Mughal
India. Babur's reign was brief, however; within four years he had died
and India passed into the hands of Humayun. The new emperor's
accession was a grand affair at which some twelve thousand rich robes
including two thousand tunics of gold brocade with gilt buttons were
distributed – largess worthy of a ruler of Hindustan.

Despite the optimistic beginning, however, Humayun proved not
to have inherited his father's prowess, a fatal flaw for an empire still in
formation. From the outset Humayun endured rebellions by his
brothers and failed to deal with them decisively. Such princely actions
came to be a feature of Mughal rule. Unlike European monarchies
where succession passed to the eldest son, any of the Mughal emperors' sons were eligible to rule and they fought for that claim.
Princely rebellions and succession wars by siblings and heirs of the
reigning emperor were regular, particularly through the seventeenth
century. During Humayun's reign, his aunt, Khanzada Begim, elder
sister to Babur, did much to mediate between her wayward princely
nephews and restore stability. Khanzada's authority within the Mughal
dynasty had been unparalleled since the reign of Babur. She bore the
title *Padshah Begim* (Lady King) and even during the feast in honour
of Humayun's accession she sat together with the newly crowned

31

emperor on the same jewel-embroidered divan, a mark of her senior-
ity. Her ambitious nephews frequently turned to her to legitimate
their claim to power. For the Padshah Begim, however, the clear
successor to Babur was Humayun. When Prince Kamran sought her
endorsement for his claim over Humayun, she retorted, 'regard him
[Humayun] as your superior and remain in obedience to him'.[6]
Throughout his reign Humayun was supported by her, and he solici-
ted her intervention repeatedly against his brothers.

While his brothers' rebellions were debilitating, it was the attacks
from outsiders that particularly rocked Humayun's rule, most notably
from the Pashtun warrior, Sher Khan. The biggest blow landed in
1540 when, following a series of battles that saw Humayun's army laid
to waste, Sher Khan successfully evicted the Mughals entirely and
claimed northern India for himself. Battered and bruised, the defeated
Humayun was left to retreat, first to Sindh before taking refuge with
the Safavid ruler of Persia, Shah Tahmasp. India's new Pashtun ruler
thereafter assumed the title of Sher Shah and established the Sur
dynasty with its capital at Delhi. Sher Shah's rule ushered in a period
of stability and prosperity, features notably absent during Humayun's
reign. What began as a glorious Mughal succession thus became a
humiliating exile. It was fortunate for Humayun that the Safavids
proved generous hosts; in 1555 they supported the exiled Mughal
with the necessary forces to secure a comeback. At the subsequent
Battle of Sirhind, Humayun's forces managed to successfully wrest
India from their Pashtun foes. After a fifteen-year exile, the kingdom
was reclaimed and the Mughal Empire was reset.

In 1556 Humayun passed away, and the empire passed to his teenage heir, Akbar. The new monarch succeeded to the throne without
challenge, his brother being a toddler at the time. While Humayun's
reign had been an anomaly in the empire's golden age, the reign of
Akbar saw Mughal consolidation in earnest. The third emperor effectively quashed what remained of the Sur dynasty, stabilised and
expanded the empire and centralised its bureaucracy. By the conclusion of his reign, Mughal India had grown from a landlocked territory in northern India to an expansive domain extending from the
Indian Ocean ports of Gujarat in the west to the Bengal coastline in
the east. Akbar instated Persian as the Mughal official language of

administration, a decision recalling Humayun's refuge and support by the Safavids. He also took care to rehabilitate his father, commissioning his scholarly and influential aunt, Princess Gulbadan Banu Begim, to compile a history of Humayun's rule. The *Ahval-i-Humayun Padshah* of Gulbadan would go on to serve as a leading primary source for Akbar's official court history. Under Akbar's rule, Mughal India attained a stability not experienced by its founding rulers. For the first time the emperor was able to spend less time firefighting and more time pursuing personal pleasures and interests. One of the interests Akbar pursued was the study of world religions.

In 1578, a year prior to the arrival of Stephens, the Viceroy of Goa sent a Portuguese embassy to Akbar's court, led by Antoine Cabral. From Cabral the emperor learnt of the Jesuit father's preaching in India. Not long after, Akbar sent letters to the viceroy, the archbishop, and the Jesuits in Goa, requesting that priests be sent to his court to explain the Catholic faith. To the Jesuits this felt like the opportunity they had all been waiting for. If the great emperor of India himself could be converted then the rest of India would surely follow. In November 1579 a group of three Jesuits was dispatched armed with a seven-volume Bible, portraits of Christ and the Virgin Mary and a giddy optimism. They arrived on 4 March 1580 at the lavish red sandstone royal court at Fatehpur Sikri, west of Agra. Leader of this group was Italian Jesuit Rodolfo Acquaviva, who had arrived in Goa the previous year. His two companions were Father Francis Henriquez and Father Antonio Monserrate, the latter of whom compiled a fascinating record of their time at Akbar's court. As Monserrate relayed, the fathers were 'inexpressibly eager to reach the King's court; for they were confident he would embrace Christianity'. Their cordial reception upon arrival only served to further their excitement, 'For they were persuaded that these signs foretold the speedy conversion of the king to the true religion and the worship of Christ'.[7] Things, the trio thought, were looking decidedly up.

What was imagined as a grand coup, however, was soon revealed as a pipedream. Conversion was far from the mind of the king, who merely harboured an interest in learning about various faiths rather than committing to any of them. Alongside the Jesuits, he also invited Jains, Muslims, Hindus and other religious groups to participate in theological discussions at a purpose-built debating hall named the Ibadat Khana (House of Worship). The emperor adopted a variety of religious practices, including installing a fire in the palace in observation of Zoroastrian tradition from Persia. Akbar was an unquenchably curious man. Combined with unimaginable wealth – and, undoubtedly, an excess of time – this often made for some rather eccentric ventures. Among his most infamous experiments is the Gong Mahal, or Deaf House, in which he tested his hypothesis that infants raised without hearing speech would not learn to verbally speak. He accordingly had a group of infants raised by non-verbal nurses at the Gong Mahal. Sure enough, upon his visit a few years later, in 1582, Akbar found none of the children could verbally speak, but communicated using visual sign.

Akbar's invitation to the Jesuits proved to be in a similar vein of feeding personal curiosity. Thus, by 1583 the three priests had returned to Goa recognising their mission would have been fruitless. Hope was not entirely lost, however; Akbar continued to invite Jesuits to his court, and the society continued to wistfully send priests, albeit without any change in their luck. Despite failing to secure their aspired conversion, Acquaviva nonetheless secured a mention in the emperor's official chronicle, the *Akbarnama*, compiled by the court historian, Abu al-Fazl ibn Mubarak. The father's contributions to discussions in the Ibadat Khana seem to have been appreciated by the Mughals, who record 'Padre Rudolph' to have been 'singular for his understanding and ability . . . making points in that feast of intelligence'.[8] The fathers were also featured in a miniature in the illustrated *Akbarnama*.

The emperor's indifference to religious conversion was also clear from another prominent and concurrent initiative: in 1578 he enthusiastically sponsored the Hajj of a community of Mughal royal women headed by his historian aunt, Princess Gulbadan. The grand journey, a pilgrimage to the holy land of Makkah that Muslims undertake at least once in their lifetime if they have the health and means, was the talk of the empire. The pilgrims were showered with gifts and riches by Akbar before they set off in a large convoy complete with a royal guard. Their pilgrimage lasted several years, coinciding with the Jesuit presence at Fatehpur Sikri. On their return, the princess and her fellow pilgrims were welcomed by Akbar with great fanfare. As Monserrate recalled, 'the king had the street-pavements covered with silken shawls' and conducted his aunt to her palace 'in a gorgeous litter, scattering largesse meanwhile to the crowds'.[9]

It was during this famous pilgrimage, as the empire still buzzed at the grand adventure, and in the early days of Akbar's invitation to the Jesuits that Thomas Stephens arrived at Goa in 1579. The charged air among the fathers of the society must have tingled with anticipation at the emperor's invitation and potential conversion, even as the empire hummed with excitement over an altogether different religious event. Stephens, however, seems to have paid attention to neither. Instead, he directed all his energies in immersing himself in remote and rural Goan communities and pursuing the rather more successful project of convincing local Hindus to turn to Christ. In the process of converting Indians, however, Stephens himself underwent a remarkable and singularly Indian transformation of his own.

Six months after his arrival at Goa, Stephens was ordained as a priest. His ordination was fast-tracked given what he described as 'the vast harvest of souls and the extremely few labourers'.[10] Thereafter he was posted to Salcete in southern Goa. The fathers had already made quite an impression on the region: a decade earlier, in 1569, they had supported the Portuguese in razing over three hundred temples there.[11] They further convinced the Portuguese viceroy to ban idolatrous practices, including the worship of the local deity, Shantadurga.[12] Salcete had faced the full force of the Jesuit mission, and by the time Stephens arrived, in 1580, the Christian community numbered eight thousand, most of whom were converted Brahmins.[13] The fathers of the society meant business, and Stephens was their latest recruit to the cause.

The Portuguese presence in Goa was no peaceful affair. Destruction of temples and oppression of local communities, often with the help of the society, was a common occurrence. In 1561 Father Xavier had helped launch the Goa Inquisition, an extension of the Portuguese Inquisition, to enforce Catholic orthodoxy. One particularly fanatical specimen was Father Pietro Berno, who accompanied the Portuguese army and not only personally set fire to the Cuncolim Temple but proceeded to slaughter a cow, a sacred animal in Hindu tradition, upon the altar of the idol, 'so as to clear the space of the superstitious people'.[14] Unsurprisingly, Hindu communities did not take such atrocities lying down; in the case of Berno, he was killed and his body mutilated. As Stephens remarks, 'the pagans, of whom there are a great many, are all of a warlike character and are the sworn foes of the Portuguese name. They are dead against the Christian faith.'[15]

It is clear that Stephens considered Portuguese and Jesuit acts of violence as par for the course. In a letter to his brother he narrates them with an entitled indifference and even admiration, describing Berno as 'a strenuous and zealous soldier of Christ'.[16] Salvation for souls by any means necessary was the order of the day, and Stephens was aligned with the theory no less than the others. In practice, however, he does not seem to have adopted the combative methods of some of his peers. Rather, he stands out for taking an immersive and scholarly approach to his ministry that centred on cultural and linguistic engagement combined with literary output. He soon mastered the main local languages of Konkani and Marathi, enabling him to communicate directly with Goans, both preaching and taking confessions in the local vernacular. He further turned his linguistic prowess to literary production to expand the reach of the mission in Hindu communities and within the society. He wrote a Konkani Catechism and, to aid fellow Jesuits in learning the local vernacular in support of their mission, compiled the first Konkani grammar book, *Arte da Lingoa Canarim*.

His greatest work, however, was far more artistic and extraordinary: an epic poem in Marathi with a sprinkling of Konkani entitled the *Kristapurana* (*Story of Christ*). Composed of 11,018 strophes of four lines each, this *magnum opus* was designed to render the biblical history of the world and coming of Christ accessible to local Hindus and Hindu converts. The poem is a stunning example of literary hybridity born of the early interaction between European Christianity and Indian Hinduism. It combines the form of Indian purana literatures and biblical teachings. Stephens structured it in two parts: the *pailem purana* or first purana, comprised of thirty-six cantos, corresponds to the Old Testament, and the *dussarem purana* or second purana, comprised of fifty-nine cantos, corresponds to the New Testament.

The *Kristapurana* was written in 1614 and first printed in 1616 at the Rachol seminary in Salcete, where Stephens served as rector. It gained popularity and a second edition was printed in 1649, followed by a third in 1654. Not long after, in 1667, England celebrated John Milton for his epic poem, *Paradise Lost*, a work still considered one of Britain's greatest literary masterpieces. The *Kristapurana* is however none too different and in some senses even more impressive, given it was written in a regional Indian language that its author had devotedly mastered to the point of literary artistry. Alongside biblical history, Stephens expresses his love of Marathi in the poem, declaring:

> As the mogra among flowers
> As musk among perfumes
> So among languages is the beauty
> Of Marathi . . .[17]

Stephens loved Indian languages. He admiringly observed to his brother that 'The phrases and constructions are of a wonderful kind'.[18] Yet, in the verses of this spiritually charged epic he expertly weaves his love of Marathi with an additional appreciation for Indian flora and fauna. As he pairs the *mogra*, or jasmine flower, with musk, one can almost experience the rich regional scenes and scents they invoke, undoubtedly drawn from the stunning rural surroundings in which Stephens resided and worked. The celebration in the verse, then, extends to more than just this Indian language, but to the beauties of India itself.

Notably, in the poem Stephens refers to himself as Patri Guru, Marathi for 'Father Teacher', thus channelling the reverential Indian figure of learning, or guru. This Catholic refugee from Wiltshire had clearly found not only his calling but his identity and home in India. He had arrived from Europe zealously committed to converting the Hindus of Goa. Yet in the process he too underwent a process of conversion: from a dissident Catholic Englishman rejected by the land of his birth to a rector of Salcete whose language, life and scholarship was wholly transformed by his adopted Indian home. In short, he became Indian, the first of many early English arrivals to do so. It was an identity that he embraced.

Stephens's work in India was a success for the society. After his arrival, he spent the remaining forty years of his life as a leading figure on the Salcete mission. He served across many parishes, converting countless Hindus along the way. In Jesuit documents he is described as 'of very good wisdom, good judgement and prudence . . . and of a very good talent for conversions'.[19] He certainly had a talent for conversion as by the time of his death in 1619 much of Salcete was Christian. The young man who had fled England rejected and lost had managed to find himself and his purpose many leagues away in India, where he lived a long and, certainly by the society's measure, productive life. His immersion in regional languages and cultures transformed him from the dissident English Catholic, Thomas Stephens, to the venerated Goan Jesuit, Patri Guru. Meanwhile his Indian writings long outlived him. The epic *Kristapurana* continues to retain its popularity and high regard to this day.

Stephens's years in India eventually coincided with the East India Company's first arrival and early efforts there, particularly in the busy port town of Surat. Whether by circumstance or design, it seems the father's engagement with the Company and its men was minimal for the most part. That the Company's primary factory was established at Surat and Stephens remained in the Portuguese stronghold of Goa undoubtedly aided this. For all his efforts, however, Stephens is a crucial yet overlooked piece in the puzzle of early English travel to the Indies, as well as the arrival of the East India Company. Much of this was down to a letter dated 10 November 1579 which he wrote to his father detailing the journey to India for the first time.

This correspondence is significant for several reasons; it is one of only two letters from Stephens in India that survives to this day and is his only extant piece of writing in English, all others being in Indian languages or Latin. Most importantly, however, it is the earliest first-hand English account of the voyage to India, and as such played a key role in enabling the first English voyages east. In 1589 noted English geographer Richard Hakluyt (d. 1616) included it in the first edition of his famed anthology of travel writing, *The Principal Navigations, Voyages, Traffiques and Discoveries of the English Nation*. Hakluyt compiled this collection to encourage the English to venture abroad in pursuit of the world's riches. It is unsurprising that he chose to include this particular dispatch rather than another of Stephens's letters that offered details of India itself and its remarkable sights and riches. The English knew full well of India's fabled wealth but had yet to voyage there, so it was details of the journey itself that mattered.

Before that could happen, however, yet another reason makes Stephens's early foray in India so significant, and it relates to the dubious misadventures of a travelling English merchant, Ralph Fitch. In 1583 Fitch and his companions stumbled off a ship at Goa, weighted by chains, to be unceremoniously thrown into a dank Portuguese dungeon. When news of the arrivals reached the lone Englishman then resident in Goa, the exiled father realised there was only one person in India who could save the captives.

3

The Grand Tour

A sailor's wife had chestnuts in her lap,
And munch'd, and munch'd, and munch'd:–
'Give me,' quoth I:
'Aroint thee, witch!' the rump-fed ronyon cries.
Her husband's to Aleppo gone, master o' the *Tiger*.
But in a sieve I'll thither sail,
And, like a rat without a tail,
I'll do, I'll do, and I'll do.
William Shakespeare, *Macbeth*, Act I, Scene iii

IN THIS OFTEN overlooked moment from Shakespeare's *Macbeth*, the three witches known as the weird sisters meet in a wasteland in preparation for the arrival of the eponymous Scottish general and his fellow general, Banquo. The witches are notoriously malicious figures in the play, engaged often in supernatural activities. Here, the First Witch narrates her encounter with a sailor's wife who refused to share chestnuts, a slight the witch intends to avenge. The exchange may seem theatrically sinister but otherwise inconsequential prattle, but it is far more than that. Here, Shakespeare recalls a famed voyage of 1583 that saw the English merchant traveller Ralph Fitch (d. 1611) journey first by sea aboard the *Tiger* to Aleppo and then overland to eventually reach India.

Fitch's journey took place over two decades prior to *Macbeth*'s likely first performance at the court of King James I, in 1606. Yet, so notable was the undertaking that years later it was referenced in this celebrated production before the monarch himself. *Macbeth* has long been viewed as a Shakespearean tribute to England's new Scottish-born king. James I, who traced his lineage to Banquo, would certainly have picked up on this. But he would also possibly have recognised the maritime reference to Fitch's journey to India slipped into this scene. While Elizabeth I had been relatively tepid on the matter of East Indies trade, preferring to prioritise her Ottoman partnerships, it was James I who oversaw a renewed energy in English travel and trade with India. During his reign not only did the first direct English voyage to Mughal India take place, but the king also appointed the first English ambassador to the Mughal court. Referencing Fitch in *Macbeth* thus tapped into James I's interest in India.

In the 1979 Royal Shakespeare Company's televised version of *Macbeth*, starring Ian McKellen in the title role, the First Witch is shown to brandish a voodoo doll presumably of the sailor husband, Fitch, journeying to Aleppo. This she pierces with a needle during the scene. Not only did the traveller's journey fascinate the English and influence Shakespeare, but his misfortunes are evoked too. Fitch's expedition had been dramatically disrupted by an encounter with the Portuguese settlers stationed at the Island of Hormuz in the Persian Gulf. As we shall see, the fallout had almost brought the English traveller's adventures to a premature halt. In the RSC *Macbeth*, the Portuguese are seemingly personified in the witches as they vindictively stab at the sailor. Yet, as the First Witch acknowledges in the same scene, 'Though his bark cannot be lost, / Yet it shall be tempest-tost'; Fitch's enterprise was ultimately neither halted nor lost, even as his journey experienced the tempest of imprisonment.

Instead, he became the first Englishman to undertake an extensive journey through India. And for his deliverance from the Portuguese that enabled this, the merchant was enormously indebted to Thomas Stephens in Goa. Additionally, building on Stephens's letter of his voyage published by Hakluyt, Fitch took the English campaign for travel and trade in Mughal lands a step further by compiling the first extensive firsthand description of India by an Englishman. His account was published in 1598 in the newly expanded second edition of the *Principal Navigations*. By this, Fitch became another key figure in the earliest foundations of English travel and mercantile enterprise in India.

While Fitch and his companions were the first English merchants to successfully reach and travel across India, they were not the first to attempt to do so. Many a botched English voyage preceded the eventually fruitful overland expedition. Prominent among these early figures of maritime failure were Martin Frobisher (d. 1594), Edward Fenton (d. 1603) and William Hawkins (d. 1613). Frobisher was an optimistic yet luckless naval commander who had led a series of unsuccessful Northwest Passage expeditions that sought to identify a northern route to the East Indies. Fenton, a similarly idealistic soldier and sea captain, participated with Frobisher, serving as captain aboard the *Gabriel* on the 1577 voyage to Baffin Island, the largest island of what is today Canada. In 1578 Fenton served as Frobisher's second-in-command on a much larger expedition to Baffin Island. The intention was to establish a minor colony – the first such English settlement outside of Europe – of which Fenton would be governor. However, poor weather amid the dangers of towering icebergs, loss of materials at sea and mutinous discord led to the abandonment of the project and return to England. The enterprise subsequently collapsed under the weight of crippling debt and the failure to live up to its promises.

In the wake of the debacle, Frobisher emerged with his reputation in tatters. Nonetheless, a few years later he and Fenton were at it again, attempting yet another ill-fated voyage this time to the Indies. In 1580 famed English explorer, privateer and notorious trader in enslaved peoples Francis Drake returned from his circumnavigation of the globe via Vasco da Gama's Cape route. Thereafter a new scheme was conceived; a joint venture between merchant investors and Drake with Frobisher appointed leader to retrace the steps of the circumnavigation and reach the East Indies. The voyage was planned for 1582. Fenton returned to join his Northwest Passage partner, Frobisher, and assist in the task. Yet, the project proved to be troubled from the start. Drake's faction sparred with the merchants; the former, hardened privateers determined to conduct violent raids during the voyage; the latter, mercantile investors seeking untroubled trade. The fallout eventually led to Frobisher stepping down and Fenton taking his place. By the time the four-vessel fleet finally departed Southampton it was May 1582. Led by the galleon *Leicester*, of which Fenton was commander, the fleet included the queen's ship *Edward Bonaventure* and two barks, the *Francis* and the *Elizabeth*. Fenton's lieutenant general aboard the galleon *Leicester* was a vivacious young adventurer by the name of William Hawkins. A cousin by marriage to Fenton, Hawkins's name would come to be prominently etched into the history of England's foundational travels to India. In this early moment, however, he proved more trouble than he was worth.

The voyage was an unmitigated disaster. Fenton and Hawkins clashed before it had even begun, with the former writing to Frobisher as early as October 1581 complaining of Hawkins. Further unrest ensued during the voyage when Drake's men returned to buccaneering form, vying to attack and loot Iberian vessels against the protestations of the dismayed merchants. Managing intrigue and conflict aboard a dangerous voyage led to Fenton's leadership becoming increasingly unstable. By the time the fleet reached the coast of Africa, the commander had been reduced to paranoia and bluster, declaring a grandiose notion to occupy St Helena and establish himself as king there. As the fleet travelled further south-west, discord was compounded by battle as they clashed with Spanish ships at São Vicente.

Ultimately, the tenuous partnership of the project broke down and the English fleet split up, the *Francis* and *Edward* departing for their own voyages. Fenton's galleon *Leicester* and the *Elizabeth* returned to England, arriving on 29 June 1583 with a chastened lieutenant Hawkins clapped in irons. Such was the humiliation of the failed expedition that several years passed before Fenton could secure employment again. Attempts to reach India around the Cape of Good Hope were abandoned for the present in favour of an older and much longer route: overland. It was Ralph Fitch who, along with a group of fellow English merchant travellers, undertook this overland journey to successfully arrive at India.

Little is known of Fitch's early life. He was born in 1550 or 1551 but thereafter disappears in the annals, only to emerge in his mid twenties when he became a member of the Leathersellers' Company in 1575. A few years later he joined the overland English expedition to India headed by fellow trader John Newberry. It was not, however, this journey alone that accounts for Fitch's significance. His true claim to fame arises from his experiences as the first Englishman to undertake a proverbial 'grand tour' across India and south-east Asia from 1583 to 1591. Some years after the fact, and with the encouragement of Richard Hakluyt, he compiled a record of his exploits that in 1598 was included in the enlarged multi-volume second edition of Hakluyt's *Principal Navigations*. Fitch's memoirs were later reissued in 1625 in a further renowned collection of travel writing, *Purchas his Pilgrimes*, compiled by yet another famed English geographical compiler, Samuel Purchas (d. 1626). Most importantly, however, Fitch's wide-ranging experiences and knowledge of India would prove invaluable to the founding and early voyages of the East India Company.

Fitch set off from Gravesend in February 1583 aboard the *Tiger* accompanied by five fellow travellers: merchants John Newberry, John Eldred and William Shales, jeweller William Leeds and painter James Story. Newberry, who had previously travelled as far as Hormuz, was leader of the group, with Fitch his deputy. Among the papers they carried was a copy of the letter from Thomas Stephens at Goa, provided by Hakluyt. The missive was undoubtedly intended as a guide, drawn by a fellow English traveller who had successfully reached India. Alongside this the travellers carried a rather more regal document: a letter of introduction from their monarch, Queen Elizabeth I, addressed to the reigning Mughal emperor Akbar. In it Elizabeth I entreats 'the most invincible, and most mightie prince, lord *Zelabdim Echebar* [Jalal al-Din Akbar]' to favourably accept her English travellers to his realms who arrive with 'good will and intention to introduce the trade of marchandize'.[1] Trade was the sole expressed aspiration of England in India and the lone dream which first drew English travellers to Mughal lands, a fact made clear by the English monarch in this respectful foundational address to Akbar. Indeed, there was hope for little else for her island nation in one of the largest and most powerful realms of the early modern world, ruled by an 'invincible' emperor.

On 20 May 1583 Fitch and his companions arrived at Aleppo, once a critically strategic city in the campaign against the Crusaders and now a bustling commercial metropolis under the aegis of the Ottomans. A key stop along the Mediterranean branch of the Silk Road, the historic city was famed for manufacturing industries ranging from woodwork and metalwork to woven textiles. Merchants arriving chiefly from the Mediterranean, Mesopotamia and central Asia converged here to avail themselves of the flourishing markets. Lengths of shimmering silk cloth woven with gold and silver, intricately hand-carved wooden goods inlaid with ivory, and delicate glassware were among the regional luxuries that went on to embellish the peoples and homes of distant lands. Venetian traders had long established a permanent factory in the city, to benefit from its bountiful offerings. The English traders too made good use of their stay, pausing for several days to avail themselves of the city's offerings before travelling on.

Thereafter the merchants reached a further commercial hub on 6 August 1583: Basra in the Persian Gulf. A crossroads of regional trade, Basra was yet another Ottoman-controlled metropolis and the largest and most prominent port city in the gulf littoral, with a population of some fifty thousand mostly Arab Muslims alongside Sabeans, Armenian Christians and Jews. In addition to overland connections with the rest of the Ottoman Empire and Safavid Persia, its maritime trade routes connected it to the Indian Ocean and, most importantly, India itself. Merchants of every description descended on Basra, tussling to trade their wares and replenish their stock of lucrative goods from across the world. European traders haggled with Persian merchants over sumptuous silks and hand-knotted rugs while Ottoman emissaries scoured central Asian stalls for distinctive diplomatic trinkets; here too, commerce was king. Trade through Basra included some of the region's most valued commodities, from prized horses, luminescent pearls, spices and dyes to vast quantities of Indian textiles, including woven cotton calicoes, delicate muslins and intricate silk brocades. Basra was also a key trading route between the Ottoman Empire and India, with Ottoman bullion employed in Indian trade regularly transited through the city.

For the English merchants this vibrant global centre of mercantile abundance and possibilities must have been thrilling. Fitch and his fellow travellers arrived with the not inconsiderable sum of £2,000 (approximately £400,000 today) worth of working capital. With this in hand they got to work in Basra's bustling markets. They sold gilded cutlery, emeralds and woollen broadcloth. Bedazzled by the commercial opportunities, Eldred and Shales subsequently decided to stay on at Basra. Fitch and the remaining Englishmen continued on their journey towards India, travelling first to the island port of Hormuz in the Persian Gulf in early September 1583.

Unfortunately for the travellers, trouble was soon to follow. Hormuz was controlled by the Portuguese and was a trading hub for countless European merchants. Within a week of their arrival the men encountered the first of their hurdles. It was Italian merchants at Hormuz who first saw in the English arrivals unwelcome competition. A resentful Venetian trader, Michael Stropeni, approached the Portuguese authorities insinuating that the English traders were spies acting in the interest of the pretender, Dom Antonio, who then lay claim to the Portuguese throne against the reigning Philip II. The response was swift; the governor of Hormuz, Dom Mathias de Albuquerque, ordered the English to be arrested and on 11 October deported them to the Viceroyalty of Goa to face charges. In this unpropitious manner the English travellers finally reached their destination of India; aboard a Portuguese carrack and weighted by chains. At Goa they were thrust on the mercy of the 13th Viceroy, Dom Francisco de Mascarenhas, a severe ruler and military man tasked with securing support for Philip II in Portuguese Asia. The prospects for Fitch and his companions seemed far from promising.

However, as the travellers' paths soon crossed with that of Father Thomas Stephens. Stephens evidently still retained an attachment to his abandoned homeland, and this emerged in his robust interventions on behalf of his compatriots. Upon discovering the plight of the Englishmen, Stephens along with fellow Jesuit Father Marco pleaded the prisoners' case with the Portuguese authorities, arguing that they were in fact good Christians in need of relief. Furthermore, he posted the considerable bond of 2,000 ducats as assurance the prisoners would not abscond if released. Thus it was by Stephens's and Marco's tireless efforts that the incarcerated Englishmen found themselves freed on 22 December 1583. If Stephens expected a modicum of gratitude for his service, however, it was not forthcoming. Although Story stayed on to paint religious murals at the Jesuit college of St Paul's and later married an Indian woman, in April 1584 Fitch, Newberry and Leeds fled Goa.

Their path took them across the Deccan Plateau, where they travelled first to Bijapur in the western Deccan and then on to Golconda
in the east. While the Mughals under Akbar succeeded in expanding
their north Indian territories as far as Gujarat in the west and Bengal
in the east, the Deccan Plateau in the south had yet to be claimed.
Bijapur at the time was in the hands of the Adil Shahi sultanate, then
ruled by Ibrahim Adil Shah II (d. 1626), while the Qutb Shahi sultanate governed Golconda with Muhammad Quli Qutb Shah (d. 1612)
then on the throne. Akbar's successors through the seventeenth
century continued Mughal expansion such that both Deccan territories were eventually brought under Mughal governance. In 1636
Akbar's heir Shah Jahan enforced Mughal suzerainty on Golconda,
with the Qutb Shahi sultans being made to pay tribute to the Mughals.
By the reign of Shah Jahan's successor, Alamgir I, both Deccan
sultanates were swept up under Mughal control. As Fitch and his
companions crossed through India they experienced the various
ruling entities that formed the mosaic of the land in the late sixteenth
century, from the Portuguese at Goa to the Adil Shahis and Qutb
Shahis of the Deccan. Through the seventeenth century, as the
Mughals expanded, subsequent English arrivals experienced India as
it transformed and consolidated under an overarching Mughal
authority.

Travel through the sultanates of the Deccan was no coincidence for
the English, even as they fled the Portuguese. Fitch and his fellow
merchants were keen on breaking into the India trade, including the
export of India's precious gemstones. This was likely the reason for
the jeweller, Leeds, being part of their group. Indeed, in the eyes of
Dutch merchant John Huighen van Linschoten (d. 1611), 'their prin-
cipall intent was to buy great quantities of precious stones, as Diamants,
Pearles, Rubies, etc.'[2] The illicit export in Indian gemstones was
banned by the Mughals and heavily policed by the Portuguese who,
along with allegations of espionage, likely suspected the mercantile
intentions of Fitch and his fellow traders.

Undoubtedly, the English travellers would have staged protest-
ations at any suggestion they were seeking illegal trade in gemstones.
Yet, at the very first town to which the fugitive travellers arrived,
Belgaum in the Western Ghats, Fitch writes of 'a great market kept of

diamants, rubies, saphires and many other soft stones'.[3] Further on, the stunning oval city of Bijapur, with its grand circular citadel, was a hub of regional commerce including in the trade of jewels. Neighbouring Golconda was no less than the global capital of diamonds. The English traders knew this well, Fitch noting that 'in the countrey of the king of Decan, bee the diamants'.[4] For the jeweller, Leeds, this would have been the most dazzling of destinations. As the merchants travelled on through Bijapur and Golconda, they enquired about diamonds and other precious stones while also longingly remarking on the 'good store of gold and silver' there.[5]

A key aim of the travellers was, of course, to reach the court of the Mughal emperor to secure royal support for English trade. Even then the Mughals reigned over the mass of India and approval from the monarch would open untold opportunities for English commerce there. Armed with the letter from their queen, the travellers continued on to Akbar's capitals of Agra and Fatehpur Sikri to wait on the emperor. The two great Indian cities enthralled them; in Fitch's words, 'either of them [were] much greater than London and very populous'. The stone-built metropolis of Agra, on the banks of the Yamuna, was especially impressive, featuring wide streets and a great sandstone fort that formed the primary residence of the Mughal monarchs. The immense wealth, influence and commercial sophistication of the Mughals were on abundant display, from the finely carved and gilded carriages draped in luxurious silk canopies that swept across the thoroughfares to the throngs of foreign merchants trading in textiles, spices, dyes, ivory and precious jewels. Fitch describes the twelve-mile stretch between Agra and Fatehpur Sikri as an uninterrupted stretch of bustling market, 'as full as though a man were still in a towne'.[6] Mughal India was a global capital and commercial hub of the early modern world, and the Englishmen were mesmerised.

Whether the merchants succeeded in securing an audience with Akbar and delivering Elizabeth I's letter is uncertain. Fitch's memoirs do not indicate a meeting, and the Mughal royal chronicles make no mention of the Englishmen whatsoever. What is clear, however, is that the traders remained for a period in this imperial and mercantile centre, until in September 1585 they decided to go their separate ways. Leeds entered Mughal service, securing the provisions of 'an house and five slaves, an horse and every day sixe S.S. [shillings] in money'.[7] Fitch and Newberry continued on their individual routes, agreeing to meet up in Bengal in two years' time. Fortune was not on Newberry's side, however. Proceeding on to Lahore, the trader seems to have met a gruesome end there as the victim of a violent robbery.

Fitch, on the other hand, undertook a spectacular solo journey lasting no less than eight years; an Asian odyssey by land, river and sea. Among the many Indian regions to which he travelled was Allahabad, where he admired the 'mightie river Ganges' into which the Yamuna flows.[8] He may well have also looked upon Abkar's magnificent fort on the banks of the Ganges, the largest such construction commissioned by the emperor. Built of red sandstone, it covers an astonishing 3.5 kilometres. Among the fort's features is the palace of Maryam al-Zamani, Akbar's chief consort and mother of his successor, Jahangir. The queen was among the many formidable royal women of the Mughal dynasty whose influence within the Mughal state extended to newcomers, including the English. This emerged a few years later when the East India Company arrived to trade in India.

Fitch managed to escape the notice of the queen, as he continued his travels across Mughal domains, continuing on to Varanasi, Patna and Bengal. Throughout his tour the merchant's mind was hard at work, noting the abundant and lucrative commodities on offer in the rich Asian lands through which he journeyed. His account often reads like an inventory of the array of goods sourced, manufactured and sold throughout India. From the dazzling jewels and diamonds 'found in divers places, as in Bisnagar [Vijaynagar], in Agra, in Delli' to the lucrative pepper that 'groweth in many parts of India, especially about Cochin' and the famed cotton textiles of which 'the best and finest' is sourced in 'Sennergan [Sonargaon]', then capital of eastern Bengal, Fitch's mercantile eye is sharp.[9] The traveller further describes the precious metals of Patna, where 'the women bee so decked with silver and copper that it is strange to see' and where 'they digge deepe pits in the earth . . . and therein they finde the gold'.[10]

Buried in his memoirs is perhaps one of the most notable yet seemingly cursory observations of the Indian market, and one which would prove valuable to later English trade efforts: the demand for ivory products by Indian women. The traveller remarks with fascinated curiosity that women of Khambhat in Gujarat 'wear upon their arms infinite numbers of rings made of elephants teeth, wherein they take so much delight'.[11] This Indian love of ivory adornments would prove an immensely valuable mercantile pathway in later years. As the early East India Company struggled to gain a foothold in Mughal trade, the burgeoning market for ivory, determined and shaped by the demands of affluent Indian women, would be key in securing English access.

Eventually, the trader arrived at Bengal where he awaited Newberry, quite unaware of the unfortunate fate of his colleague. By November 1586, with no Newberry in sight, Fitch ventured on, his travels taking him as far as Siam (Thailand), Malacca and Macao, whence, after seven weeks, he returned to Bengal by way of Ceylon and Cochin. Having spent over eight years traversing India, observing its peoples and traditions, admiring its cities and, of course, noting its commercial offerings, he finally made his way back to England. Retracing his steps first through the perilous routes of Portuguese Goa and Hormuz, he continued overland, returning via Basra and Aleppo and then onboard ship to London. He reached English shores at the end of April 1591. So long was his absence that the previous year, in February 1590, he had been given over for dead and his property in England had been divided among his heirs.

But the traveller was very much alive and would spend the remaining decades of his life engaged in trade, primarily in the Mediterranean, and, armed with a lengthy experience in India, as a valuable resource of knowledge for London's trading community. His written account, published in Hakluyt, would prove yet another useful resource for English traders venturing east. Furthermore, in 1600 when the East India Company secured its royal charter, Fitch acted as a consultant on India for the new enterprise. In this capacity he translated documents, offered guidance on the lading of East Indies-bound vessels and provided the appropriate titles for the Mughal emperors. Although not listed on the rolls of EIC founders, he nonetheless played a prominent role in the Company's creation, early years and subsequent efforts in India. For that he would be remembered, his travel account still with us to this day offering a glimpse of sixteenth–century Mughal India through the fascinated eyes of a lone English merchant venturing across an empire many leagues from home.

In October 1611 Fitch passed away in London having spent his final days in the parish of St Katharine Cree off Leadenhall Street. Perhaps fittingly, in later years Leadenhall Street would house the headquarters of the East India Company. While their first attempts to reach India were replete with setbacks, the English ploughed on in their endeavours to access Mughal commerce and wealth. Fitch's grand tour of India was a key moment, when an early English traveller acquired firsthand experience of late sixteenth–century India and the rule of Akbar, to the benefit of merchant compatriots who looked to follow. Yet, it was nearly two decades after the return of Fitch that the sluggish path of concerted English travel to and trade in Mughal India made tangible progress under the aegis of the East India Company. To trace that event, we must return to Fenton's catastrophic Cape route enterprise, and particularly to his lieutenant general, William Hawkins.

4

Indias of Spice and Mine

I T TAKES A strong constitution to travel across desert plains at the height of summer. But on 7 July 1600 a large caravan embarked from the bustling trade city of Aleppo to undertake precisely such a journey. Hosting anywhere between six hundred and a thousand travellers, like its city of departure the caravan was an immensely cosmopolitan collective. Christian Armenian travellers broke bread with Safavid Shia traders, Turkish Ottomans exchanged pleasantries with Venetian merchants, and Arab traders rode alongside Portuguese fortune seekers. Then there were the impressive steeds; prized Persian horses bearing wealthy masters brushed flanks with regal camels pulling carts or carrying goods as they slowly wove a trail between countless cities and across miles of desert. Camels were chosen as much for endurance across long distances as for strength in carrying immense loads: luggage and commodities teetered high upon their humps or were loaded on to panniers slung on either side of the powerful beasts.

Amid this sea of peoples, merchandise and mounts was a curious pair of travellers from a rather more far-flung land. They were two Englishmen. One was a self-styled preacher by the name of John Cartwright, whose travels would lead him to Isfahan in Persia and then across the Middle East. He would later collate his experiences in a memoir, *The Preacher's Travels*. The other was a merchant by the name of John Mildenhall. Although travelling partway with Cartwright, Mildenhall's sights were set on the more distant and potentially lucrative destination of India. Following close on the heels of his predecessor Fitch, Mildenhall too carved an early mercantile path seeking his fortune and, as he would claim, that of his monarch and nation, in the lands of the Great Mughal.

John Mildenhall was a merchant who travelled extensively, spending time in the Levant and further into Asia, chiefly Persia and India. Earliest records of him emerge in *Purchas His Pilgrimes* and comprises two key materials on the traveller: one an account of his journey from London to Kandahar via Constantinople that includes his account of joining the great caravan from Aleppo; the second, a letter dated 3 October 1606 from Mildenhall to London merchant Richard Staper, relating the former's travels to India and his dealings at the court of Emperor Akbar. What is clear about Mildenhall is he was a lone and bold adventurer, exuberantly seeking a share in Indian riches, and not always via creditable means. This may account for his failure to secure employment with the East India Company when it directed its attentions to Mughal lands. Nonetheless, Mildenhall's brief appearance was impactful and laid the foundations for future formal English interactions at the Mughal *darbar*.

On 12 February 1599 Mildenhall boarded the *Hector* from London, arriving on 29 October at Istanbul, the Ottoman capital and a global centre of trade and diplomacy. English post-Reformation partnerships with the powerful Ottoman Empire were now decades old. Queen Elizabeth I's successive ambassadors had built strong diplomatic relations with the Ottoman sultans, and the Sublime Porte had become by then a regular haunt of English emissaries and traders. At the time of Mildenhall's arrival, the English ambassador was Henry Lello, who had famously begun his term by presenting an elaborate organ clock from his queen to the sultan. Mildenhall spent six months in Constantinople engaging in trade. Relations with the Ottomans in some way proved a foundational experience to England's subsequent interactions with India, and this was true for Mildenhall too. This Turkish residency subsequently coloured his later engagements in India.

It is likely during Mildenhall's sojourn in Constantinople that he learnt of an initiative to found a trading company directed to the Indies. News of the September 1599 Founders' Hall meeting to establish the East India Company had spread like wildfire through London's mercantile community, eventually reaching the Mediterranean shores where Mildenhall was residing. For the ambitious merchant, it presented a promising opportunity. Securing experience, knowledge and a trading foothold in India could make him indispensable to the East India

Company when it finally sought to enter the Mughal market. The potential for personal profit was substantial. And so in July 1600 he joined the vast caravan from Aleppo, his sights set on India.

The journey was slow and sure, and it would not be until 1603 that Mildenhall finally reached Lahore. From there he travelled on to Agra, to wait upon Akbar. Unlike Fitch, it would seem Mildenhall did secure an audience with the emperor. Gifts were an indispensable diplomatic currency at the Mughal court, and the English merchant claims to have lavishly catered to it. In his letter to Staper he professes to have presented the emperor with twenty-nine horses, 'some of them cost me fifty or threescore pounde an horse', precious jewels and a range of rings and earrings.[1] If true, Mildenhall had read his hosts well. Horses, particularly those of Persia, were greatly prized by the Mughals and would prove a key import for later East India Company trading efforts in India.

The gifts had the desired effect, and Akbar invited the newly arrived Englishman to state his case. Alone, thousands of miles away from home and with no official backing, he proceeded to position himself as an envoy of Queen Elizabeth I, proclaiming on her behalf that she desired friendship with the Mughals and free trade for her nation in India. The queen for whom Mildenhall so confidently spoke likely didn't know he existed, even less that he presented himself as her envoy at one of the seventeenth century's most power- ful courts. The merchant was not done, however: he further declared to Akbar that since the Mughals had warred with the Portuguese, they should not take issue if the English were to capture Portuguese ships and ports in and around India. This demand was an especially bold if not foolhardy one, unprotected as he was and given the century-long hold the Portuguese enjoyed in the Indian Ocean and parts of India.

Since his invitation to Jesuit missionaries from Goa in 1579, Akbar had retained a relatively regular Portuguese presence at court. Predictably, the proclamation of this brash Englishman enraged the missionaries then in attendance. The escapades of Fitch and his fellows meant English travellers in India were far from trusted by the Portuguese, and Mildenhall's demands only fuelled the enmity further. In response, the Portuguese actively campaigned against this latest

English arrival and his nation, declaring to Akbar that they were untrustworthy thieves and spies who sought to occupy Mughal ports. Negotiations thus stalled. Whatever Mildenhall had hoped to achieve for his country in India, he had successfully aggravated sensitive and very well-established European rivals there. The merchant continued for several months at Agra, seeking to secure an agreement with the emperor, yet being undercut at every turn. He conducted negotiations via an Armenian interpreter he had hired at Aleppo, yet this man too was soon turned against him by the Portuguese.

Eventually, Mildenhall took matters into his own hands. Hiring a tutor, he spent six months learning Persian, the official Mughal state language, until he could engage directly at court. He then returned to court to defend his case, asserting that the English were not thieves and had absolutely no intention of invading or annexing Mughal territory. His robust defence once again established the essential terms of England's early entry and efforts in India: trade was the sole impetus and remained so throughout this formative period of Anglo-Mughal relations. Mildenhall further drew on the Ottoman example in his assertions to Akbar, describing the flourishing relations between England and the Sublime Porte and how Elizabeth I sent regular ambassadors to the sultan bearing lavish gifts and would do the same for the Mughals. Once again, the merchant had no authority to make such proclamations, but that certainly didn't stop him. Akbar's son and heir, Crown Prince Salim, later Emperor Jahangir, was present at this audience. The speech had the desired effect: Mildenhall had raised expectations and, as he claimed, favour for his English nation. Writing from Qazvin in Persia in 1606, he asserted that he had successfully secured an agreement in writing from both Akbar and Selim, which he retained with him.

The East India Company was formed primarily to trade in East Indies spices, which were sourced in the Indonesian archipelago. It was not until the Company's third voyage of 1607 that direct travel to Mughal India was contemplated. This was the point at which Mildenhall made his move. Writing to the EIC directors, he offered his services for the staggering sum of £1,500. The EIC, however, chose not to work with Mildenhall on the grounds that not only were his demands unreasonable but he was 'for divers respects . . . not fitting to be ymployed in the service of the Companie'.[2] Mildenhall's chutzpah in Mughal courtly negotiations had been established, but questions around his character remained. Reportedly, he was heavily engaged in bribery in India and in 1611 attempted to steal a mass of merchandise and cash during a further expedition east. During that infamous attempt, he absconded with merchandise belonging to several merchants including Staper, in the direction of India. Two men were swiftly dispatched in pursuit, capturing Mildenhall with some £9,000 worth of loot near Persia. However, perhaps the biggest factor in play in Mildenhall's rejection by the EIC was that his offer of services was too late. His letter reached the EIC directors in 1608, and at that point the third voyage direct to India was already under way, with one Captain William Hawkins at its helm.

The key reasons for the EIC directing their first two voyages to what was then known as the Spice Islands of the Moluccas were twofold. Firstly, spices, the most prized and lucrative commodity of the early modern world, were the primary target of the East India Company, who had lobbied for a royal charter in the name of 'trade in the East-India, to bring into this realm spices and other commodities'.[3] The Spanish historian Bartolomé Leonardo de Argensola (d. 1631) reports that during his circumnavigation of the globe, Francis Drake had reached an agreement with the sultan of Ternate to establish English trade on the island.[4] The Spice Islands were the world's source of the delicate yet immensely valuable commodities of cloves, nutmeg and mace, among other desired spices. Traders from around the world voyaged to and competed, often violently, to access and secure a monopoly over these goods, and none more so than the western Europeans arriving around the Cape. The most active of European traders targeting Moluccan spices were the Dutch East India Company, or Vereenigde Oostindische Compagnie (VOC).

The second reason for the EIC's early restraint in voyaging to Mughal India was a political one. England was at war with Spain and Portugal, so India was avoided to evade conflict with the Portuguese settlers there. However, in 1604 the Treaty of London ended hostilities with the Iberians, allowing the English at last to venture into Indian trade. Nonetheless, it would still be another three years before a voyage was undertaken in that direction. Peace with their rivals alone did not alert the English to the value of Mughal trade; it took more practical challenges in their primary markets of the Moluccas to trigger the move.

The first EIC voyage to the Indies, led by Captain James Lancaster, departed on April 1601, travelling directly to the Spice Islands and arriving in Aceh in June 1602. A second voyage followed in 1604, led by Captain Henry Middleton, setting off in March and arriving at Bantam in December. Both expeditions focused on securing direct access to East Indies spices. The luxury commodity had long been subject to price inflations by the time they reached Europe, due to the long distances and countless intermediaries through which it journeyed. A direct route securing the products at source was deemed the solution, and a potentially hugely profitable one at that. It was this that motivated Portuguese explorer Vasco da Gama (d. 1524) to seek a direct seaward route to India in the first place. Over a century after the Portuguese, the same motivation fuelled England's first voyagers along that very same route.

However, the EIC, like its European rivals, soon discovered that trade in the Moluccas was inseparable from the textile trade in India. English woollens proved of little interest in the humid climate of the Moluccas, where the airy cottons of India were the key commodity of barter. Established regional traders, such as Gujarati merchants from India's western coast, actively traded in Indian textiles for Moluccan spices. Furthermore, the trade in spices proved more costly than it was worth for the English. Violent dangers from European rivals such as the Dutch and Portuguese made it necessary to send costly fortified English fleets that could withstand attacks, yet the home market for spice was too small to turn a decent profit. A single ship could carry the entire spice cargo required. Breaking into the thriving 'country trade', as inter-Asian trade was termed, became necessary to adequately profit from the spice trade. And so the EIC turned its attentions to India in an incidental move motivated by its original purpose of trading in spices. By importing the textiles of India to the Moluccas, English traders hoped to barter cottons for spices just as the Gujarati traders did. With peace secured with Spain and Portugal, this diversification of trade was now conceivable. The world-changing ramifications of England's cautiously pragmatic turn to India in this moment could never have been predicted.

Accessing Mughal markets was not going to be easy, however. Mughal India, among the wealthiest realms of the early modern world, needed little from their new English arrivals. The Mughals' primary source of revenue was an agrarian system of land taxation over their vast and ever-expanding empire. The immense income this brought in meant the Mughals were financially self-sustaining and not dependent on international trade. This was very different from the debt-riddled western European states for whom trade was often a lifeline. Furthermore, not only did Mughal India have well-developed manufacturing industries capable of producing the empire's needs, but where they did engage in trade, they prioritised long-standing Asian trade networks and partners over the newcomers from distant Europe. And, like the islanders of the Moluccas, no one in sweltering India wanted English woollen broadcloth. As such breaking into Mughal markets was a singular challenge. There was much the English keenly desired in India's markets, but very few enticements they could offer in return.

Besides the primary export of broadcloth, English offerings also included sword blades, mirrors, paintings, furs and cutlery, but these too the Company struggled to sell. EIC merchants complained of having 'sold but three pieces of cloth for ready money and a few swordblades; all the coney skins, loo[king] glasses, and pictures remain as last year, unsold and little worth', further remarking on the 'Inconveniences attending the sale of the Company's cloth [broad-cloth]; it is so unvendible that they are glad to be rid of it on almost any terms; the Company will do well not to send any more for a year or two.'[5] The few commodities English merchants found saleable on the Indian markets were spices, ivory, coral and Persian horses, all of which had to be imported from elsewhere. Ivory was especially valued by Indian women for jewellery and sold substantially. The English therefore imported considerable quantities of it from East and West Africa. By this, Indian women became among the foremost customers to shape the early English trade in Mughal India.

The markets of India were a treasure chest for the English and their European rivals as they vied for an astonishing array of spices, dyes, jewels and textiles. Delicately patterned cotton calicoes and chintz to Bengal silk brocades, plush hand-woven carpets and rich indigo dyes dazzled the English. Imports of these treasures triggered an increase in demand, and by 1620 the EIC was selling a quarter of a million pieces of Indian cloth in London. Indian goods began to change the material landscape of England and also its continental cousins. However, as merchants plying Indian markets and mercantile petitioners at the Mughal court, the English offered little, a fact which only served to further skew an already unequal exchange. This fact inevitably played out in the earliest English efforts to both formally secure a trade agreement at the Mughal court and trade in India's markets. When the first EIC fleet docked near Surat, hopes were high for a trade partnership and, led by a self-assured Captain William Hawkins, they were unaware of the troubles that lay ahead.

In the absence of adequate English goods with which to barter, the EIC was forced to trade for the most part in specie rather than commodities. Trade with Mughal India was therefore a costly and rather one-sided affair. Silver would be imported from the mines of the Americas direct to Surat in India, chests often transiting through London unopened. In India they were minted at local imperial mints into Mughal coins of silver rupia, which were then employed in the purchase of Indian goods at local markets. India's already overflowing coffers were thereby further enriched by this ever-increasing injection of silver from English trade.

As the English realised the centrality of silver to their Indian trade, they sought more proximate sources of the precious metal. This led the Company to turn to the silver-rich land of Japan. In 1611 experienced EIC trader John Saris embarked as head of a three-vessel Company flotilla on a lengthy voyage via Yemen and Java that eventually reached the Japanese port of Hirado in June 1613. Armed with yet more hefty bolts of broadcloth to trade, and a nifty gift of a telescope 'cast in silver gilte' to woo the shogun, Saris set out to establish mutual accord with Japan's rulers and set up an English trading factory. This was all in the service of his foremost task: to acquire Japanese silver to aid the Indies trade.[6] During a stay of several months the trader met with the shogun, delivering the telescope and receiving a set of luxurious screens for James I in return. He set up an English factory at Hirado before departing at the end of the year. Back in England he drew on his experience to advise the Company on the best exports to dispatch to Japan to secure silver specie, specifying brazilwood from Thailand, Javanese pepper and Chinese raw silk. The English project in Japan did not ultimately succeed, however, and after a decade of abortive trade the Company withdrew in 1623.

Perhaps what is most notable about these early enterprises, however mixed their outcome, is how England honed an internationalist strategy to address its many disadvantages in India. While Mughal India was turned to support the trade in Moluccan spices, the markets of East and West Africa and Persia and the mines of the Americas and Japan were tapped to facilitate trade in India. The formative threads of a gradually woven global English network was beginning to take shape, with trade in Mughal lands at its centre.

There is some slight speculation that William Hawkins is the sea captain and privateer who led the first direct English voyage to Mughal India. If he is the Hawkins of the famed Hawkins of Plymouth, as is most likely the case, then his ancestry prepared him well for his seafaring adventures, yet was steeped in blood and infamy. Born around 1560, William Hawkins (d. 1613) was the eldest child of Plymouth shipowner William Hawkins (d. 1589), also a sea captain, merchant and privateer. His grandfather, yet another William Hawkins (d. 1544/55), was similarly a merchant and sea captain, who served as MP for Plymouth and rose to be one of the richest men in the town. Yet it is perhaps the uncle of our William Hawkins, Sir John Hawkins (d. 1595), who is most notable and notorious. Among the most renowned English naval commanders of the sixteenth century, John Hawkins was one of the Sea Dogs quartet of privateers, along with Sir Walter Raleigh, Sir Martin Frobisher and Sir Francis Drake, who were commissioned by Queen Elizabeth I to plunder Spanish ships. As royally commissioned privateers, a portion of their profits from this piracy would go to the English crown.

Most significantly, however, John Hawkins was a founder of the global trade in enslaved peoples, who set the foundations for the triangular trade. By this system Europeans traded manufactured goods for West African peoples who were then transported and enslaved in the Americas. His expeditions included four to Sierra Leone between 1564 and 1569, in which he violently captured and trafficked some twelve hundred people into devastating enslavement in Spanish plantations of the Americas in exchange for raw materials such as sugar, cotton and tobacco. These brutal enterprises rewarded him well, not only by direct profit but from the monarch herself: Queen Elizabeth I sponsored his journeys, providing ships, supplies and guns. In 1565 she bestowed on him a coat of arms, featuring a bound and captive Black enslaved person, a reward for his immense profiteering from the slave trade. By this sponsorship England's monarchy became key in the foundations and future of the transatlantic slave trade. Elizabeth I's later Stuart successors Charles II and James II established the Royal African Company (RAC) that shipped more enslaved African men, women and children to the Americas than any other company in the history of the transatlantic slave trade.

William Hawkins, the father of Hawkins of India, was an active partner with his brother John on his expeditions. His engagements included being a lead investor in at least three of John's voyages to Sierra Leone and the West Indies in the 1560s. In addition to this elder William's role in the life of his India-bound son, John was attentive to the progress of his nephew. It was likely at the uncle's request that Francis Drake took the young William on for the 1577–80 circumnavigation of the globe. It was also at the uncle's request that the nephew was nominated in October 1581 to join Edward Fenton as lieutenant on that first attempt to reach the East Indies via the Cape route, from which Hawkins returned clapped in irons for drunken and mutinous behaviour. On his death, John Hawkins left his nephew a share in the profits of his last voyage and an annuity of £10. Born into a family foundational to the slave trade and raised in the care of its patriarchs, it is from this blood-stained heritage that William Hawkins, the first Englishman to navigate directly to Mughal India, sprang.

Like Mildenhall, Hawkins also travelled and traded in the Levant prior to India. In Ottoman lands he picked up Turkish, a language actively used at the Mughal court. This may have been a factor in his selection to captain the *Hector* – the same ship by which Mildenhall had voyaged to the Levant some years earlier – as part of the third East India Company voyage, and first direct to Mughal India. In this role he was charged with not only successfully navigating to India but also delivering a letter from his monarch, King James I, to the Mughal emperor and undertaking negotiations for English trade in India. Hawkins was further furnished with numerous gifts for the emperor, including plate and broadcloth.

The third voyage fleet was comprised of three ships: in addition to the *Hector* was the *Consent*, captained by David Middleton, brother of Henry Middleton, and the *Red Dragon*, captained by William Keeling, who also served as commander of the fleet. The ships set off from England on 1 April 1607, but soon after the *Consent* was separated on the tumultuous journey, never to rejoin; instead, it made directly for Bantam. Eventually the remaining ships arrived at the island of Socotra in April 1608. There they split up, Keeling in the direction of Bantam and Hawkins in the direction of India. Four months later, at the height of the monsoon season, on 24 August 1608, the *Hector* reached the Mughal coast, dropping anchor at the entrance of the Tapti River a few miles shy of the bustling port city of Surat. England's first ship had finally reached Mughal lands, following the route carved by Vasco da Gama over a hundred years earlier. Finally, efforts to forge Anglo-Mughal relations could formally begin, and Hawkins would lead the way.

Surat was a vibrant, international metropolis and commercial hub. Situated along the heavily silted banks of the lower Tapti, it is over-looked by an impressive fort. A mid-sixteenth-century construction commissioned by the sultan of Ahmedabad, Mahmud Shah III (d. 1554), the fort is a brick-built square structure with imposing circular towers at its four corners. In 1573 Surat was captured by Akbar as part of his conquest of wider Gujarat. Thereafter the city grew to become the leading maritime port and commercial centre of Mughal India, a status it retained throughout the seventeenth century. As much as it was a Mughal metropolis, however, Surat lacked the order and archi-tectural grandeur of India's political and religious capitals. Its streets were narrow and flanked by low-built homes primarily constructed of wood or bamboo. The wealthier classes resided in homes built of brick with flat plastered roofs where evenings were spent sipping tea in the cooling air. Beyond the city gates picturesque villages, housing the weavers, spinners and dyers that catered to Surat's mercantile communities, dotted the surrounding countryside.

The city attracted traders from across the globe, rendering its population hugely diverse even by Indian standards. Merchants of every description plied their trade in its markets, from Europeans, including the Dutch and Portuguese, to Arabs, Turks, Persians, Armenians and Indians of every denomination. And now Hawkins joined the throng. The task before him was daunting: to secure audience with the Mughal emperor and negotiate a trade agreement for England. To ease his path, James I had furnished him with a letter of introduction addressed to the Mughal emperor. There was one slight problem, however: the letter was addressed to Akbar, but it was an entirely different monarch who then ruled India.

Nur al-Din Muhammad Salim Jahangir, son of Akbar and fourth emperor of Mughal India, very nearly did not gain the throne. Years of rebellion against his reigning father had soured their relationship almost beyond repair. Matters had come to a head in 1599 when Salim seized the fort of Allahabad and established himself as ruler in the region. Akbar's efforts at mediation fell on deaf ears, and in 1601 the prince went so far as to conduct a provocative march at the head of a large army to Agra's precincts before returning to Allahabad where he proclaimed independence and declared himself sultan. By this time Akbar's officers too had had enough and began encouraging the emperor to overlook Salim entirely for succession and instead pass the throne on to the prince's eldest son, Khusraw. The options were few: of Akbar's other sons, Murad had died and Danyal was a drunkard whose health was failing. As such, young Prince Khusraw became an increasingly tempting alternative.

Once again it took the level-headed intervention of the empire's royal women to resolve matters. In 1603 Empress Salima Begim, one of Akbar's chief consorts, offered to bring about a reconciliation with the prince. Akbar agreed and the Empress immediately travelled to Allahabad where she managed to convince Salim to return with her. At the gates of Agra they were joined by the queen mother, Hamida Banu Begim, whose presence, Akbar's chroniclers report, 'soothed the prince's terrified soul'.[7] When the trio finally arrived before the emperor's throne, the two queens flung the prince at the feet of Akbar in a symbolic gesture of contrition. The emperor then lifted the prince, lovingly embraced him and placed his own turban upon Salim's head. Reconciliation was thus secured, as was the succession. Two years later, when Akbar passed away in 1605, Salim was able to mount the Mughal throne as the new emperor, taking for himself the title Jahangir (Conqueror of the World).

Despite his grandiose title, Jahangir did not venture far into the world. Just like his father, however, his *darbar* was a microcosm of the globe. Mughal power and wealth attracted people from lands near and distant, such that the court and the administration was a veritable collage of ethnicities, religions and races. It was during Jahangir's reign that unprecedented Englishmen, including the newly disembarked Hawkins, began arriving in India, keen on a share of the empire's fabulous riches. Like Akbar, the English found Jahangir a genial and hospitable yet otherwise largely indifferent host. While England's travellers to India kept minutely detailed records of their adventures and encounters, Jahangir did not trouble himself to include a single mention of Hawkins or his fellow travellers in his royal memoirs. In this itself is revealed the dynamics of the encounter; the English were very eager for a partnership, the Mughals were singularly not. The reality was that the Mughals were simply in no need of English trade and the English struggled to capture their interest enough to convince them otherwise.

As in previous reigns, Jahangir was guided and supported by powerful imperial Mughal women. For the increasing numbers of English arrivals, these royal women directly impacted England's entry into India. They included Jahangir's chief consort, Empress Nur Jahan Begim (d. 1645), also known as Nur Mahal, an astute woman of great intellect and authority who ruled as co-sovereign with Jahangir. Most prominent however, during Hawkins's residence, was the illustrious queen mother, Maryam al-Zamani (d. 1623), who was also previously chief consort to Akbar. As queen mother, the respect and regard with which al-Zamani was held was unparalleled, and the impact of it would be felt not only by English traders but also by their western European rivals, including the Portuguese. Her titles included Shah

Begim (Queen Lady) and among her prerogatives was the right to issue official documents, a privilege normally the preserve of the emperor.[8]

In her presence, Jahangir offered exceptional deference, conducting 'the rites of *korunush* [a central Asian greeting], *sijda* [prostration], and *Taslim* [a greeting usually performed before the emperor], and after observing the formalities the young owe their elders under the terms of the Genghis code and Timurid law'.[9] Before the queen mother, Jahangir thus performed an elaborate range of ritual greetings in an extraordinary display of obeisance that the emperor offered none other but would usually be accustomed to receiving himself. As Jahangir dotingly wrote, 'I hope that the shadow of her protection and affection will always be over the head of this supplicant.'[10] Like many royal Mughal women, the queen mother enjoyed immense wealth with which she built palaces, gardens, mosques, wells and caravanserais. English traveller William Finch (d. 1613) records lodging 'at Menhapoore, a great saray by which is a garden and moholl or summer house of the Queene Mothers, very curiously contrived'.[11] Among her surviving architectural commissions is the Begum Shahi Mosque in Lahore. Built during the early reign of Jahangir, this stunning building features wide archways and short domes with interiors intricately embellished with frescoes in floral and geometric motifs. For worshippers, the mosque was and continues to be a symbol of the queen's wealth and generosity.

Significantly, Maryam al-Zamani was also among Mughal India's foremost traders and shipping magnates. The queen mother's agents were active across the empire and well beyond, and her vast vessels were recognisable in the Indian Ocean. English traders in India noted how 'there are many buyers, and never so many great ones as now, viz. the Queen' and how the queen's commerce impacted the price and supply of commodities at market.[12] Foreign traders found their access to the Mughal market often determined by the queen mother, and particularly the smooth running of her trading operations. Arriving as Hawkins was in pursuit of trade for his nation, it would be interactions with the queen mother's mercantile pursuits that would prove among the chief factors influencing England's formal entry to India.

★

Within days of his arrival in Surat in April 1608, Hawkins met the man who would prove to be his Indian nemesis. Muqarrab Khan was the Mughal official appointed to oversee the ports of the state of Gujarat, and Surat therefore lay within his jurisdiction. The English were met by Khan and his officials, who soon impounded their goods, including most of the courtly gifts sent for Jahangir. There was little Hawkins could do, being a new arrival, largely alone and unprotected with only his fellow trader William Finch and two English servants with him. Their ship the *Hector* had by then voyaged on to the Moluccas. The Portuguese in India were also displeased to see more English arrivals. It was not long before they staged two attempts on Hawkins's life. According to Hawkins, Muqarrab Khan was also in league with the Iberians.

Hawkins and Finch eventually decided to split up, the latter remaining in Surat to trade, the former to travel on to the Mughal court at Agra. In February 1609 Hawkins set off on the six-hundred-mile journey, taking the precaution of being accompanied by Pathan guards along the way. Ten weeks later, on 16 April, this first official English merchant envoy to India bearing letters from the English monarch arrived at the Mughal capital, ready to meet with one of the most powerful rulers of the seventeenth century.

Hawkins was a brash and daring spirit with a tendency for tipple, and his heady personality emerged no less rambunctiously in his forays at the court of Jahangir. This was further embellished by his EIC sponsors, who sought to make an unforgettable impression. For his attendance at the *darbar*, the merchant was furnished with an astonishing outfit of vibrant scarlet complete with a cloak lined in taffeta and bordered with striking silver lace. Even for the colourful surroundings of the Mughal court, the merchant must have cut quite the dazzling figure. As he sweated profusely in the Indian heat beneath his many layers, Hawkins nonetheless felt appropriately suited and booted for the grand part he intended to play.

From the moment of his arrival at Surat, Hawkins positioned himself as an ambassador of his monarch. While he may have carried a letter from James I, he was at best a merchant envoy or messenger sent to make preliminary headway for trade in India. However, like Mildenhall before him, Hawkins's efforts combined a desire to impress with an absence of anyone to keep him in check. And so, at Agra too, he declared himself as the newly arrived official representative of James I. The Mughal court duly received him as such and Jahangir sent for him with an entourage 'as an Embassador of a king ought to be'.[13]

The *darbar* of the Mughal emperor was an impressive and well-regulated affair. In a large hall supported by towering columns, the emperor rested upon sumptuous hand-knotted carpets and silk brocade cushions by a *jharokha* or interview window-cum-balcony. Smartly uniformed royal standard bearers stood to attention to the left while behind were stationed eunuchs who, with fans of peacock feathers and fly whisks of dyed yak hair, kept the monarch cool and the insects at bay. Security was maintained by burly Uzbek bodyguards, who surrounded the emperor. Before the *jharokha*, attendees were arranged by rank, high officials and nobility positioned nearest the monarch. Courtly protocol and etiquette was minutely managed: no one was permitted to sit in the emperor's presence nor leave without his permission. When permitted to approach, formal greetings had to be enacted, such as the *zaminbus* ('kissing the ground') where a petitioner laid their right hand on the ground and kissed the back of it.

Courtly gifts presented to the emperor were particularly important and expected, especially from foreign emissaries, for as French traveller François Bernier (d. 1688) remarked, 'one does not approach the Great One empty handed'.[14] For Hawkins, this could have been a problem given he had lost the best of his gifts for Jahangir to the caprices of Muqarrab Khan. Luckily, he was received cordially and, by his own account, initially impressed and ingratiated himself. His command of Turkish did much to assist this; the merchant notes that Jahangir, 'perceiving I had the Turkish tongue, which himselfe well understood', invited him to a private audience. It is likely Jahangir had also anticipated the arrival of an English ambassador given he had been present when Mildenhall had made the promises of emissaries bearing gifts to Akbar. For Jahangir, Hawkins was the fulfilment of that promise and expectations were high.

Yet, there was more to Hawkins's initial welcome and tentative rise at the *darbar*. Jahangir, the son of Akbar of Gong Mahal fame, was no less a man of insatiable curiosity, and similar traces of Akbar's fascination and playfulness emerge in Jahangir's dealings with Hawkins. This is,

however, unsurprising; a white English *firingi* from a distant and unfamiliar island nation arriving at the *darbar* speaking the Islamicate
lingua franca of Turkish would have been a most curious sight for many,
not least the Mughal and his court. And so, it seems, Jahangir decided
to explore this culturally hybrid Englishman, and see how far his willing malleability could be taken. Before long, the emperor offered
Hawkins the title of khan – a status of minor nobility – an Indian
household, four hundred Indian cavalry, a generous annual stipend and,
eventually, an Indian wife. In short, he sought to make Hawkins Indian.

The thrilled merchant embraced all offered privileges with gusto,
undoubtedly to the delight of his host. He became known as the
English Khan, managed his new household and staff wholly according
to Indian traditions, dressed in Indian attire and observed halal meals
in line with the Muslim Mughals. Like Thomas Stephens in Goa,
Hawkins too became enthusiastically Indian. Yet this was far from
surprising; the power and wealth of India made it a land and culture to
which a great many aspired and willingly assimilated in a bid to rise.
For Hawkins, the doorway opened to a respected station in a leading
empire of the world was an opportunity not to be missed. Not all his
English compatriots were impressed, however. For the horrified John
Jourdain (d. 1619), a fellow merchant in India, Hawkins's Indian turn
reflected the man as 'very fickle in his resolucion, as alsoe in his religion'.[15] With his new-found favour, Hawkins petitioned the emperor
for the English cause, seeking permission for English trade at Mughal
ports and a permit to establish an English factory at Surat, requests
Jahangir did not initially resist. Hawkins even claims Jahangir expressed
an interest in sending an Indian ambassador to England, although such
an embassy certainly did not materialise.

Unfortunately, intrigue and his own blunders meant the merchant's
initial successes were short-lived. Conflicts with Muqarrab Khan
continued at court, culminating in a public falling out over English
stock Muqarrab Khan had failed to pay fairly for. This only fuelled
Khan's animosity continued with vigour he and his supporters actively
lobbied the emperor against the English merchant. Meanwhile, the
Portuguese courtly campaigns against English trade fervently continued. Before long the sands beneath Hawkins's feet began to shift
and the emperor's support faltered. A couple of years into Hawkins's

residence, Jahangir married Nur Jahan, who became his chief consort. Her father, Ghiyas Beg, was appointed vizier and her brother Asaf Khan also rose at court. Seeing an opportunity, Hawkins acquired gifts for all three to gain favour, a prudent move given Ghiyas Beg in turn managed to gain Hawkins an audience before Jahangir. There the merchant succeeded in securing an agreement for an English factory in Surat. Yet this too was soon undone by Muqarrab Khan, and a formal document of the agreement was never issued.

The year 1611 ultimately proved the unmaking of Hawkins. In September 1610 the English vessel the *Ascension* from the fourth EIC voyage was wrecked off the Indian coast, its crew escaping in boats to dry land. The drunken and disorderly behaviour of the latest English arrivals, however, predictably enraged locals and officials. Although news travels fast, the distance may have offered scope to contain the embarrassment had the sailors not then decided to travel to Agra, where they arrived in January the following year. In the capital too they managed to make quite the drunken spectacle, a matter of deep embarrassment and indignity for Hawkins at court. Yet it was not only the drunkenness of his compatriots that lost Hawkins favour. Although usually a heavy drinker himself, that year Jahangir had commanded that none should appear at his *darbar* with the smell of alcohol about their person. Hawkins, ill suited to abstinence at the best of times, made the blunder of arriving smelling strongly of his latest indulgence. He was promptly sent home in disgrace, never to regain the close position to the emperor he had hitherto held.

Yet perhaps what most disgraced Hawkins was an unfortunate English entanglement with the queen mother's trade that same year. While Hawkins was resident at court, William Finch was actively trading for the Company, and at Bayana, a centre for indigo dye, he inadvertently came into conflict with al-Zamani's agent, who was also there purchasing indigo to take aboard one of the many royal trading vessels. Just as the agent was about to make his purchase, Finch appeared and outbid him. News of this reached al-Zamani who, incensed at Finch's temerity, reported the incident to her reigning son. Jahangir was enraged and the unfortunate Hawkins found himself in public 'disgrace' at court, the emperor informing him to 'not looke for any thinge att the Kings hands, alledginge unto him that hee had sent to Biana to buye the indico out of the Queenes Mothers hand, her factour havinge made price for itt'.[16] For the English, this gave a sharp signal that the queen mother and her trade were inviolable on pain of losing mercantile access and privileges in India. Thereafter, EIC traders took immense care to tread carefully around al-Zamani's ventures.

For Hawkins, however, the damage was done and the already faltering merchant found his cause swiftly toppled. Eventually, his allowance and provisions were stopped; of the £3,200 annual allowance allegedly promised, he seems to have only received some £300. Jahangir, who had once found in the newly arrived Englishman a curiosity and toy, had now tired of and discarded his playful distraction. Hawkins pleaded with the emperor to either reinstate him in his provisions or permit him to depart, likely in the hope he would relent. Instead, Jahangir informed Hawkins that he had free leave to depart, dismissing the merchant with neither trade agreement nor treaty for a factory to show for his years of trouble.

Returning to Surat empty-handed and with little to detain him on Mughal shores, the defeated merchant looked to return to England. He joined, along with his Indian wife, the fleet of Henry Middleton, sailing to Java, before transferring to the *Hector*, the ship he had led to India five years previously. In April 1613 the *Hector* arrived at the Cape. Throughout the journey Hawkins continued with his journal, however sometime after 20 May the entries come to an abrupt halt. Disease had struck and England's first official merchant envoy to India was among the many on the ship to succumb. His remains were subsequently taken on to Ireland where they were buried.

Hawkins's efforts in India, although initially promising, ultimately proved an unfortunate failure that ended in tragedy. Nonetheless, it was a significant step in the many England took towards establishing trade there. While his dramatic forays at the Mughal court are fascinating, the most captivating part of his residence remains to be told. The brash merchant navigator may not have secured a trade treaty at the Mughal court yet he did secure the affections of and marry a Mughal noblewoman. The union, arranged by Jahangir himself, was happy if tragically brief. Maryam Khan is among the most intriguing yet overlooked figures in the early history of England and India.

5

A Mughal Lady and an English Khan

I T WAS FAR from an auspicious occasion that prompted the Emperor Jahangir to take counsel with his most senior nobles. His eldest son, Prince Khusraw, had rebelled against the throne, seeking to claim it for himself. Neither was the prince alone in the intrigue, encouraged as he had been by his father-in-law, Mirza Aziz Koka, a senior noble-man and foster-brother of the late Emperor Akbar. For Jahangir, his son's treacherous exploits must have provoked markedly mixed feelings; betrayal no doubt, but also guilt. Jahangir had hardly spent his own years as crown prince in perfect obedience. Rebellion and an attempt to usurp Akbar's throne in 1599 remained fresh in his mind, and haunting echoes were now emanating from his own ambitious son. During Jahangir's rebellion a notable figure of authority in the Mughal royal household had intervened to save him from his father's wrath: Akbar's leading consort Empress Salima Begim had reminded the emperor of how desperately he had prayed for the birth of the prince and offered to manage a reconciliation between father and son. Akbar had relented, and Salima had gone on to seek out the wayward son and reunite him with his father.

Seven years later history seemed to have repeated itself, and Jahangir was less than keen on this bitter lesson. Khusraw certainly had not made too fine a point of it, declaring: 'I shall certainly not become more criminal by taking arms against Jahangir than he himself was in revolting against Akbar. If I offend, it will only be by following the example of my father.'[1] Upon defeat, his followers had been brutally punished while Khusraw's punishment had been meted out in kind: paraded in chains among his executed companions and then impris-oned, albeit later to be granted a degree of freedom to roam within the confines of the court.

71

Now his father sat among his courtiers at the *darbar* to seek counsel for the rebellion, and attention had turned to Mirza Aziz Koka. Some of the noblemen felt Koka deserved a swift execution for his role in the revolt. Like a repeat of the princely rebellion, reconciliation also found itself echoed in this moment as a voice rang out from within the palace: 'Your Majesty, all the Begims are assembled in the *zenana* for the purpose of interceding for Mirza Koka. It will be better if you come here. Otherwise, they will come to you!'[2] Salima Begim had arrived, complete with an entourage of leading Mughal royal women. Jahangir could hardly ignore the summons of so senior a figure and her formidable lobby, and immediately withdrew to wait on them. Their intervention and counsel prevailed as they convinced the emperor to overlook the recommendations of his courtiers and pardon Koka. No doubt the nobleman's closeness to Salima's husband Akbar played a role in the support given him from within the *zenana*.

Once again, Salima and her companions reveal the authority and influence of Mughal imperial women both throughout the empire and at court. From wielding immense wealth and economic author-ity to influencing imperial decisions, managing conflicts and broker-ing reconciliations, the Mughal *zenana* was a formidable force. And it would be within its walls that a particularly intriguing figure in England's historic relationship with India would be nurtured. Maryam Khan, a ward of the *zenana*, was the first Mughal noblewoman to marry an Englishman and travel between India and England. The traditions of the powerful household in which she was forged clearly emerged in her marital alliances.

Maryam Khan was a Mughal lady of Christian Armenian heritage. Her father, Mubarak Khan, was a respected merchant and courtier at Akbar's *darbar* bearing the rank of a thousand cavalry. Upon his death, relatives reportedly seized most of his wealth, leaving her a collection of jewels. She was taken in by the *zenana* as a ward of the imperial household; Salima Begim too may have kept the young girl under her watchful eye and care. Although bereaved of her father, Khan was far from friendless as she grew up. In addition to her networks in the *zenana*, she had a brother, mother, aunt and numerous other relatives to look out for her. She was a figure of noble descent and well connected.

Early in his residence at Agra, the intrepid traveller William Hawkins had gained increasing favour at Jahangir's court. This was fuelled by the emperor's insatiable curiosity over the cultural fluidity of a *firingi* hailing from distant northern lands who spoke Turkish. It was further bolstered by Hawkins's own admiration for the wealth and vibrancy of Mughal lands and his willingness to ingratiate himself at the *darbar* to further his prospects, including personally transforming himself at the emperor's behest. Like a puppeteer, Jahangir refashioned the English merchant into an Indian with titles and privileges, which Hawkins seized and embodied to proudly become the English Khan. Then in 1610 the emperor sought to complete the transformation with a further offering: an Indian bride. At this, Hawkins initially faltered, answering: 'In regard she was a Moore [Muslim], I refused; but if there could be a Christian found, I would accept it.'[3] In his ignorance, Hawkins admitted he 'little thought a Christian daughter could be found'. However, Mughal India and its imperial court were immensely cosmopolitan, home to vastly diverse religious, ethnic and linguistic communities, as is India today. Among them was a sizeable Armenian Christian community, from whom Maryam Khan's family hailed. Akbar had invited Armenians to settle in Mughal lands during his reign, and an Armenian church was established at Agra in 1562. It was far from difficult to identify a potential Christian partner for the English merchant when such an individual was then resident in the Mughal *zenana*. Khan was soon proposed as the match.

For Hawkins, the offer of marriage to an Indian noblewoman of the imperial household was a tremendous honour. Not only was it an opportunity for him to climb further socially in India, but it also presented the potential for making inroads in EIC trade negotiations via the connections of an elite Indian wife. Hawkins therefore readily agreed. Although records are silent on the matter, Khan would also have been asked and duly consented to the marriage. Mughal noblewomen exercised considerable personal independence and were forthright in their opinions on matrimony. Humayun's principal wife, Hamida Banu Begim, mother to Akbar, initially refused his proposal; it took forty days of persuasion, and the intervention and counsel of Humayun's stepmother, Dildar Begim, to finally gain her acceptance. Meanwhile, Babur's first wife, Aisha Sultana Begim, ultimately decided to leave him altogether. Like other

73

noblewomen of India, Maryam Khan too could have turned down the proposal of marriage to Hawkins.

With the couple's agreement secured, the marriage soon took place, Hawkins's serving companion Nicholas Ufflet leading the ceremony. Later, upon the arrival of a priest aboard an English ship captained by Henry Middleton, they remarried with the priest officiating to ensure a lawfully Christian union. The marriage of an Englishman and an Indian woman was not new, even for those early days of English travel to India. But the marriage of Maryam Khan and William Hawkins had a further distinction: not only was it likely to be the first instance of a union between an Englishman and an Indian noblewoman but in due course was the first case of an Indian noblewoman emigrating to England.

English travellers had been marrying Asian women from the moment they set foot in those lands. Although their travels were aimed primarily at forging trade partnerships, personal and romantic alliances were also often formed, and growing numbers of families born. This was true not only of senior EIC captains, such as Hawkins, but of wider EIC factors and employees as well as individual travellers and traders. Ralph Fitch's companion, the painter John Story, married an Indian lady and settled in Goa soon after his release from the Portuguese viceroy's prison. John Mildenhall had an Indian wife resident in Persia, with whom he had a son and daughter. On his deathbed in India, Mildenhall had beseeched a French companion to marry his daughter, although whether the Frenchman followed through on the promise is uncertain. Englishmen were not alone in marrying Indian women either; of Maryam Khan's own family, her mother married a Dutch merchant while her aunt married a Portuguese merchant. Meanwhile, of the Persian women who married Englishmen is one Lady Tomasin Powell, wife of Sir Thomas Powell; the latter had travelled to Persia and been in the employ of the Safavid shah, during which time it is likely that he met his wife.

While these unions crossed cultural and ethnic divides, they usually took place on the basis of shared faith. Hawkins had made a point of seeking a Christian spouse of Jahangir, subsequently marrying the Armenian Maryam Khan. Maryam Khan's mother and aunt would also have been Christian, like her, and accordingly married their European husbands on the basis of a shared faith. Although little is known of John Story's wife, that he was in the employ of the Jesuit order who were vociferously converting local Hindus suggests his wife was a Hindu convert.

Details of these early Asian wives generally tend to be sparse in the archives beyond the fact of their existence. Maryam Khan stands out as a case of an Indian wife about whom enough is known to construct a picture of her life and marriages. However, there is also the factor of class privilege; senior women married to senior men tended to be more visible in the historical records. Their presences emerge in the memoirs and letters maintained by spouses and colleagues, as well as the discussions and court minutes of EIC officials and directors, privileges less available to lower-ranking employees and travellers.

Written materials of the wives themselves may also survive, such as petitions to the English court. Of Tomasin Powell, sufficient historical fragments survive to construct a picture of her marriage to Powell, travels aboard the English ship the *Expedition* and birth of her first child, believed to be the first English infant born in India. It is also possible to identify Powell's associations with fellow English travellers and their wives, including another contemporary and prominent Persian wife whose historical presence is especially pronounced: Teresa Sampsonia (d. 1668). Sampsonia was the daughter of a Circassian Christian nobleman of Persia called Ismail Khan. Born around 1589, from the age of four she was raised in the Safavid royal household. On 2 February 1608 Sampsonia was baptised by the Carmelites, following which she married an English merchant and diplomat in Persia, Robert Sherley (d. 1628). Together they had a son named Henry, born in autumn 1611, whose godparents included the Prince of Wales.

Notably, Sampsonia's visibility in the historical records has less to do with her English husband, whom she outlived by a good forty years, than with her many formidable accomplishments over a long life. She was a polyglot fluent in up to ten languages, including English, an accomplished equestrian and a skilled archer. She travelled extensively between Europe and Asia; an impressive feat at a time when travel was especially treacherous and deadly. Her travels across Europe took her to Russia, Poland, Germany, France, Spain,

Portugal and Italy. In Rome she not only met privately with the Pope but had her portrait painted by the famed Flemish Baroque artist Anthony van Dyck, who would go on to be the chief court painter for England's Charles I. She travelled between Persia and Europe five times – one instance following the birth of Henry whom she and Sherley left in the care of Sherley's parents in England. She also travelled to India between 1613 and 1615, spending time in both the Portuguese and Mughal capitals.

In her capacity as a wife she deployed her skills in combat to save Sherley's life at least twice, once from Persian would-be assassins and a second time from hostile Portuguese traders. Not without reason did English traveller and state official Thomas Herbert (d. 1682) describe Sampsonia as the 'thrice worthy and undaunted lady'.[4] In England, she petitioned the court in favour of her husband when he was accused of imposture. Being fluent in English, it is probable the written petition was in her own writing. Although Sherley was officially a diplomat, she was referred to as 'Ambassadress of the King of Persia', placing her on an equal footing with her spouse.[5]

Significantly, Sampsonia's itinerant path crossed with that of a fellow Asian English wife, Khan. It is unlikely that the two women met in person, however. Khan voyaged from India to England in 1613 with Hawkins, the same year Sampsonia voyaged with Sherley from England to Persia. What is almost certain, however, is that during her stay in England Khan visited Sherley's parents, where she met Henry, Sampsonia and Sherley's son. These were women of a small and exclusive cosmopolitan circle with a commonality in their interracial marriages to travelling Englishmen. Their husbands often knew each other as part of a shared mercantile community. At the time of Khan's immigration to England, she was married to Hawkins. However, by the time she visited the young Henry Sherley she was partnered with a wholly different English merchant.

Hawkins and Khan seem to have had a happy marriage. This was certainly the case for Hawkins, who glowingly wrote of his new wife, 'So ever after I lived content and without feare, she being willing to goe where I went, and live as I lived.'[6] For Maryam Khan too, the union seemed a contented one, a fact particularly reflected in her willingness to remain by Hawkins whatever the circumstances. As her husband's standing at court started to decline from 1611, so too did the privileges he had enjoyed at the hands of Jahangir. Humiliation at the arrival of drunken English merchants in Agra and his own drunkenness at court combined with the mishaps of William Finch's conflict with the queen mother's trade to see Hawkins dramatically lose favour with the emperor. With this came the loss of allowance and provisions, a matter that would have profoundly affected Khan no less than Hawkins. For Khan, an erstwhile ward of the Mughal imperial household, a life of comfort would have been the norm and the loss of it would have been felt deeply. When Jahangir subsequently directed Hawkins to depart the court, the merchant left in some disgrace, his wife accompanying him. It was not the ending Hawkins had hoped for, nor likely one Khan had anticipated when she consented to the match arranged by the emperor himself. Nonetheless, she departed with her husband in a dignified manner.

Although Hawkins was intent on returning to England, members of Khan's family, including her brother and mother, were decidedly opposed to the prospect of losing her to so distant a land. Fearing they might never see her again, they insisted Hawkins take his wife no further than Goa. They also, somewhat presciently, pressed him to include Khan in his will should anything befall him, although it does not seem that Hawkins did so. Faced with this opposition, the couple – for one as strong-willed as Khan would certainly have been in on the plan – initially pretended to head for Goa before changing route and making for Surat where they joined the fleet of Captain Henry Middleton. The decision to voyage many leagues to a distant, entirely unknown and markedly smaller and less powerful kingdom, that too against one's family's will, would have been a particularly bold undertaking for anyone, let alone a privileged Indian woman who had enjoyed a life of luxury in the Mughal *zenana*. Khan's choice was certainly an indication of her attachment to her spouse. It was on this voyage that the couple were remarried by the ship's Anglican chaplain.

Upon reaching the Red Sea, they met with the fleet of Captain John Saris on its first English voyage directed to Japan. Hawkins, fresh from the first voyage to Mughal India and residence at the Mughal *darbar*, Saris on the first voyage to the court of the shogun in pursuit of silver for the Indies trade: theirs would have been a fascinating meeting. From the Red Sea Hawkins and Khan journeyed on to Bantam, arriving soon after Christmas, where they found the *Hector*, *Thomas* and *Solomon* preparing to depart for England. They joined the *Thomas*. Meanwhile, Middleton appointed another English merchant voyager to captain the *Hector*: a certain Gabriel Towerson. When the two fleets had met in the Red Sea Hawkins had encountered Towerson, and it is not unlikely that the latter also met Maryam Khan. It was a chance meeting that must certainly have left an impression.

The fleet headed for England in January 1613, reaching the Cape of Good Hope by April. From there it departed in May. Tragedy soon struck, however, as devastating disease swept through the *Thomas* with countless travellers succumbing. Among the fatalities was William Hawkins. Maryam Khan had experienced much tumult in her marriage, from disgrace at court to a surreptitious departure. Having weathered all with great devotion, she now found herself facing her greatest trial as a bereaved young widow aboard a foreign vessel en route to an unknown land many leagues from home. The prospect would ordinarily have seemed immensely daunting, but not for this resourceful Mughal woman.

By autumn the *Thomas* had reached Ireland. There Hawkins was buried at Waterford, the ceremony attended by Khan as well as the original officiator of their marriage, Nicholas Ufflet. The arrival of the first Indian noblewoman to those parts was thus overshadowed by the pall of bereavement. From Ireland Khan journeyed on to London where she forthrightly petitioned the EIC directors for financial support as Hawkins's widow and rightful heir. Yet while she may have arrived as a solitary Asian woman in these northern isles, Khan was not alone for long. Sometime between the burial of Hawkins and her meeting with the EIC directors to discuss her case, in the late winter, she had acquired a new fiancé. It was none other than Gabriel Towerson, captain of the *Hector*.

It is difficult to not conclude that the marriage of Khan and Towerson was predicated on a considerable degree of convenience. For Khan, a lone Indian woman in a distant foreign land, partnership with an English EIC captain similar to her late husband, and indeed one who was on friendly terms with Hawkins, must have offered a sense of security and support. For Towerson, a merchant seeking to advance trading prospects in the east, Khan presented an opportunity as a Mughal noblewoman who likely enjoyed connections and networks in India that could be of immense benefit to English trading efforts.

Towerson possibly also believed Khan to be a woman of wealth. Speculation already surrounded her fortune as a woman of the Mughal *zenana*, including her alleged possession of lucrative jewels and connections to the Mughal king. This notion was further bolstered by the potential of her inheriting from her late husband. Hawkins had made a great show of wealth, not only claiming the Mughal had bestowed on him £3,200 (£430,000 today) as an annual stipend and that he had profited substantially from trade, but that the Company owed him extensive payments. Further, unlike in India, women in seventeenth-century England were subject to the system of coverture, whereby all personal property was handed over to their husband upon marriage. It is no surprise, then, that Towerson was present to endorse Khan's cause as heir to Hawkins before the EIC directors.

On February 1614 the EIC Committee of Committees sat down to consider Khan's claim. Widows of EIC employees frequently petitioned the Company, particularly since wives and children were not permitted to join their spouses on the journeys east. This meant many families left behind in England ended up destitute or bereaved, turning to the EIC to relieve their circumstances or pay outstanding wages. Khan's, however, was no ordinary case. Not only was she a foreign Indian widow but she sought to claim the then astonishing sum of £2,000 (£268,000 today) for her late husband's expenses in India. In addition to drawing on Hawkins's prior claims of vast sums owed by the Company, as a noblewoman of India Khan would have been accustomed to a level of wealth not usual for the average EIC widowed petitioner. Her claim for so substantial an amount is therefore not all too surprising.

In her claim Khan was supported by Hawkins's brother, Charles Hawkins, who himself was submitting a more modest petition for £300, and her fiancé, Towerson. However, in opposition was none other than Ufflet, who had now turned against Khan and claimed that he knew her to be in possession of a collection of gemstones, including a diamond worth no less than £2,000, several smaller diamonds amounting to a princely £4,000 and numerous other precious stones.[7] Although initially believing him, the directors later withdrew their support for these assertions. Ufflet had been in service to Hawkins and the idea of a jealous spying servant who betrays his EIC merchant employer seems to have troubled the committee, who now called Ufflet's employment into question. Subsequently, the Company sent Ufflet to Jakarta as a scribe, with firm warning that he conduct himself honestly or he would be swiftly returned to England in reduced circumstances.[8]

Maryam's petition was not successful either. The directors rejected the 'extraordinary charges' demanded and declared that, despite Hawkins's claims, he was not owed substantial sums but was in fact indebted to the EIC to the tune of £300 for bringing his wife and household to England from Agra. Instead, professing their 'being charitably affected towards the widow, who is to be married very shortly', the EIC offered Khan a purse of two hundred gold sovereigns 'as a token of their love' with the caveat that 'a general release being given for all matters depending between herself and the Company'.[9] In short, she was to cease all claims in exchange for the payout. Having determined that this was the best that could be managed, Khan accepted the offer.

A week later, on 21 February, Khan and Towerson married at St Nicholas Acons parish church, the same day the two hundred gold sovereigns from the EIC arrived. In keeping with English law, Towerson likely pocketed the payout. Furthermore, although disappointed in her potentially substantial inheritance, Khan still presented an opportunity for productive networking in India, an aspect Towerson would seek to make use of a few years later. As the Company officials themselves noted, 'it may be for the honour of the Company if she shall signify their bounty and kind resort towards her, unto her friends in those parts'.[10] The potential to benefit from her influence in India was clearly a factor in the Company payout.

In the meantime, the newly married couple remained in England, Khan settling into a new life in a very different land. Although little is known of this period, it would seem that the marriage began well. Towerson was on friendly terms with Sir Robert Sherley, whose parents he visited at Wiston, West Sussex, almost certainly accompanied by Khan. That Sherley's wife, Teresa Sampsonia was, like Khan, a woman of an Asian royal household must have influenced the decision to make the visit. Khan and Towerson resided in England until 1617. It would have been an extraordinary and likely unsettling experience for the Indian lady. London was a far cry from the grand cities and tropical climes of Mughal India. Having been raised within the opulent halls of the *zenana* in one of the most imposing empires in the world, for Maryam Khan the dank and diseased capital of an underdeveloped island nation must have been a culture shock in the extreme. Gone were the carved red sandstone forts and marble palaces. Here she faced diminutive wood and plaster houses jutting out in awkward shapes. Sweeping tree-lined roads were replaced by narrow streets and crowded alleyways where sewage ran freely. Where humid Indian climes meant light cottons and airy silks were the foundations of a wardrobe, Khan now had to wrap herself in layers of stiff taffeta and heavy woollen cloaks to keep out the biting cold. The first year at least may well have been quite miserable as she attempted to acclimatise to living on an island where the warmest days of summer resembled the coolest days of an Indian winter.

On top of this, Maryam Khan would probably have felt quite alone and alien as an Indian woman in England. Maritime capitals like London did offer a degree of diversity as ships voyaging from distant parts came to port bearing travellers from across the world. English vessels alone were sufficient to see to this; travel by sea was such a perilous affair that by the time ships reached their destinations, many sailors had perished. New men would then be hired from foreign ports for the voyage back to England. By this a growing diversity of people converged in London drawn from the many destinations of the English fleets. East India Company vessels would have returned with crews hired from regions as far flung as Japan, Indonesia, India, Sri Lanka and Africa; in short, wherever they travelled, ported and traded.

Still, in the early seventeenth century Maryam Khan would have cut a largely unfamiliar figure among the English populace, particularly as a foreign woman. English maritime employees were men, and women aboard English vessels were a rarity. This was especially true in the early years and ventures of the EIC when the Company usually prohibited wives and families from voyages and limited their female employees to domestic roles on land rather than at sea. Fortunately,

Khan succeeded in making some friends, among them one Mrs Hudson, widow of EIC factor William Hudson (d. 1610). Her friendship with Hudson has been interpreted by some as an indication that the fellow widow was also an Indian lady. However, years of residency in England and marriage successively to two Englishmen would clearly have given Khan a command of English language and culture. There is little reason to think she would not have managed to engage with and befriend a fellow EIC English wife, like the similarly widowed Mrs Hudson with whom she had much in common.

In 1617, some three years after arriving in London, Khan and Towerson determined to return to India, taking passage aboard the *Anne*. Towerson was to resume his work as an EIC trader, this time hoping that his Indian wife's connections would prove profitable. For Khan it would have been a long-awaited opportunity to return home and visit family. On the voyage Khan was joined by two other women: her friend Mrs Hudson and her young maidservant, Frances Webbe. With women not ordinarily permitted on EIC voyages, the presence of the three was something of an anomaly. In the case of Khan, her marriage to a Company captain and the EIC's recognition of her as a potential networking asset likely eased her admittance on the voyage. Khan, however, would not wait until India to make the weight of her presence known.

Travel to India in the seventeenth century was dramatic enough on a normal day. A journey around the entire African continent and across the vast Indian Ocean was replete with perils, from treacherous elements to the violence of piracy and the ravages of disease. The voyage bearing Khan and her companions, however, was additionally marked for scandal of a proportion worthy of the stage. By the time the *Anne* reached the Cape of Good Hope, several months into the voyage, it became unavoidably apparent that Khan's servant, Frances Webbe, was pregnant and heavily so. The revelation caused uproar, not least because Webbe was unmarried and the culprit was clearly aboard the ship. In a profession worthy of Shakespeare, Webbe declared that she was betrothed to Richard Steele, an EIC factor on the voyage, who was father of the child. The exposed Steele dutifully stepped forward to claim his bride and child while the fleet's captains looked on aghast. Nathaniel Salmon, captain of the *Gift*, another ship of the fleet, recorded the 'strange accident which hath happened' where Webbe's 'belly told a tale that could no longer be hid under the name of a timpani [bloating]' such that 'I fear if she have not twins, she will hardly hold out to Surat'.[11] A remedy to the situation was swiftly found: with the support of Khan and overseen by Towerson, Webbe and Steele were married. The union was solemnised by the Reverend Golding, chaplain of the *Anne*.

Khan's support was critical in this outcome. As a senior figure, the wife of a captain and mistress of Webbe, her position held a weight that neither Webbe nor Steele likely enjoyed. Rather than be penalised for engaging in an illicit affair on Company time, Khan instead saw to it that the couple enjoyed a tropical on-location wedding hosted aboard an adventuring EIC ship. It would be quite the tale to tell the grandchildren. Khan hailed from a culture where women's marital agency was upheld, and this she must have channelled in her backing of Webbe as the latter announced her betrothal and child. The attachment of the two women continued well after the marriage, and in India they remained close.

The new Mrs Steele did ultimately manage to hold out until Surat, where she gave birth to a boy. The infant is believed to have been the second English child to be born in India. He was not to be the last; the Steeles were a fecund couple, and Mrs Steele bore consecutive children during her stay there. This was much to the chagrin of the English ambassador then posted to India, Sir Thomas Roe, who was struggling to ensure the besotted Richard Steele pulled his weight as EIC factor rather than be constantly distracted by his wife and family. For the Company and its ambassador, this was precisely the reason why employees were not permitted spouses while on their ventures east. As Roe bitterly wrote, 'she hath one child sucking (as they say) forward of another'.[12] The ambassador demanded that Steele return his wife to the service of Khan, to keep her out of the way of Company work. Steele overtly promised to do so, then secretly carried her off and set up house, complete with coach, seven horses, ten servants and even a palanquin. Roe, who detained Steele in his residence to extract an explanation, tersely reported that 'The excuse of all is affection'; there was truly no separating the smitten pair.[13]

The Steeles were not, however, the only source of chagrin for the EIC and Roe; a second related scandal was to emerge soon after the *Anne*'s arrival at Surat. The Reverend Golding had developed an intractable attachment for the three women who had voyaged on the *Anne*, and was now desperate to remain by their side in Surat. Whether the attachment was anything more than platonic friendship is unclear, but the pursuit of three women by a man of the cloth was sufficient to cause a stir. Golding was ordered back to the ship while Khan, Hudson and Webbe travelled on to Ahmedabad. Yet such was the chaplain's devotion that he went so far as to disguise himself as an Indian and sneak away unnoticed to join the women. For an English chaplain, tasked with ensuring the religious constancy of Company merchants in distant lands, transforming himself into an Indian in pursuit of three women was quite a scene. His was perhaps not quite the assimilative act of becoming Indian undertaken by Stephens and Hawkins, but it was diverting enough. The appalled Roe promptly sent Golding back to Surat, this time accompanied by other EIC factors. Yet, once again the priest gave them the slip and was away. 'The woemen and the indiscretions of Mr Goulding will suffer mee,' the exasperated ambassador lamented.[14] Golding seemed to have eventually cooled his ardour and sought pardon for his behaviour. The damage was done, however, and news of his indiscretions alongside those of Khan, Webbe and Hudson subsequently reached London.

Meanwhile, things were not well in the Towerson household. The captain, now accompanied by an Indian wife, expected to be a man of substance in Mughal lands, capable of making significant inroads in trade and amassing great wealth. His estimation of his wife's networks was high. Since departure from the Mughal *zenana* several years back, including an extended residence in England, Khan's royal connections seemed to have waned. No longer a ward of the imperial court, her respected father long passed and her remaining family not as consequential, Khan did not have as much to offer as her husband anticipated. Furthermore, she was no longer happy with her marriage, and the relationship grew markedly strained. The couple were described to 'fence one upon another, and are both weary'.[15]

By 1618, Towerson had tired of India and was determined to return to England. Although having willingly voyaged with Hawkins, this time Khan refused to join her husband, insisting on remaining behind in India with her family. This was much to the displeasure of Towerson, who subsequently returned to England alone. His wife was left the nominal sum of 200 rupias for her needs. The funds soon exhausted, Khan then turned to vociferously petitioning the EIC at Surat for maintenance as a wife of an employee. This reached such a point that EIC factors warned the Company that 'shee will breed much trouble to your factors at Agra and the court . . . is needful you take some course with hir husband for hir maytaynnance, or send for hir to him to avoid expence, trouble and scandall'.[16] However, the couple were never to reunite and Towerson never sent Khan any further support.

Some years later when Towerson died and his estate was adminis-tered, in November 1624, the merchant captain was described as unmarried. Khan, now widowed for the second time, was left with no recognition, no inheritance and no support. What had begun as a marriage of convenience had progressed to discontent and concluded in absolute estrangement. Nonetheless, while Towerson and his family failed to recognise Khan in his final days, her profound impact and larger-than-life presence in the early days of the EIC offers a fascinating insight into both the social dynamics of the Company and its factors in India, and the cultural transformations under way in England as a result of its increasing travel to India.

Maryam Khan was a product of the Mughal *zenana*. Even as a ward of the royal household, a respected if not notably prominent figure, her forthright confidence and will strikingly emerges through the annals. She and her fellow EIC wives provoked much grief for the English ambassador, for whom women were distractions and 'encum-brances' to be left in England.[17] Back home Roe himself had secretly married Eleanor Beeston not long before his departure to India, yet had left her behind in the care of an uncle. Yet, while the EIC wives and what he saw as their disruptive activities were a steady source of annoyance for Roe, the source of the ambassador's agitation lay with an entirely different woman in India. Throughout his embassy, Roe was at the mercy of the most powerful and influential woman Mughal India had ever known: the Empress Nur Jahan. Khan and her compan-ions were nothing compared with this most imperious of Mughal queens.

6

A Queen's Ransom

THE GREAT CENTRAL hall of Banqueting House in Whitehall, half a mile from the Palace of Westminster, hummed with intrigue on a frosty evening in February 1635. Designed by the celebrated architect Inigo Jones (d. 1652), the imposing Palladian-style venue was a centre of courtly entertainments performed for the monarch, his consort and the English elite. Performances at court were unique as often the monarch or consort themself performed in the lavish productions. Lit by the flickering glow of candlelight, that evening an elaborately conceived stage, also designed by Jones, had been erected ready to host a much anticipated masque. The gathered crowd of England's aristocracy and political class cast long shadows across the columns that lined the space as they craned their necks to get the clearest possible view of a shimmering stage of silver and gold. On that evening it was Queen Henrietta Maria, consort to the reigning King Charles I, who was to lead a cast of her ladies upon this stage. The production was an elaborate mythical offering from the queen's favoured playwright, William Davenant: *The Temple of Love*.

Charles I's reign was already facing the ominous rumbles of discontent. The king had a combative relationship with his parliament that often resulted in his suspending proceedings. In 1629 he had suspended it for an extended period, continuing as absolute monarch under what is now known as Personal Rule. This would continue until an uneasy and short-lived recall of Parliament in 1640. Discontent nonetheless continued to grow, eventually triggering the outbreak of the English Civil War, which would conclude with the dramatic execution of the king in 1649 upon a scaffold built outside that very same Palladian hall where he now sat eagerly awaiting the evening's festivities led by his queen.

Of the many things held against Charles I by his opponents was his choice of wife. Henrietta Maria was French and Catholic, and both facts marked her for suspicion in Protestant England. Over the years Charles I and Henrietta Maria sought to counter their critics by portraying an image of blissful domesticity; a king and queen in devoted harmony, a kingdom secure. The burgeoning fertility of the royal household served that narrative well; together they had no fewer than nine children. Portraits of the royal family were regularly commissioned, to be displayed in pride of place in key state buildings. For many in the kingdom, however, the king's evident attachment to his foreign and heretical wife was less than comforting.

Court entertainments were another means to further the credibility of the royal household, particularly among the social elite. These performances were often a political affair, the productions commissioned by monarchs to advance support for their rule. This was certainly true of Maria's performance that February evening in Davenant's sumptuous production. Interestingly, this beleaguered queen of England, distrusted as a foreigner and disdained as a Catholic, made a particularly noteworthy choice in the character she chose to endorse her right of rule in England: she performed as Indamora, a queen of India. While a French and Catholic consort was deeply distrusted by her English subjects, Maria knew an Indian queen was a figure sufficiently fabled and admired in English society as to be one worth channelling in her quest for validation. England had by then marked some decades of travel and trade with India. The wealth and commodities of the Mughals had become proverbial and well recognised. Alongside that, there was growing recognition not only of the political and imperial authority of the Mughal Empire but specifically of that wielded by their powerful queens. It was a recognition and respect that Maria sought to harness.

Among the attendees of *The Temple of Love* that evening was one particularly surly English politician and diplomat. 'The masque was yesternight performed with much trouble and wearisomeness,' grumbled Sir Thomas Roe the next day.[1] Roe perhaps had fair cause for such feelings, having served four abortive years from 1615 to 1619 as English ambassador at the court of Jahangir. His opinion of the masque echoes that often expressed during his residence in India.

Clearly the production struck a pained chord for the diplomat. Roe's embassy had been particularly marked for its struggles with the then reigning Mughal chief consort, Empress Nur Jahan. Recognised as Mughal India's most influential queen and co-sovereign with her husband, Jahangir, she directed the full force of her authority at Roe in his stunted attempts to further the English mercantile cause. The ambassador painstakingly recorded in his memoirs and letters his many struggles with the imperious queen whose imagination he consistently struggled to capture. It is no doubt, then, that the sight of the Indian queen Indamora, performed by England's Queen Henrietta Maria no less, did much to rekindle humiliating memories he'd much prefer to forget.

Of the many realities both John Mildenhall's and William Hawkins's residencies in India had established was the fact that the Portuguese were a considerable threat to English efforts there. From briefing the emperor and court against the English to attempts on Hawkins's life, the EIC soon recognised that more robust means would be required to make headway with the Mughals. The stumbling efforts of Hawkins were followed by those of EIC Captain Henry Middleton in 1610, which also failed to secure a trading permit. Following the arrival of Captain Thomas Best two years later, a limited permit was fortuitously received in January 1613. This allowed the English factory in Surat that had been tentatively established in 1608 to become permanent, and in due course factories in this and the surrounding regions formed the local bases from which the Company worked. The walled compounds housed storage facilities for goods as well as living quarters for EIC merchants. With a permanent base, the EIC finally had the foundation from which to establish itself in the Mughal marketplace.

Meanwhile, the adversarial Portuguese proved to be as capable of harming English efforts as they were at shooting themselves in the foot. The same year the English received their permit, the Portuguese lashed out by attacking the commercial enterprises of none other than Maryam al-Zamani. The queen mother, whose authority had been illustrated in minor fashion during Hawkins's residency when the outbidding of al-Zamani's agent at Bayana led to the English merchant's disgrace at court, would impose herself in far more resounding terms in face of the foolhardy actions of the Portuguese upon her vessel, the *Rahimi*.

Maryam al-Zamani, the most famous of the Mughal women ship-owners running vessels at time, was described by the English as 'a great adventurer'.[2] The *Rahimi* was her most renowned vessel and the largest and most recognisable of the Mughal ships crossing the Indian Ocean. Its home port was Surat, where the main English factory was based. John Jourdain records the ship to be of 1,000 tonnes, capable of boarding 1,400 passengers and carrying vast cargoes of merchandise. The Portuguese controlled the maritime routes of the Indian Ocean, enforcing a *cartaz* system whereby ships voyaging there were required to purchase a pass. Such was the size and influence of the *Rahimi* that the *cartaz* rate levied on her determined the going rate for other vessels. As one English trader responsible for setting rates observed, 'The ground that I had to work by was the sum formerly agreed on by general consent and that in the forenoon agreed on for the Remee [*Rahimi*].'[3]

From the earliest arrival of the English, the Portuguese had actively lobbied against them before the Mughals. Yet seeing the English continuing to slowly but surely edge their way in, the Iberian rivals became increasingly desperate. Things came to a head in 1613 with the Mughal approval of the English factory at Surat. The Mughal navy was the weakest of its military branches, a factor which aided the Portuguese imposition of the *cartaz* even on imperial vessels. On 13 September that year the Portuguese decided to show their hand in the realm where they held most sway: the Indian Ocean. Portuguese carracks seized the *Rahimi* along with all its cargo and some seven hundred passengers and carried it off to Goa. What made the move all the more audacious was that the *Rahimi* already possessed a previously negotiated *cartaz* which should have rendered it immune from attack. The Portuguese knew full well of the queen mother's standing and the significance of her commerce, and sought to leverage that in their competition for Mughal trade.

However, true to al-Zamani's status, the incident backfired spectacularly. EIC factor Nicholas Withington gleefully reported that the capture was 'soe odious that it is like to bee the utter undoing of the

Portungales in their parts, the King taking yt soe haynosly that they should doe such a thinge, contrarye to theire passe'.[4] Jahangir was livid, and his response was swift. He ordered a halt to all Portuguese trade through Surat, the capture of the Portuguese-held town of Daman and closure of their church at Agra. Further still, he suspended state allowances to all Jesuit priests in Mughal realms. Although piracy was a common reality of voyaging in the high seas, and Mughal ships were far from immune, the effrontery of the Portuguese attack on the queen mother's vessel, more so while a *cartaz* was in place, was not to be tolerated. The incident is the first on record to elicit such a harsh response from the Mughals, a reflection of the authority of al-Zamani in Mughal realms and especially in Mughal and Indian Ocean commerce.

Notably, although the Portuguese offered the return of the *Rahimi* on condition that the Mughals 'deliver the English that were here into their hands', they were refused.[5] The emperor was in no mood to negotiate on a breach that was beyond reckoning. Furthermore, Jahangir seems to have realised that the Portuguese threat at sea was in need of a check which the Mughals were not yet in a position to undertake. The emperor wrote an extensive personal memoir of his rule, in which he mentions the English only twice. One of these references remarks on their success in battle at sea against the Portuguese: 'Good news! . . . the defeat of the vice-rei . . . most of whose ships were burned up by English fire. Unable to resist, he had fled.'[6] It seems Jahangir had found his way to check the reckless Iberians. Although the Portuguese did eventually achieve 'a truce rather than a peace' with the emperor that involved the former paying the hefty sum of 300,000 rupees as compensation for their crime, the Iberian influence in India struggled to recover from the fallout. Conversely, the English presence grew; the fall of one saw the growth of another as balances were tipped. For the English, one lesson was profoundly learnt at the expense of their competitors; that one does not infringe on the queen mother's trade. It was a warning they never forgot.

Yet, even as the English benefited from the foibles of the Portuguese, making substantial headway at the Mughal court in securing a permanent trade treaty remained a challenge. Merchant envoys, such as Hawkins, who lacked formal authority, necessary resources, and indeed appropriate diplomatic comportment that did not involve drunkenness, met with little success. A suitable representative seemed necessary to lobby for the English cause. So, in 1613 Company merchant Thomas Aldworth, writing from Ahmednagar, advised London to send a formal ambassador from the English crown to Jahangir's court to negotiate a trade agreement. The following year the decision was finally taken, on 7 October 1614, to send 'an Embassadour of extraordinarye Countenance and respect' to represent the English cause at the Mughal *darbar*.[7] Sir Thomas Roe, who had previously served as MP for Tamworth and was a member of James I's privy chamber, was selected for the role.

News of events between the Portuguese and Maryam al-Zamani had certainly reached the Company in London and Roe would have been well aware of it. What he was probably not aware of, however, was that the queen mother was far from the only powerful Mughal empress then controlling the reins of Indian commerce. While the Portuguese had faced a formidable matriarch in Maryam al-Zamani, she nonetheless paled before the reigning Empress Nur Jahan.

At St Stephen's Hall in the Palace of Westminster eight striking murals adorn the walls. Based around the theme 'The Building of Britain', the murals were curated to reflect great foundational moments in history that defined and built Britain's glory. Given they were commissioned in 1927, at a time when the British Empire was at its zenith, they speak to a contemporary sense of national greatness and exceptionalism. Among the vast works is one that perhaps speaks to a notion of where the foundations of Britain's greatest jewel in its imperial crown – India – reside: a portrait of Thomas Roe at the court of Jahangir.

This mural imagines and memorialises in a distinctive manner Roe's first presentation at the Mughal *darbar*, in January 1616. The English ambassador is presented with a confident and poised gait, standing almost level to Jahangir and looking him resolutely in the eye. In his hand is a letter from King James I, elaborately rolled into a scroll, which he is offering to Jahangir. Even as he is alone in a new land, standing before a powerful emperor and surrounded and watched by armed Indians, the ambassador is composed and proud. Meanwhile,

Jahangir, seated upon a strikingly low throne, is attentive, looking directly at Roe from his dais and reaching out with interest for the scroll being offered. The impression given is of a robust and confident embassy successfully establishing England's foothold in India. Furthermore, the suggestion is that these foundations were established solely by the actions of powerful men. In reality, neither perception is true.

Thomas Roe was a politician and diplomat, the son of a haberdasher and landowner. In 1601 he became an esquire of the body to Queen Elizabeth, and over the years his royal associations continued to grow. Upon James I's accession, he joined the household of Prince Henry and Princess Elizabeth, whom he served devotedly, becoming particularly close to the latter. His services clearly made an impression as by 1605 he had secured a knighthood and before long was appointed a gentleman of James I's privy chamber. He went on to be elected MP for Tamworth in 1614 during the short-lived Addled Parliament. Later that year the invitation arrived to become England's first official ambassador to Mughal India. In October Roe accepted the position, and within a few months the newly appointed English ambassador was ready to undertake the perilous voyage around the Cape.

The following February Roe embarked at Tilbury aboard the *Lion* as part of a four-ship EIC fleet. Contrary winds plagued the early months of the voyage, but the fleet eventually reached the Cape of Good Hope where it paused for a fortnight. Thereafter it continued on the final leg of the journey across the Indian Ocean. Finally, in the moist heat of high noon, on 18 September 1615, the ships dropped anchors in the warm water of the Tapti River off the coast of Surat. It was the final month of the monsoon season, and clammy moisture mingled with the searing rays of a sun at its height. An arduous voyage of some eight months had been exhausting, and the sight of land brought some comfort to the weary ambassador and his fellow travellers. Yet, they could not immediately disembark, for this was no ordinary EIC fleet. It bore England's first official ambassador and first impressions were key, especially for the austere figure who carried that title.

In his perfectly starched linen ruff and fine fitted doublet, Roe was a man of stiff morals and high ideals. He was deeply aware of his own respectability and especially that of his beloved monarch whom he represented. An oppressive voyage was no reason to let standards slide, and so the English fleet proudly marked the arrival of the ambassador with due pageantry. For the English in India, it was a momentous occasion. The ships displayed their most splendid regalia: striking crimson waist clothes were draped across the upper works and English flags flown with pride. As Roe's boat put off for shore, the fleet fired rounds while a guard of honour announced the ambassador's arrival with trumpeted fanfare. The crews stood to attention on the decks, reverentially acknowledging the ambassador as he passed accompanied by an entourage of the general, captains and principal merchants. Whatever the eventual outcome of this embassy, Roe had certainly aspired to the dignified portrayal crafted centuries later upon the wall in Westminster.

For the observing Indian officials, however, the event was an altogether different affair. Upon arrival, a mollified Roe complained that 'at this name of an ambassador, they laughed one upon another: it being become so ridiculous, so many having assumed that title and not performed the office'.[8] Roe may have been the first authentic ambassador to the Mughal court, but the English traders who had preceded him had often falsely claimed the ambassadorial role, then spectacularly failed to perform it. Perhaps the biggest culprit in this respect was Hawkins, whose ambassadorial pretence had lasted years, but he was by no means the only one. From Mildenhall to Middleton, many had tried their luck with the Mughals. To the Surat officials, then, Roe was merely one more in a line of imposters hailing from an obscure and distant island to fumblingly seek mercantile favours in India. Indignity continued to beset the ambassador as Surat port officials first failed to show interest in receiving him, then repeatedly, even forcefully, sought to search the English crew and their belongings. Flustered attempts to exert diplomatic immunity ignored, Roe protested at 'how meanly an ambassador was esteemed at my landing'.[9]

It was not the most successful of arrivals, yet Roe continued with fortitude, travelling on to the imperial court in Ajmer. Although state officials had treated the ambassador with scant regard, Roe would be gratified to find civil respect, if not accord, at the *darbar*. Following a period of illness, on 10 January 1616 the ambassador presented himself before Jahangir. The surroundings of the Mughal court were characteristically lavish – and considerably distinct from that later depicted in Westminster: the emperor was seated at his decorative raised *jharokha* high above his subjects, resting upon soft carpets and silk cushions. Beneath him, court attendees were organised by rails according to rank. At the innermost, most privileged rail directly beneath the *jharokha*, shaded by velvet canopies, high officials and ambassadors awaited audience. Behind this, a second rail was set for Indian gentry, close to the emperor but of a lesser degree. Finally, an outer rail beyond the immediate court precincts was reserved for regular subjects.

In this hierarchy of access, however, was a fourth, less visible but most privileged space: the imperial household, or *zenana*, within the palace. A space exclusive to the royal family, including queens, princesses, princes, children and the emperor himself, it comprised the vast living quarters where the imperial household and its most trusted staff resided. Most significantly, it was the emperor's home where he rested and spent his nights. Guarded by armed female retainers and eunuchs and administered by a vast network of female staff, the royal household was perhaps the most exclusive and protected space in the entirety of the Mughal realms. None could enter it apart from those who resided or worked there; even the emperor's most senior ministers and officials were not permitted within its inner sanctum. Crucially, this meant the royal women of the Mughal household enjoyed exclusive influence over the emperor when he was at his most accessible, enabling the queens and princesses to advise and guide his decisions to the exclusion of his high officials. In this way Mughal queens and princesses wielded an overarching power behind the throne. The *zenana*'s prominent residents included the aforementioned queen mother, Maryam al-Zamani, and Salima Begim. The most renowned and formidable figure, however, was the Empress Nur Jahan Begim, chief consort and co-sovereign with Jahangir. Even at Ambassador Roe's very first audience at court, he witnessed Nur Jahan's overarching hand in Mughal affairs.

As emissary, Roe brought with him a selection of gifts from James I to present to Jahangir at the *darbar*. There was a set of virginals, knives, an embroidered scarf and a sword, but the principal item was a coach, lined in crimson China velvet, harnessed for four horses and complete with an English coachman. However, this costliest of English gifts proved inadequate by the Mughal's lofty standards. The emperor humiliatingly questioned 'whether the King of England were a great King that sent presents of so small value'.[10] He had the coach first keenly examined, both by his men and himself, and then proceeded to have it comprehensively refurbished to match the opulence of his court. Royal craftsmen pulled out the fading China velvet and replaced it with plush floral silk, lining the footwell with silver and replacing the brass nails with solid silver nails. The luxuriously refitted English coach was then presented to none other than Nur Jahan.

Not only was Mughal India's status as one of the wealthiest empires in the world visible in this deeply embarassing encounter; the rank of the empress – as true recipient of James I's gift – was also clearly established. It became clear that while Roe had been sent to Jahangir, it would in fact be Nur Jahan from whom he would need approval to further England's cause. This was additionally impressed on him when two days after Roe's appearance at court a royal messenger visited the ambassador at his residences to request the seal from James I for the empress to examine. Nur Jahan kept the document overnight, returning it the following day, in Roe's words 'with such care that the bringer does not deliver it but to my own hands'.[11] While the *zenana*'s chief resident may not have been visible to the ambassador, her influence most certainly was.

Mihr al-Nisa had married Jahangir in 1611, making her the twentieth and final wife of the emperor. Following their marriage, Jahangir granted her the titles Nur Mahal (Light of the Palace) and Nur Jahan (Light of the World). Aged thirty-four, widow of a governor of Bengal and mother to a daughter, she was experienced, astute and mature, characteristics she deployed as she rose to the position of chief consort. Her marriage had taken place during Hawkins's residency at court, and it would not be long before the latter felt the effects of the union. Within a year he reported that he had 'to seeke out for jewels fitting for the king's . . . new paramour [Nur Jahan]' to secure favour at court as 'without gifts and bribes nothing could either goe forward or bee accomplished'.[12] Roe referred to Nur Jahan as Jahangir's 'beloued wife . . . that wholly gouerneth him'.[13] Not only was she chief consort but her father Ghiyas Beg was grand vizier to the emperor and her brother Asaf Khan was a senior Mughal court official whose daughter was married to Prince Khurram, heir apparent to Jahangir. Collectively, the queen, her father, brother and Prince Khurram formed a formidable group, with Nur Jahan at the helm, that held sway over the emperor, the court and the state.

In Mughal India three acts were particularly identified as the exclusive privilege of the emperor, to be conducted in his name: the issuing of imperial *farman* (decrees), the minting of coins and the delivery of the *khutba* (sermon) at Friday prayers. Of these, Nur Jahan engaged in the former two. From their marriage in 1611 the royal couple ruled in partnership, and from 1622 to 1627, when the emperor's health declined, Nur Jahan took many administrative matters into her own hands. The empress's rise has often been associated by historians with Jahangir's ineffectiveness as ruler, a woman's rise being deemed a reflection of a man's inadequacy. This idea is probably drawn from Roe, who remarked as much in his memoirs. However, the authority of royal women in Mughal India was nothing new, a fact established from the many prominent and influential Mughal women who enabled and secured the empire, several of whom have already been mentioned in these pages. For Nur Jahan to rise to prominence and influence was therefore not unusual and all the more so given the devotion she and her emperor shared. Jahangir's memoirs are replete with references to his beloved queen, in his eyes 'the one I thought had more affection for me than any other'.[14] The emperor was content to share authority with Nur Jahan, who not only doted on him but was singularly intelligent, resourceful and capable.

In addition to her imperial authority, Nur Jahan's mercantile engagements were extensive. That she enjoyed great wealth is perhaps no surprise. She possessed vast swathes of land from which she collected tax revenue. She engaged in extensive domestic and international trade, and her officials collected duties at key locations including on goods transiting Sikandra before reaching Agra. Upon the death of her father, Jahangir ensured all the late grand vizier's lands, household and titles were bestowed on Nur Jahan rather than her brother. This mass of wealth and authority served to further establish her influence. She deployed her fortune and influence via, among other things, impressive architectural projects. A prominent example is the Serai Nurmahal constructed by commission of the empress in 1618 while the English embassy was then at court. A vast caravanserai located in Jalandhar, Punjab, en route to Lahore, the Serai Nurmahal is named after the queen who built it and lives up to her grandeur. It is built of brick and carved red sandstone, with a large and exquisitely embellished western gateway decorated with floral motifs, animals and birds. Its premises included an enormous court-yard to house animals and surrounding rooms to accommodate over two thousand travellers. The serai mosque is similar in design to the Begum Shahi Mosque of Maryam al-Zamani in Lahore, bearing a flat dome, arched entrance and arched windows covered with fretwork panels. The serai also included royal quarters for the emperor, who spent a few days there at Nur Jahan's invitation. An impressed Jahangir would describe the site as 'a fine palace and regal garden'.[15] For Dutch merchant Francisco Palsaert (d. 1630), the queen had a singular aim for such commissions: 'she [Nur Jahan] erects very expensive build-ings in all directions – serais, or halting-places for travellers and merchants, intending thereby to establish an enduring reputation.'[16] Patronage of architecture was certainly an expression of authority, and Nur Jahan knew this well. But in sponsoring grand caravanserais in particular, catering to merchants in their thousands at any given time, she also established a keen interest and investment in commerce. And this reality also fed her involvement in the affairs of the English trade.

Perhaps the most significant marker of the imperial and mercantile influence of the empress was an unprecedented minting of coins in her name, a practice no other Mughal queen undertook. These bore the celebratory superscription: 'By order of the King Jahangir, gold has a hundred splendours added to it by receiving the impression of the name of Nur Jahan, the Queen Begam'.[17] The coins began circulating in 1617, issued at royal mints across the empire, including at Surat where the English factory was headquartered, to join the bloodstream of the Mughal economy and indeed that of English trade in India. For the English, who struggled to trade in English goods, cash purchases were the primary mode of commerce. The Company imported silver specie which was then converted into coins at local Mughal mints and spent in India's markets. The empress's coins too would certainly have been among those minted and used by Company merchants as they plied their trade. Nur Jahan was therefore at the tangible centre of India's trade with the English, her rupias active in English enterprises and pulsing through India's commercial arteries.

Roe had initially believed himself subject to Jahangir, but soon discovered the embassy was in fact at the mercy of Nur Jahan. Not only did she acquire the carriage and procure the English royal seal to examine, but in October 1617 she declared herself official 'protectoresse' of the English, writing to Roe to declare his goods under her aegis, while her brother was appointed chief negotiator.[18] The English embassy became beholden to the empress and Roe's energies would be spent desperately seeking to secure favour by catering to Nur Jahan's demands. Fretfully the ambassador wrote:

> I feard I should drawe upon me the hate of Normall [Nur Jahan] the beloved queen, Ante to Sultan corrons [Khurram] wife, sister of Asaph Chan [Asaf Khan], whose daughter the Prince married, and all that powerful faction . . . the Power of a wife, a sonne, and a favorite, would produce revenge.[19]

He was not wrong in his observations of the 'powerful faction'; Nur Jahan, Khurram and Asaf Khan were indeed the most influential group in Jahangir's India. In his keenness to keep that faction at bay, Roe would direct the English factory to 'sell to the seruants of Normahall and her brother whatsoeuer may bee spared'.[20] Catering to the empress was central to gaining her approval and accessing Mughal trade, a reality Roe understood well.

An area that would play a prominent role in English negotiations was gift diplomacy at the Mughal *darbar*. In the highly regulated Mughal court, this tradition required the presentation of a gift to the emperor during an audience. Such was its importance that while Jahangir makes no mention of Roe in his memoirs, the English carriage the ambassador gifted is mentioned – the only other instance where the English are mentioned aside from their defeat of the Portuguese at sea. In fact, the *Jahangirnama* is replete with accounts of gifts, from those bestowed and received by Jahangir and Nur Jahan to those exchanged with wider members of the royal family, state officials, nobility, emissaries and beyond.

Unfortunately, in his four years in India, Roe's foremost struggle would be in impressing the Mughals with suitable gifts. The carriage was the single most valuable item afforded him, and thereafter he spent his time scraping together items in the fleeting hope of impressing the Mughals and gaining traction for his negotiations while desperately writing to the Company to send appropriate gifts. In misery Roe wrote that 'Here are nothing esteemed but of the best sort: good Cloth and fine, rich Pictures', lamenting at the 'little and meane' offerings the East India Company sent him.[21] To the ambassador's shame Jahangir would express amazement that Roe should be furnished with so 'little, meane and inferiour' presents.[22]

As the carriage proved, Nur Jahan was a central recipient for diplomatic gifts. Her brother, Asaf Khan, accordingly directed Roe to 'giue his sister Normahall some toy' to gain favour.[23] Roe in turn wrote to the Company that 'the Queene must be presented', listing favoured 'toyes' to send, including 'fine needle worke toyes, fayre bone lace, cuttworke and some handsome wrought wastcote'.[24] It did not help that given Roe's official status as ambassador, the expectations of gifts were 'ten times as much . . . now an ambassador was come, a great man, they should receive proportionable gifts'.[25] In short, it was simply not possible for the English embassy to cater to the demands; the English crown, presiding over already severely depleted coffers thanks to the extravagance of James I, offered nothing more while the Company could scarce match the expected standards. Meanwhile, the perils of failing were profound: the ambassador would be met with coldness from the empress, his diplomatic enterprise threatened. His despondence emerged in his writings: 'the neglect of her . . . I have felt heavily'.[26]

Ultimately, the presentation of gifts would be a prominent factor in the embassy's undoing. Roe's material inability to fulfil a custom so crucial to securing Nur Jahan's favour consistently served to undermine negotiations. And so, after just a few stumbling years plying the Mughal court with little success, Roe returned home without the official trade treaty that was the sole purpose of his mission. While back in England the Company sought to make much of their ambassador and his first embassy, in reality the mission was so unsuccessful that it would be eighty years before England attempted another.

Nonetheless, three centuries later Roe's troubled efforts in India would be idealised in mural form in a British hall of power; portrayed as a defining historic moment for England's foothold in India and a triumph of patriarchal diplomacy and power. Had Roe been in a position to be consulted, there is little doubt he would have disabused the curators of such notions.

A lack of means before an imperious queen was key to the failure of Roe's embassy, but true also was the fact that Roe possessed an intractable disposition that did little to further his cause. Throughout his embassy he refused to engage or entertain Mughal customs or cultures, insisting on retaining a thoroughbred Englishness regardless of the pitfalls. He resisted customary courtly greetings, rejecting them 'with some mislike' and 'saluted after my owne manner'.[27] Unlike Hawkins, he spoke no Turkish or Persian, relying on interpreters throughout his stay. He insisted on dressing in English attire, from stiff ruffs to taffetas that were wholly unsuited to sweltering Indian climate and frequently made him unwell. And, notably, he dismissed the courtly gifting tradition as bribery rather than recognising it as a cornerstone of Mughal diplomacy. This approach did little to appeal to the Mughals whose disposition towards Roe remained civil but otherwise indifferent. For Roe, however, representing his monarch was a matter of duty and pride and he was unwilling to compromise on what he saw as an English identity and comportment that appropriately reflected James I. Unlike Hawkins and Stephens, this was an Englishman in India who was singularly resistant to becoming Indian.

While the ambassador resolutely maintained his starched English self, during his stay in India another rather more eccentric traveller unexpectedly arrived from London. Thomas Coryate was a man familiar to Roe from their days spent at the Stuart court. Yet, where Roe was the embodiment of the stiff Englishman abroad, Coryate was a veritable chameleon adapting to his surroundings with an ease most unsettling for the ambassador. Hawkins himself paled before the transformative capacities of this latest arrival. Before long, Roe found himself deeply affronted – and somewhat jealous – of his guest. For the adaptable Coryate was soon showing Roe up at the imperial *darbar.*

7

The Fakir of Odcombe

IT WAS WITH astonishing speed that a decades-long crisis was dissi-pated. In the early hours of 24 March 1603 Queen Elizabeth I finally breathed her last. Sixty-nine years of age and having ruled for near half a century, for many of her subjects her lengthy reign was all they knew. More critically at this juncture, much of that reign had been spent fearing its end. Because the queen was unmarried and childless, and with at least a dozen claimants to the English throne, her passing could trigger civil war.

The queen's leading privy counsellor, Sir Robert Cecil, can take a fair share of the credit for what came next. For some years he had maintained a secret correspondence with Elizabeth I's godson and only child of Mary Queen of Scots, James VI of Scotland. Cecil recognised that James VI's claim to the English throne was strongest and that smoothing his transition was the best chance of avoiding bloodshed. As the queen's health failed, Cecil had the proclamation announcing the king's accession drafted by early March. On the day the queen passed, it would be he who read it at Whitehall and the gates of the City of London: the erstwhile James VI of Scotland was now James I of England. As the new monarch made his slow progress towards his seat in London, Cecil remained in the capital overseeing the queen's funeral and ensuring no outbreak of unrest before going ahead to meet the king at York.

James I reached London on 7 May to cheering crowds. The relief was palpable; a crisis of succession had been averted and the transition of power had been peaceful. The new monarch represented more than stability for the kingdom; he also offered continuity. Unlike his predecessor, James I was not in want of an heir. His firstborn, Prince Henry Frederick, for now at least, bore the promise of a stable monarchy and kingdom. While the king travelled ahead, the queen and crown prince were soon to follow. On 1 June, Henry, now Duke of Cornwall, and Queen Anne departed for England. Meeting with the king along the way, they reached Windsor Castle on 30 June where the prince was invested as a Knight of the Garter on 2 July. With the plague raging in the capital, Henry was then removed to the relative safety of Oatlands Palace in Surrey where his father set up the heir's first household. By the end of the year the trusted men and youths surrounding Henry numbered 141 with Sir Thomas Challoner as his governor.

It was at some point that year that a rather curious fellow also joined Henry's household. Thomas Coryate cut an interesting figure. Short with a small torso paired with a conversely large head and bulbous eyes, for playwright Ben Jonson (d. 1637) the diminutive man was 'an engine wholly consisting of extremes, a Head, Fingers and Toes'.[1] Appearances were matched with personality; Coryate was not only excitable in nature but given to extraordinarily dramatic and lengthy orations – extended speeches delivered complete with theatrical hand gestures and facial expressions. Hailing from Odcombe in Somerset, to his friends he inevitably became known as Odd Tom.

How Odd Tom ended up in the retinue of so valued a prince is anyone's guess. One suggestion is that he secured the position through the support of one of his patrons, Sir Edward Phelips, serjeant-at-law supported by James I and later Speaker of the House of Commons. However he came about it, Coryate's role in Henry's household bore little gravity; he was an informal, and likely unpaid, court jester. In that role his entertainments consisted as much in histrionics as wordplay. The young prince may well have found his energetic companion an amusement, but James I dismissed Coryate as little more than 'that fool'.[2] A fool he may have been, but hardly one to dismiss. For while Coryate began a jester he rose to be a remarkable traveller whose combined audacity and eccentricity made him unforgettable.

Among the countless taverns that dotted England's capital, one sought – and arguably succeeded – in distinguishing itself. The Mermaid, located on the north bank of the Thames in what is today central London's Cannon Street, was known as much for the quality of its food as for its exclusive clientele. The tavern benefited from its central position; near Bread Street, where many a rich merchant resided, and the famed Blackfriars Theatre, home to celebrated playwrights such as Christopher Marlowe and Ben Jonson. The landlord, William Johnson, was himself a business associate of Shakespeare. Although it isn't certain whether Shakespeare dined there, the Mermaid was a haunt of many of his most famed colleagues or 'wits', including Jonson as well as Francis Beaumont and Shakespeare collaborator and successor, John Fletcher. The literary elite dined, drank and mingled with worldly merchants; it is perhaps here that Fletcher conceived his play, *The Island Princess*, the first English drama to be set in the East Indies.

The Mermaid was particularly popular for guild banquets and with drinking societies, among them one aptly named Sereniacal fraternity, a society of wits. Deriving its name from the French for 'siren' or 'mermaid', the Sereniacs met on the first Friday of every month. Among the stewards was Laurence Whitaker, who had served as secretary to Sir Edward Phelips. On an evening in 1612 the food was abundant as the fraternity made merry in welcoming one of their more animated companions. Coryate had in all likelihood just completed one of his customary orations where he regaled his companions on the grand tour of the Continent he had undertaken in recent years. The journey, conducted largely on foot over five months and featuring everything from enraged gondola chases to a fascination for umbrellas, had been compiled by the self-styled Odcombian Legge-stretcher and published the previous year as *Coryat's Crudities*. It was prefaced by dozens of eulogies – including one by Jonson for 'Tom of Odcombe, that odde Joviall Author'. So popular was the publication that it enjoyed several editions and Coryate went on to produce a supplement within the year entitled *Coryat's Crambe, or his Colwort twise sodden*. While the *Crudities* was a primarily English publication, Coryate's oration at the tavern that evening may well have been delivered in a mix of the several languages he spoke – English, Latin, Greek and, most recently acquired during his continental travels, Italian. He was a performer by nature and did not undertake his calling by halves.

Desire for fame was like a burning flame beneath Odd Tom's outsized feet. His restless travels across the world in pursuit of it would be described by a companion as 'footsteps and flittings, up and down, to and fro', and the success of the *Crudities* did little to abate that fervour.[3] Having delivered this latest oration to the delighted roars and jeers of his companions, he was now to set forth on his most daring travels yet. It was at this dinner in 1612 that the Sereniacs created a mock passport for the traveller, complete with company seal and identifying Coryate as their beadle, this time to travel east. By the autumn Coryate was at Odcombe Cross announcing by yet another dramatic oration this latest and most daring of adventures: he was to travel for a full decade, walking – quite literally – across Asia. The aspiration was to follow in the famed footsteps of Tamburlaine. It would be a journey that led him to the lands of that great conqueror's descendants: Mughal India.

For Edward Terry, the East India Company chaplain who spent a period sharing accommodation with Coryate in India, 'while he lived [Coryate] was like a perpetual motion' and 'if [he] had not fall'n into the smart hands of the wits of those times he might have passed better'.[4] Coryate was indeed an excitable oddity who spent his life committed to restless movement across continents. While he travelled to many places, it was his sojourn in India that truly stood out. For one thing, he reflected the diversity of English travellers adventuring to Mughal lands. It was rare in those days of turbulent travel to venture far without a purpose that involved trade or diplomacy. Coryate stood out for seeking neither and in this respect he shared common ground with Father Thomas Stephens. Rather, the excitement of Tom of Odcombe and the encouragement of the Mermaid wits combined to create that most unique of historic figures: England's first tourist in India. Furthermore, like both Stephens and William Hawkins, Coryate was yet another early Englishman in India who sought to adapt, assimilate and identify with that fabulous land of cultural and material richness. In short, he too became Indian. But where Patri Guru and the English Khan walked, Coryate ran. The history of this traveller thus speaks as sonorously as his orations both to the range of impulses that inspired seventeenth-century English travel to India and to India's transformative qualities upon the English who managed to arrive there.

Coryate was a pioneer of travel writing. He made a career of travel for pleasure propelled by an insatiable thirst to see the world and secure personal fame in its dramatic retelling. And he was avaricious in his pursuit: in his *Crudities* he describes having 'Hastily Gobbled up' the countries he saw. As the son of Odcombe's rector, he was devoutedly Protestant and did not shirk from proclaiming it, making for some rather awkward encounters during his travels. Among Roman Catholics and Jews in Europe, he was wont to exuberantly proselytise to the point of personal danger. Similar outbursts in India led bemused locals to dismiss him as a madman. In this is perhaps another echo of Stephens, albeit while Patri Guru was a solemn missionary who brought many into his fold, Coryate's clamorous declarations did little to convince anyone.

Born around 1577 in Odcombe, Somerset, to George (d. 1607) and Gertrude Coryate, he completed his schooling and went on to matriculate at Gloucester Hall, Oxford, in June 1596, where he remained for three years. He had already established himself as an eccentric and a performer, and not long after entered the household of Prince Henry. Years later, in recognition of his benefactor, Coryate dedicated his *Crudities* to Henry and presented the prince with a copy. By 1607 courtly life seemed to no longer satisfy the Odcombian. Leaving Henry's household, in 1608 he undertook his first major expedition, the walking tour of Europe. His journey took him to France, Italy, Switzerland, Holland and Germany. In addition to a newly acquired command of Italian, he returned home five months later skilled in using a fork, a practice new to England. The pair of shoes with which he travelled – and was proud to point out as having only been mended once at Zurich – he solemnly presented accompanied by a grand oration to his local church of St Peter and St Paul in Odcombe, where they were hung up.

Coryate also carried with him the copious notes he took during his travels. He now settled down in Odcombe to carefully compile these into a mammoth 665-page travelogue, bearing the sensational title *Coryat's crudities; hastily gobled vp in five moneths trauells in France, Sauoy, Italy, Rhetia co[m]monly called the Grisons country, Heluetia alia`s Switzerland, some parts of high Germany, and the Netherlands; newly digested in the hungry aire of Odcombe in the county of Somerset, & now dispersed to the nourishment of the trauelling members of this kingdome.* The elaborate title page featured illustrations of his continental pursuits, from riding a sedan chair to being pelted with eggs. The enormous success of this book, both in England but also among English travellers abroad, brought about a new realisation for Coryate: while orations attracted attention, the true path to great renown was in adventurous travel and the publication of his experiences for the consumption of an enthusiastic audience. Europe, on his doorstep, had elicited an encouraging response; but the world was a vast place indeed.

In the latter part of 1614 Teresa Sampsonia and her husband Robert Sherley were to be found travelling out of Lahore in great state. Their entourage included two great elephants and no less than eight antelopes, and the dust billowed in great swirling plumes. They had just returned from visiting Mughal India and were now journeying to the Safavid court. As they neared the Persian frontier they were met by a squat, ragged and positively dishevelled man who seemed quite ecstatic to see them. Peering beneath the layers of dust they heard a familiar voice speaking the English tongue. The man was none other than Thomas Coryate, the famed Odcombian legge-stretcher and celebrity author of the *Crudities*. Whether they were quite as giddy to see him is uncertain, but the couple were certainly very pleased.

Sherley must have been especially enthused as he soon produced both the *Crudities* and the *Crambe* to show off, much to Coryate's delight. Such was the popularity of the publications that they now accompanied the diplomat on his travels in Asia. Coryate was also very excited to encounter the Sherleys' elephants. He had determined that as part of his wandering travels in India he would ride this great eastern creature and have an illustration depicting it in his next book.[5] In 1616 four of his letters from India were published as a pamphlet, *Thomas Coriate traveller for the English wits: greeting. From the court of the Great Mogvl, resident at the towne of Asmere, in easterne India*, complete with the now well-known woodcut of Coryate riding an elephant.

While Sherley flattered Coryate, Sampsonia, an accomplished and singularly astute woman, was far more practical. Surmising the straitened circumstances of the unkempt traveller, she generously bestowed on Odd Tom 40 shillings in Persian money (the equivalent of £268 today). At this the latter was more than a little appreciative, writing,

'both he [Sherley] and his lady used me with singular respect, especially his lady'.[6] He had been robbed of most of his money early on,
and this small windfall was like manna from heaven. Nonetheless, the
indefatigable traveller prided himself on his singular frugality, adapt-
ability to every circumstance and cheerful willingness to rough it
when necessary, often living on as little as a penny a day. As he travelled he had adapted to the region he crossed, learning its languages,
adopting its attire, customs and cuisine and befriending its peoples.
Nothing less would have sufficed for the extensive and difficult overland journey he undertook on a pauper's budget, from England's
familiar shores to the fabled Mughal *darbar*.

He had begun his journey on 20 October 1612, sailing for
Constantinople. Visiting numerous sites along the way, he finally
reached that destination in late March the following year. There he
developed a cordial relationship with the English consul, Paul Pindar,
who often included Coryate in state occasions. Spending ten months
in the Ottoman capital, the traveller developed a command of the
Turkish language that would serve him well on his continuing journey. In January 1614 he then voyaged to Iskenderun in southern
Turkey and from there travelled on to Aleppo. Next he journeyed to
Jerusalem accompanied by a fellow Englishman hailing from Kent,
Henry Allare. It must have been exhilarating for Coryate to undertake this greatest of sacred pilgrimages. No doubt his elation frequently
emerged in histrionic outbursts; his companion Allare must have had
quite a journey. Reaching Jerusalem in time for Easter on 12 April
1614, he remained there in the care of a Franciscan order of monks
visiting sacred and historic sites including Nazareth and Bethlehem.
He also had crosses tattooed on his wrists, as was common among
Christian pilgrims. By May he was back in Aleppo where he remained
until September to compile his notes on his travels thus far. This first
batch he sent back to England where they were later heavily edited
and published in 1625 in *Purchas his Pilgrimes*.

By late 1614 Coryate was ready to continue on his adventure, this
time through Persia towards India. He journeyed via caravans, a
common mode of travel in the region and an immense blessing for
Coryate as he traversed vast and often sparsely inhabited and mountainous terrain. Bandits and highwaymen were as abundant here in

Asia as in Europe, and often the caravans included armed guards or military personnel to ensure safe passage. Careful to avail himself of these roving groups, he travelled as far as they took him, then paused at major cities for the next available convoy. The caravan that took him to Persia was an astonishingly vast affair; 'a great mixt multitude of people from divers parts' – Ottoman officers to Portuguese traders, Egyptian priests and Syrian potters – snaking their way across thousands of miles of varying terrain.[7] No doubt Coryate flexed his linguistic muscles in such diverse company; that he also descended into his self-described 'linsie-woolsie orations' or 'extravagant discourses' is similarly likely.[8] For travellers wearied by extensive journeying, an entertainer in their midst must have been welcome amusement. Beasts of every description, horses and camels to mules and asses, were also among the vast numbers, bearing travellers by the thousands along with luggage, merchandise and tents. Where this moving mass paused, canvas cities mushroomed as tents and pavilions were erected and people made itinerant homes in the open fields. By this convoy Coryate made slow but safe passage, eventually reaching Tabriz, Qazvin and then Isfahan where he paused for a period of two months once again to collate his notes. These he left in that Safavid city, where they would be lost to history.

On 15 February 1615 he joined yet another caravan, this time destined for India. This too was enormous; by the traveller's own reckoning, 6,000 people were joined by 2,000 camels, 1,500 horses and 1,000 mules.[9] Progressing through central Asia in its company, he finally entered Mughal dominions where he met the Sherleys on the way to Lahore. Buoyed by the encounter, and furnished with Sampsonia's gift, Coryate was now quite ready to embark on his explorations in Mughal India.

Although Queen Elizabeth had granted the East India Company its charter in 1600, during her reign her attentions were directed, as we have seen, more towards the Levant trade. In addition to hosting an emissary from Morocco she also forged strong partnerships with the Ottomans, including appointing a succession of ambassadors to the Sublime Porte and maintaining correspondence with the sultan and his chief consort, or *haseki sultan*. It would be during the reign of James I that increasing attention was apportioned to the Indian trade, including the appointment of Thomas Roe as first official ambassador.

Within weeks of his arrival in Surat in mid September 1615, Roe set off for the Mughal court. Jahangir was at this time based in Ajmer and in the midst of overseeing military campaigns. Although not a committed expansionist like his father Akbar, Jahangir did direct more limited efforts, particularly in the Deccan, Mewar and Kangra. Campaigns were conducted by his generals and sons while he oversaw proceedings from his roving court. He had been based at Ajmer since November 1613, with a view to finally bringing to heel Amar Singh, the rebel Rajput king of Mewar, to the south. Jahangir had history with this maharana; his father Akbar had failed to successfully conquer Mewar due in no small part to Jahangir's own rebellions as crown prince. Now as emperor he sought to finally complete Akbar's vision – and perhaps assuage a little of his own guilt. Soon after his accession, Jahangir had dispatched his son Parviz to take on the Rajput rana without success. Subsequent campaigns over the years had also proved fruitless until now, declaring his intention 'to deal with the damn Rana Amar Singh', he had shifted his court from Agra to the nearer location of Ajmer.[10] From here he dispatched his son Khurram alongside veteran general Mirza Aziz Koka in a campaign that would eventually subdue the indefatigable rana.

Ajmer was some seven hundred kilometres from Surat, and the ambassador's journey was a protracted and difficult one, made lengthier by a detour stop at Burhanpur and the court of Jahangir's second son, Prince Parviz. Thereafter the small English convoy navigated its way through the extensive mountainous terrain of Rajasthan towards its destination, couched amid the ancient peaks of the Aravalli Range. By the time they arrived in late December, two weary months later, Roe was in such a state of failing health that he was carried in a palanquin and almost given over for dead.

Rest and recovery were undoubtedly foremost in his mind as he was borne to an awaiting English encampment on the outskirts of the town. It would have to wait, however, because among the East India Company factors there was none other than an ebullient Thomas Coryate. Since July the Odcombian tourist had been enjoying the hospitality of this EIC cohort in Ajmer. When news of the ambassador's arrival at Surat reached him, Coryate was delighted. 'Wee received newes', he wrote, 'of the arrivall of foure goodly English ships at the haven of Surat in India, and in the same of a very generous and worthy English knight, a deare friend of mine, Sir Thomas Rowe.'[11]

Roe and Coryate moved in similar courtly circles in London. While the latter had served in the household of Prince Henry, Roe was a gentleman of the king's privy chamber. Later, upon the marriage of Princess Elizabeth to the Elector Palatine, Roe had accompanied her entourage to Heidelberg. Coryate and Roe were thus well acquainted, and for Coryate at least it was a most welcome sight to encounter a colleague so far from home. It is difficult to say whether those sentiments were shared by Roe at this first meeting in India; as the ailing ambassador arrived, Coryate was ready with yet another lengthy oration to inflict upon his old friend. Not that Roe regarded Coryate's tendency towards histrionics as always disadvantageous; on one occasion Coryate took on the ambassador's mercurial Indian laundress who inclined to 'scold, rail and brawl from the sun-rising to the sun-set'. Subjected to Coryate's verbal barrage, within a morning she was 'so silenced that she had not one more word to speak'.[12] Indeed, Roe would later write warmly of 'Thom Coryat . . . whom the fates have hither sent to ease me, and now lives in my house'.[13]

Since his meeting with the Sherleys, Coryate had made steady progress through the Mughal territories, passing through Lahore and Delhi before reaching the capital at Agra. His accounts of this passage betray immense wonder; Lahore is 'one of the largest cities in the whole universe', he effusively declares, while the long tree-lined road to the 'verie great citie' of Agra is 'a delicate and eeven tract of ground as I never saw before and doubt whether the like bee to be found within the circumference of the habitable world'.[14] Just as India made a lasting impression on the traveller, so too was he intent on leaving an impression of his own. Five times a day the Muslim call to prayer, or Adhan, would be sonorously recited by muezzins (those who call to prayer) from the slender minarets that tower beside India's countless domed mosques. Predictably piquing the devoutly Christian orator, at Agra he took the opportunity to climb atop a building adjacent to a minaret, just as the Adhan was being recited, and bellowed in response 'La Allah illa Allah, Hazarat Isa Bin Allah!' ('There is no God, but one God, and

Christ is the Son of God!'), adding for good measure that Muhammad is an imposter.[15] Bewildered Indian spectators, for whom religious diversity and coexistence was as common as the rain, dismissed him for a lunatic. Terry later remarked with palpable relief, 'Happily . . . everyone there [in India] hath liberty to profess his own religion freely, and if he please may argue against theirs, without fear of an inquisition.'[16]

At Agra Coryate learnt that Jahangir and his itinerant court were then posted at Ajmer, and the traveller immediately hastened in that direction. It was upon reaching that town that he encountered his fellow countrymen, the small group of East India Company factors headed by one William Edwards. So far from English shores, a fellow Englishman was always a welcome sight, and Coryate was something of a celebrity thanks to the *Crudities*. Edwards and his cohort warmly welcomed the famed traveller, who was happy to take full advantage of their kindness. So much so that he took up residence with the factors and didn't shift for a full fourteen months. 'I abode in the house of the English merchants, my deare countrimen, not spending one little peece of money, either for diet, washing, lodging or any other thing,' he cheerfully wrote to his mother.[17]

Meeting with his friend Roe was a welcome delight, and the oration for that reunion was composed with care. But his long residence in Ajmer was in aid of another rather more distinguished audience and performance. Coryate had spent the year mastering the Mughal official language of Persian in preparation for his greatest oration yet; the one he would give before the Emperor Jahangir.

As he travelled many leagues from home, Coryate wrote letters to England in the hope that he would not be forgotten among his friends. The wits of the Mermaid Club, who had bestowed on him his passport east, remained especially high in his mind. Few of the Odcombian's writings from India survive, but among the handful of letters that reach us is one addressed to 'the High Seneschall of the Right Worshipfull Fraternitie of Sereniacal Gentlemen'. In it his signature is particularly wonderful: 'Your Generosities most obliged countryman, ever to be commanded by you, the Heirosolymitan-Syrian-Mesopotamian-Armenian-Median-Parthian-Persian-Indian Leggestretcher of Odcomb in Somerset'.[18]

Coryate was not simply a committed tourist but a shape-shifter, absorbing the cultures, languages and norms surrounding him, often to become almost indistinguishable. As he travelled so he assumed a degree of local identity; the Odcombian becoming Syrian, Persian and, finally, Indian. This we see indicated in his tongue-twister of a signature. To be so fluid served him well as the often destitute travel-ler depended on the generosity of strangers and the cheapest of local cuisine to survive his tireless eastern tour. Echoing his predecessors Patri Guru and the English Khan, in India he learnt several local languages, dressed in regional attire and partook enthusiastically of Indian fare. And like Hawkins, Coryate's chameleon-like tendencies seem to have appealed to Jahangir when a meeting finally took place.

Even as military campaigns raged, Jahangir maintained a daily audience with his subjects at Ajmer's Akbari Fort. One September day, three years after his move to the city, he entered the small *jharokha* as usual. Monsoon rains had eased the summer heat but brought with them an uncomfortable humidity. Attendants on either side gently fanned him with peacock feather fans, offering some much needed relief. Jahangir spent much of these audiences in a degree of boredom as a steady stream of petitioners of every description approached below. Businessmen to beggars patiently waited before being admit-ted to make their case as their monarch looked impassively on. If anything, Jahangir's mind was on the battlefield, anxious that his generals and princes were making the advances he expected.

Today, yet another bedraggled figure was making his way up to the *jharokha*. The fellow seemed one of the sprightly ones, an unmistak-able spring visible in his step as he eagerly approached from below. Meeting the emperor and the potential for largesse was often cause for excitement. However, when the man finally spoke, he stood out as a curiosity; his accent was foreign, akin to those English *firangis* who travelled to India from the far north. But, unlike many of them, this Englishman was dressed in Indian garb and spouted enthusiastic, if broken, Persian. Furthermore, he didn't seem the least interested in trade. As Jahangir watched the intriguing figure, he may well have recalled that other Englishman once resident at his court who dressed as an Indian, spoke a regional language and for whom the emperor had procured an Indian wife.

As Coryate stood before one of the most powerful monarchs in the world, many emotions must have overcome him, but stage fright was certainly not one of them. With dramatic flourish he proceeded to deliver a winding oration in ill-constructed Persian, his well-practised sonorous voice rising and dipping as his arms dramatically swept through the air. Ingratiatingly praising the emperor, the traveller proceeded to present himself as a *faqir-darvish*, proudly declaring the latest local identities he had assumed: a pauper and a travelling ascetic. Just as it had been with Hawkins, Jahangir's curiosity for this slippery Englishman was piqued and he was undoubtedly amused. Once Coryate had completed his lengthy performance the emperor rewarded him liberally, dropping a bag clinking with a hundred silver rupees, the equivalent of twelve pounds and ten shillings (£1,676.20 today), down to the gleefully awaiting orator.

Coryate could not have been more pleased; not only had he succeeded in mastering Persian enough to entertain the emperor of India himself but he had also made a tidy sum into the bargain. His friend, Roe, however, was horrified. While the Odcombian embraced performance and a chameleon-like propensity to assimilate, to the stiff and proper ambassador to do so was nothing short of undignified. Roe soon gave Coryate a sharp dressing down, declaring it to be 'to the dishonour of our nation, that one of our countrey should present himselfe in that beggerly and poore fashion to the King . . . to crave money of him'. Unsurprisingly, Coryate did not take it well, retorting 'in that stout and resolute manner . . . that he was contented to cease nibbling at me'. It is perhaps unsurprising that a single performance saw a windfall for Odd Tom while four years of desperate efforts bore little fruit for the ambassador. While one traveller performed to his audience, the other singularly failed to do so. Had their roles been reversed, perhaps England's early fortunes in India might have been better assisted.

While Coryate held much hope for his continued journey and eventual return to England, it was not to be. Much as he proudly wrote of his strong constitution in his letters, lengthy travel in destitute conditions had inevitably taken their toll. In July 1617 he joined Roe at Mandu, where the ambassador and his entourage had taken up residence in an abandoned mosque. There a much weakened Coryate fainted by a pillar, Roe and his colleagues taking great pains to revive him.

By November the traveller determined to return to Surat, arriving the following month severely weakened by raging dysentery. Unfortunately, the ever-inebriated EIC merchants resident there extended their hospitality by plying him with English sack. Coryate, not accustomed to heavy drinking even in health, indulged freely in the long-missed beverage from home and deteriorated swiftly as a result. In December 1617 Odcombe's favourite son passed away long before he could embark on the final leg of his travels. The loss of the traveller was also the loss of his Indian notes. But the materials that do reach us, including his letters and accounts from fellow travellers, tell a remarkable tale of England's first tourist in India; a histrionic performer, rambler, shape-shifter and indefatigable seeker of fame who walked into the court of the Mughal as the latest Englishman to have transformed himself into an Indian. Some years after, English physician and traveller John Fryer (d. 1733) would write of a grave in Surat where lies 'Tom Coriat, our English Fakier'.[19]

PART II

Rivals and Riches

8

Amboyna

Thus have you heard what bloody deeds,
were late in *Indi* done:
To make us all in *England* heere,
with sorrow to thinke upon,
What sad misfortune should be hap,
To take our friends in such a trap.
Yet heaven lookes downe,
Upon poore innocent soules.
>   *Newes out of East India: Of the cruell and bloody usage*
>   *of our English Merchants and others at Amboyna, by*
>   *the Netherlandish Governour and Councell there* (1625)[1]

IT MUST HAVE been with mixed emotions that in 1618 Captain Gabriel Towerson watched the Indian coastline recede into the horizon. He had returned to the land of the Mughals the previous year with an Indian bride on his arm and immeasurable hope of good fortune. Maryam Khan was cause for much of his optimism. The captain had surmised that his wife, erstwhile ward of the Mughal royal household, would bring him abundant opportunities for elevation and enrichment by way of her royal connections in her homeland.

On arrival he soon discovered he had been sorely mistaken. Khan's connections with the imperial household had lapsed. Meanwhile, rather than finding riches and opportunities among her other friends, they pestered *him* for gifts. 'I am sorie for him and his little vanitie,' Ambassador Roe grimly remarked, 'hee thought to be esteemed here a great man.'[2] Poor prospects spelt discontent in the marital home and this became increasingly noticeable to those around them. Towerson's entitlement and disappointment met with Khan's frustration at a husband who built ambition at her expense. The couple sniped at each other and made scant attempt to conceal how little they enjoyed one another's company. When a dejected Towerson determined to return to England, Khan refused point blank to join him. And so he now travelled alone aboard an East-Indiaman, as Company ships were called, no doubt harbouring a fair amount of bitterness. Although leaving a small sum for Khan's expenses, once back in England he failed to send any further support despite Khan's vociferous petitioning, and they were never reunited. When he died, his will failed to even acknowledge his Indian wife, let alone leave her anything. Hell hath no fury like an English merchant disappointed.

Towerson did not return to Mughal India, but in 1620 he would be found on yet another voyage east, this time directed to the Indonesian archipelago. Initially based in Jakarta, he was eventually posted to Ambon, then known as Amboyna among the English. India may have been a disappointment, but nothing was to prepare the merchant for the events that took place on that tiny island on the north side of the Banda Sea.

Trade in the East Indies – a capacious term in that period that encompassed everywhere from Mughal India to Japan – was from the beginning a matter of European competition. Portugal had beaten its continental cousins when Vasco da Gama opened the route around the Cape of Good Hope in 1498. Once there, the Portuguese concertedly sought to control maritime trade in the region, retaining a hold for over a century. They proved a particularly formidable force in the Indian Ocean, where they conducted their protection racket in the form of the *cartaz* on all ships sailing there. Crucially, they controlled the trade in spices, those most lucrative and coveted of early modern commodities, which then grew exclusively in the East Indies. The most sought-after spice, pepper, was to be found along the Malabar Coast of south-west India as well as in Sumatra and Siam (Thailand). Cinnamon was the preserve of Sri Lanka's west coast. Nutmeg, mace and cloves were the rich crop of the Spice Islands, the volcanic archipelago of the Moluccas in present-day Indonesia. It was the pursuit of these fragrant treasures that had originally brought the Portuguese to those distant parts. And it would be these same treasures that brought their European rivals.

The East India Company proved to be a critical challenge in Mughal India, and the Portuguese were aggressive in their resistance, from lobbying the Mughal authorities to outright warfare. Nonetheless, the English made headway, defeating their rivals in a series of waterborne battles off the Indian coast with the result that even the Mughal emperor was forced to sit up. Of the rare mentions the English are granted in Jahangir's memoirs, their defeat of a Portuguese fleet is one. The rivalry – to the attentiveness of regional monarchs – continued in neighbouring kingdoms too. Since 1515, when Afonso de Albuquerque captured it, the Portuguese had controlled the strategic island of Hormuz. Located in the Persian Gulf off the Safavid coast, this holding allowed the Portuguese to control trade with Persia. In 1622 the East India Company partnered with the forces of the Safavid shah to overthrow the Portuguese at Hormuz. It was a remarkable victory, improving the prospects for English trade in Safavid lands, particularly in the lucrative commodity of Persian silks. Although England was then formally at peace with Portugal, the East India Company characteristically dodged accountability with its monarch for risking the accord by slipping James I a generous gift of some £10,000.

However, while progressively succeeding against the Portuguese, another European competitor was proving a far greater adversary for the English enterprise in the Indies, particularly in the Moluccan spice trade. The Dutch East India Company was a formidable adversary. Established in 1602, it out-resourced the English East India Company by a country mile. Founded with a permanent capital of £14 million, from the outset the VOC was granted extensive privileges by the Dutch government. It enjoyed an exclusive monopoly in Dutch trade in Asia, was exempted from import taxes and had been granted the right to establish armed forces, erect forts, engage in diplomacy and war as well as mint its own money. The VOC was tasked with targeting the competition from the very beginning; their first fleet was dispatched with instructions to lay siege to Portuguese strongholds, including at Goa and Malacca.

By contrast the EIC was a decidedly modest affair. Established by a collective of private merchants, it began with a petition to Elizabeth

I for a royal charter that took a year to approve. The Company went on to raise the comparatively paltry sum of £68,000 for its first voyage to Asia, of which nearly £40,000 was spent in the purchase and refitting of four second-hand merchant and privateer vessels for the voyage.[3] It would not be until 1657 that the Company secured a permanent stock and later still, after the Restoration, for its charter to be extended to the right to command armies, make treaties, wage war, acquire territory and issue its own money.

Superior fleets were another reason for the Dutch advance. The Portuguese had long benefited from the might and force of their fortified carracks that lorded over the Indian Ocean like floating castles. English fleets paled before a single grand *nau*. The VOC, however, commandeered a large and technologically diverse fleet of vessels fit to navigate a range of maritime terrains, engage in tactical warfare and take on the bulky nau. Here too extensive state backing emerged in a manner the English could only dream of. Until 1625 the Dutch government provided the VOC with all its required military vessels and equipment, directly seconded from an admiralty that was regularly instructed to hand vessels over to the trading Company. At its height, the VOC commanded 40 warships and 10,000 soldiers and controlled a fleet of 150 merchant ships.

In the theatre of trade and war, the disparity showed. Although Portugal had enjoyed a century of dominance in the East Indies spice trade, the seventeenth century saw that control shift decisively to the Dutch and its zealous VOC merchants. The loss of control in the early modern world's most lucrative commodity was keenly felt. In 1678 King Afonso VI directed his viceroy at Goa to send East Indies spices to colonies in Brazil in what would prove a largely unsuccessful effort to cultivate them there. Meanwhile, certainly in the first part of the century, the diminutive EIC struggled to match the VOC's advance. Arguably the Dutch had more to lose; the United Provinces was a fledgling nation seeking to establish itself independently of western Europe's greatest power, Hapsburg Spain. Trading companies became a means for the newly formed republic to establish, enrich and empower itself – as it certainly did. State and public backing combined with a consciousness of the costs of failure to produce a Dutch vigour that often eclipsed the competition from its European rivals.

Throughout the seventeenth century, much like their Portuguese predecessors, the VOC did whatever was deemed necessary to secure and retain a cut-throat monopoly in the East Indies spice trade. Producers were ruthlessly exploited to keep costs low while violently crushing resistance and competition was par for the course. Much blood was spilt in pursuit of the delicate prized commodities. Lush evergreen clove trees, several metres high, grew on the islands of Ambon, Ternate, Tidore and Seram. Spherical nutmeg and its crimson-laced wrapper, mace, were to be found sprouting from verdant trees in the Banda Islands. The greatest victims of these European colonisers and their pursuit of spice were inevitably the largely Muslim indigenous communities that endured brutal invasions of their lands and genocidal attacks on their people.

It took a particular kind of person to be mad enough to travel to the East Indies from Europe. The perilous voyage could take six months, during which time if storms or piracy didn't get you, disease often would. Shakespeare's Venetian merchant Antonio knew the dangers well as he fretted over whether his ships would be taken by corsairs or caught in a tempest,

> Which, touching by my gentle vessel's side,
> Would scatter all her spices on the stream . . .[4]

Overland, the journey was even longer and all the more treacherous. Desperation at his own religious persecution combined with a missionary zeal to lead Thomas Stephens on a voyage to Mughal shores. The sheer eccentricity of Thomas Coryate had the orater plodding cheerfully overland to India. Jan Pieterszoon Coen, governor general of the VOC (1617–23 and 1627–9), however, was an outright sociopath. In the early years, between 1605 and 1609, the VOC aggressively extracted agreements from local authorities at Amboyna, Ternate and Banda obliging suppliers to sell cloves, nutmeg and mace exclusively to them at cut prices. The Dutch Company also destroyed crop surpluses to their own requirements. These practices were taken to new heights by Coen, who added genocidal zeal to his colonial talents. In 1619 he occupied Jakarta, decimating the city and renamed it Batavia, the Roman name for Holland. Two years later

Coen took his butchery to the Banda Islands. The conquest he led there saw the slaughter, displacement or enslavement of some fifteen thousand Bandanese, the majority of the island population. This veritable extermination was among the largest massacres of indigenous peoples by Europeans in the period; an all the more shocking feat for a time when colonial depradations raged in the Americas.[5]

As they brutalised and burnt their way to a monopoly, the VOC established posts throughout the Spice Islands, including Malacca, Amboyna and Ternate, while establishing its headquarters at the rechristened Batavia. It further set up a fortified base at the Cape of Good Hope to oversee the safe passage of Dutch ships. Often these posts and fortifications were the uprooted existing bases of European competitors, usually the Portuguese. In 1623, as the English celebrated their victory over Hormuz just the previous year, the Dutch took the battle to the EIC.

By the second decade of the seventeenth century Gabriel Towerson was an old hand in the English eastern trade, particularly in the Spice Islands. Adventuring ran in his blood: his father, William Towerson, was a respected merchant and member of the Skinners' Company who had led three voyages to Guinea in the mid sixteenth century and was a principal promoter of the failed Fenton expedition; his brother, William the younger, a privateer who later served as director of the Spanish Company and the East India Company.

In early 1601 he had joined the first fleet of the East India Company, headed to the Spice Islands. The five ships commanded by James Lancaster were the flagship *Red Dragon*, *Hector*, *Ascension*, *Susan* and *Gift*. They voyaged in the hope of trading iron, lead and broadcloth in exchange for the fine spices that were exclusive to that tiny archipelago of the Far East. Soon after reaching their destination, the Company set up a factory at Bantam, in 1602. Towerson became one of the first resident English factors there, going on to serve as chief of the Bantam factory from 1605 to 1608. In 1609 he returned to England aboard the *Red Dragon*. He had clearly cultivated a taste for the spiced east as it was not long before he returned to Bantam, in 1611 as captain of the *Hector*. There he remained until 1613, when he returned, once again aboard the *Hector*, joining the voyage taken by William Hawkins and Maryam Khan, whom Towerson would later marry.

In 1618, as he returned to England from India leaving behind his wife and a fair amount of personal dignity, perhaps he thought of his earlier more successful expeditions. The first East India Company fleet he had joined had returned with an abundance of spices that spelt a windfall in profits. So, on 24 January 1620, when he was directed to proceed to Jakarta as principal factor, he must have been quite ready for the appointment, even as ominous rumblings of Dutch perfidies there were reaching English shores. In early 1622 Towerson was posted to Ambon where, by his own account, he was graciously received by the resident VOC governor, Herman van Speult. Towerson could not have been more approving of the man, declaring: 'I doe him butt ordinary right to place him in the first ranke of all the Dutch that I have bin accquainted with for an honest and upright man.'[6] The EIC president at Batavia, however, was prescient in his response to Towerson; van Speult was 'a subtle man therefore be carefull you be not circumvented in matters of importance through his desembling friendship'.[7]

Although competition in the east was rife, English conflict with the Dutch was by no means a foregone conclusion. Rather, the relationship was born in friendship; a shared Protestant faith and a concordant animosity for Spain often saw alliances forged between the two nations. During the Dutch Revolt against Spain that precipitated the Eighty Years' War, Queen Elizabeth I had vocally supported the Low Countries and many Englishmen signed up to fight for their cause. By 1586 English troops comprised up to 32 per cent of the army fighting for the United Provinces. Protestant Dutch refugees from the war sought and found refuge in England, becoming one of the largest foreign communities in London. By the end of the Twelve Years' Truce in 1621, English troops still comprised 23 per cent of the Dutch forces. For many in England, they were the saviours of the Dutch. No doubt this only furthered the English grievance and sense of betrayal at the events on the island of Ambon.

Aggressive competition erupted into outright hostilities between the EIC and VOC in 1618. The following year the traders were forced into an uneasy alliance by the Treaty of Defence forged in Europe in which the English were decidedly the worse off. In addition to being denied the right to build fortifications of their own, the EIC were granted only a third of the spice trade in the islands and half the pepper in Java, and further were expected to pay a third of the cost of maintaining regional Dutch garrisons. It was a humiliation, and an expensive one. The costs of maintaining VOC garrisons were exceedingly high and far from offset by the profits from trade. Between 1621 and 1622 the EIC procured cloves to the value of approximately £12,000 but their costs towards VOC maintenance stood at a crippling £28,000. The 1619 treaty proved so ruinous that the EIC was forced to begin contemplating a withdrawal from the spice trade. By December 1622 EIC regional president Fursland had directed the closure of several Company factories in the region and wrote to Towerson to prepare for imminent withdrawal unless conditions improved. Yet for the Dutch even this limited competition was too much; in the view of Governor Coen, the English had 'no claim to a single grain of sand on the coast of the Moluccas, Amboyna or Banda'.[8] Furthermore, while Anglo-Dutch violence was paused by the Treaty of Defence, deep-seated animosity and suspicion were only further entrenched. In 1623 that mistrust descended into bloodshed that turned the erstwhile allies into resolute enemies.

The Portuguese loved a good fort. As they voyaged towards the East Indies they populated their path with them. The brick structures sprouted along the African coast including at Guinea-Bissau, Ghana, Angola and Mozambique. Across the Arabian Sea and into the Indian Ocean, castles continued to spring up from Muscat to Mumbai. And on the paradisiacal coastline of Ambon bay was yet another fort, built by the Portuguese in 1576. In 1605, when the VOC captured it, they proceeded to transform it. The outcome was an imposing and well-fortified structure complete with four bastions, two gates and surrounded by a moat one and a half metres deep. The newly rebuilt and renamed Fort Victoria became the official residence of the regional Dutch governor, and in 1623 this was van Speult, the man so praised by Towerson. Within months of Towerson's glowing testimony, however, van Speult would conduct a bloody campaign against the English. The trigger for this turn of events was enquiries made of the Victoria Fort itself.

Among the men in the VOC's employ was a brigade of Japanese troops. On the night of 22 February 1623 a soldier named Shichizo felt the need to ask questions about the strength of the defences at Fort Victoria. It wasn't the first time either; the fort seemed to fascinate the man. By the next morning word had reached the governor and Shichizo was hauled before him. The terrified soldier's immediate response was to deny everything. When witnesses from the guard were produced, however, Shichizo was forced to concede; he had indeed been asking questions, but it was just out of curiosity and nothing more. For the governor, however, contorted in long-standing and deep-seated suspicion of his English competitors and jealous of his monopoly over cloves, far more was afoot. Why else would this man make repeated enquiries of his fort's defences? It was a conspiracy – it had to be – and the names of the co-conspirators must be extracted from the soldier at any cost.

Waterboarding, infamous today as a form of torture inflicted by the CIA in the so-called War on Terror, is far from new.[9] At that tropical fort four centuries ago a struggling Shichizo was tied spreadeagled to a doorframe. A cloth tightly bound across his mouth, VOC soldiers proceeded to pour water over his face. It would not be long before the young guard, spluttering and gasping for breath, submitted to a 'confession'. He was indeed part of a conspiracy to overthrow the Dutch. The plot was the brainchild of the English at Ambon, who were intent on taking the cloves trade for themselves. The main intermediary in the conspiracy between the English and the Japanese was an EIC factor named Abel Price.

With the confession now in his hands, van Speult assigned the investigation to his chief legal officer, Isaac de Bruyn, who proceeded to round up the remaining ten Japanese officers in the VOC's employ. He then tortured and bribed the men into corroborating Shichizo's account. On 26 February de Bruyn then went to work on the English, beginning with Abel Price, from whom a confession was soon extracted. The story that emerged was the fulfilment of Dutch fears; on New Year's Day the Japanese soldiers had taken an oath at an English house in a plot against the VOC. The aim was to murder the Dutch and overtake the fort. The chief instigator was none other than Gabriel Towerson, then head of the EIC at Ambon.

Rather than take the case to the capital at Batavia, as was standard procedure, van Speult decided to take matters into his own hands. On 8 March a tribunal was set up, presided over by VOC officials, to judge the case. Twenty-one men – ten English EIC employees, ten Japanese soldiers and erstwhile employees of the VOC and one man of mixed Indo-Portuguese descent responsible for overseeing the VOC's enslaved workers – were, predictably, found guilty and condemned to death. The very next morning the broken and weary men were marched to the front of the fort to the dull beat of drums. There they were executed by beheading, the work made swift by an executioner handy with a sword. The last thing they felt were the warm gusts of a promised tropical storm, which arrived later in the day to wash away their spilt blood. Most of the bodies were tossed into a mass grave while three Japanese and one English head were affixed to pikes as a stark warning to those who might ever consider threatening the VOC's pre-eminence. Among them was Towerson, once a rising star of the EIC efforts in the Indies, now a martyr for the Company in what would thereafter be known to the English as the massacre at Amboyna.

Imam Rijali (c.1590–after 1653), an exiled member of Ambon's north coast aristocracy and an Islamic scholar, well recalled the conflict between the Europeans resident on his island. In his *Hikayat Tanah Hitu* (*History of Hitu*) he wrote of how the 'English and Japanese's plan to betray the Dutch and their fort became known to the Dutch, who then killed them all'. For this Ambonese at least, there was some credence to the Dutch claims against the English and Japanese. For the indigenous Ambonese exile who had suffered much at the hands of the European settlers, the conflict was a welcome 'divine tribulation', particularly against a 'very cruel' Dutch governor whose brutality only resulted in further 'wars'.[10] Rijali had unfortunate familiarity with Dutch aggression. Following protracted resistance against the VOC, he had been forced to flee to the sultanate of Macassar. In his recollections he was clearly referring to the indigenous resistance at Ambon as the wars precipitated by van Speult's cruelty. However, his words were no less true for Anglo-Dutch relations, not only in the Moluccas but also back in Europe.

The incident at Ambon sent shockwaves through both England, where it was termed a 'massacre', and the Low Countries, where it was deemed a conspiracy. News reached English shores on 29 May 1624. It was poor timing for James I, who was then about to renew an Anglo-Dutch alliance against Spain. While he angrily railed over the murder of Englishmen, the king nonetheless chose diplomacy over war. It was an approach his heir Charles supported but his subjects and later historians derided. Instead, the battle was taken to the presses by the companies in protracted pamphlet wars.

The VOC were the first to print – and translate into English – their account in *A True Declaration of the Newes that came out of the East-Indies* (1624), which they distributed both at home and in England. In it they vociferously decried the English conspiracy against their colleagues. The EIC swiftly responded with several publications of their own, condemning the Dutch-inflicted massacre. Their pamphlet, *A true relation of the unjust, cruell, and barbarous proceedings against the English at Amboyna in the East-Indies* (1624), was supplemented with graphic woodcuts depicting EIC factors being tortured. Gabriel Towerson was portrayed as an honest man manifestly wronged by the brutal Dutch.

The incident turned into a cause around which English nationalist outrage rallied. Grievance and betrayal came together in the single loaded term, 'Amboyna'. It rebirthed the term 'massacre', previously referring to executions associated with religious persecution, as a broad term for mass murder in general, a usage that continues to this day. The fallout was enduring, ultimately turning the committed allies into sworn enemies and precipitating no less than three Anglo-Dutch Wars throughout the seventeenth century. Such was its afterlife that decades later, in 1654, Oliver Cromwell brokered a deal with the Dutch to finally compensate the descendants of the Ambon incident.

In the East Indies, however, the impact was of another kind entirely. Since the ruinous 1619 treaty the English had been contemplating a departure from the spice trade. The incident at Ambon only served to further this resolve. Although trade in the Moluccas did continue through the century, the EIC withdrew from Ambon and several other factories such that by the end of 1623 only the factories at Aceh, Jambi, Jepara, Macassar and Machilipatnam, on India's Coromandel

Coast, remained under the aegis of the English council at Batavia. Macassar was an especially valuable base; post Amboyna, the English switched to procuring cloves from this sultanate, where they were smuggled by indigenous traders rebelling against Dutch colonial enterprises in Ambon. This too was brought to an eventual halt when the Dutch defeated the Ambonese rebellion some years later. Between attacking its English competitors and crushing indigenous resistance, the Dutch retained a stronghold in the spice trade with an iron fist.

All was not lost for the English, however. The spice trade was just one part of their nascent mercantile mission in the East Indies. While the Dutch proved, for now at least, an indomitable force in the Moluccas, the Portuguese were on the retreat in India. Hormuz was cause for much optimism as the English now redoubled their efforts in Mughal lands.

9

Christians and Spices

THOMAS AND JOHN Smith – so they had named themselves – were exhausted. For 'John', the exhaustion showed, as did more than a little degree of boredom. France was familiar territory for a man educated there, and galloping across it at full pelt for a fortnight astride a less than desirable hired mount was challenging on a normal day. To do so disguised with a scratchy periwig and the simplest homespun French coat was quite another matter. His was the sullen discomfort of England's most glamorous fashion icon, whose ostentatious wardrobes were awash with intricate lace standing collars, sleek satin doublets encrusted with pearls and hats bearing magnificent plumes of heron feathers and glittering diamonds. It was a mercy that it was only March and the scenic south of France was enjoying the mild temperatures of spring. The height of a Mediterranean summer would have made an undignified journey all the more unbearable.

Not that the small matter of the weather would have prevented the two from their undertaking. This was a matter of the heart, after all – or so 'Thomas' spiritedly assured himself – and one must suffer gallantly for love. Unlike his fatigued friend, Thomas had remained decidedly chipper throughout their travels. Having lived a sheltered life in England, this was his first foray abroad, and he was enjoying every minute of it. After arriving at the French coast, the pair had passed through Paris, taking in the sights including that of the French king and his queen, sister to the powerful king of Spain. They'd also glimpsed – without very much interest – the king's sister, the petite and pale young Henrietta Maria. Continuing south past Bordeaux, they'd managed to reach the foothills of the Pyrenees on the Spanish border where a craving for meat saw them hopelessly chase after a herd of goats. Eventually, Thomas managed to make use of his skilled upbringing by shooting one down from astride his horse. Boosted by a hearty meal, the men soon cleared the border, eventually reaching their destination of Madrid. By 5 o'clock on Friday, 7 March 1623 the 'Smiths' were standing upon an unfamiliar doorstep owned by a very familiar English gentleman. Thomas rapped smartly upon the knocker while John lingered in the shadows.

When John Digby (d. 1653), English ambassador to the Spanish court, arrived at his front door, he nearly jumped out of his skin. There on his doorstep in Madrid stood none other than a positively ecstatic Prince Charles Stuart, heir to the English throne. With the giddy prince was the dashing and indefatigable meddler George Villiers, Duke of Buckingham, favourite of James I and boon companion of Charles. Their mission: for Charles to personally woo and marry the Spanish infanta Maria, thus bringing to a conclusion more than a decade of tedious negotiations to secure a powerful alliance with Europe's most influential royal house.

Born a younger son, the English throne was far from Charles's horizons as a child. His early years had been spent enjoying the attentions of a doting mother without having to bear the pressures of becoming king. Days before his twelfth birthday, however, all that was to change with the unexpected death in 1612 of his older brother and erstwhile heir, Prince Henry. Overnight the spare became the heir, and the hopes and fears of a nation descended on young Charles. This included the question of marriage, ever a matter of politics and bloodline rather than affection among western Europe's royal houses. James I had his hopes pinned on securing a Spanish infanta for his heir, and discussions with the powerful Hapsburgs had already been under way when Henry lived. These now shifted to young Charles and as early as 1613 efforts began to secure a Spanish match for the new crown prince. Inevitably for a political alliance – that too between leading Protestant and Catholic royal houses – the negotiations dragged, testing his patience and emotions. Each ebb and flow noticeably lowered and raised the prince's hopes for his prospective bride. Eventually he imagined himself quite in love, and by 1622 was finally out of patience.

The notion to undertake a mission worthy of a Shakespearean romance requires a wild self-assurance, and this Charles had in abundance. It was only furthered by an equally bold companion, who probably originated the idea in the first place and certainly egged the prince on. Between them they had decided that the obvious answer to the stalled formal marriage negotiations was to don wigs, dash across Europe to Madrid and win the infanta in person. Somehow, they even managed to convince James I, who followed the progress of his son and favourite with an indulgent eye, sending on robes for the pair, jewels for the princess and even preparing a ship with the wistful commission of bringing home the prince and his Spanish bride. And so, on that evening of 7 March a thoroughly bewildered Digby was left wondering what on earth to do with the royal heir he now had hastily hidden away in his bedchamber. Yet, the ambassador was soon to realise that, although securing a Spanish match in this manner was dubious at best, the diversion the English prince offered him in Madrid would prove useful in other ways.

News travels fast, and it wasn't long before the Spanish were aware of the arrival of their infanta's royal suitor. Both the Hapsburgs and the Stuart prince sprang into action, the next six months occupying them in a decidedly awkward royal courtship. It was, however, a fruitless pursuit for a Catholic princess who point blank refused to marry outside the faith and a Protestant prince with no intention of converting. For Digby, however, the courtship had proven a valuable distraction from a rather tricky situation. Not long before Charles and Buckingham's arrival, news had reached the Spanish court of the joint Anglo-Persian assault that had displaced the Portuguese from their holding at Hormuz in the Persian Gulf. It was a sizeable blow to Portugal's Estado da Índia, the pride of the Iberian nation. Philip IV, king of Spain and Portugal, had promptly hauled Digby before him for an explanation. The ambassador had done his best to smooth things over, insisting that the English had acted under duress from the Safavids. It was at the height of these tensions that Charles arrived on his star-crossed mission, proceeding to overshadow all discussions of Hormuz for the duration of his stay. By the time the dejected prince had returned to England, the prospective Spanish match was in tatters, relations with Spain strained anyway and Hormuz just one of many Hapsburg grievances.

For England, however, while a coveted royal alliance may not have materialised, the conflict many leagues away in the Persian Gulf was significant to their trade in Asia. The capture of Hormuz proved a key moment in the downward turn of the Estado da Índia. The subsequent decline of Portuguese power spelt a rise in English opportunities.

It is hardly a surprise that Portugal saw India as something of a birthright: it was the first Western nation to reach India by sea, spending the best part of a century to achieve the immense feat of navigating around the entirety of Africa to reach the coveted destination. Portugal's pursuit of India had been fuelled by a combination of mercantile aspiration and missionary zeal. An alliance of religious brotherhood was imagined with the fabled Prester John, Christian ruler of Ethiopia, and the Thomas Christians along India's Malabar Coast. Most importantly, however, it sought the most coveted commodity of the time, which was exclusively to be found in the East Indies: spices.

Europe had long been a consumer of the fragrant riches of the East. Spices were employed as much in culinary seasoning as in medical practice, their virtues extolled in a range of therapies. By the time the commodity had navigated the ancient trade routes to reach western Europe's spice capital at Venice, however, the cost of what was already a luxury product had inflated to excess. The overland route taken was lengthy and laborious, involving multiple intermediaries. Asian ships carried the goods from the Indonesian islands across the Indian Ocean and up the Persian Gulf or Red Sea. Reaching land, it was transported by Arab traders across the Ottoman territories and North Africa; and then via Genoese or Venetian galleys across the Mediterranean to Italy, to finally be distributed across Europe. Each stage in this journey saw the price buffeted upwards until western Europeans – at the bottom of the world's most lucrative food chain – paid the highest price. Held to ransom by Asian and North African merchants, western European traders dreamed of direct access to the spices at source, and of the untold riches to be made by those that opened up the route.

Portuguese explorations began in the early fifteenth century when Prince Henry the Navigator (d. 1460) oversaw an annual dispatch of exploratory expeditions to the Atlantic and the African coast. The aim was to identify a direct route by sea to the Indies, whether that be by circumnavigating the globe in a westward direction – Europe was still ignorant of the existence of the Americas – or circumnavigating the vast African continent. Portuguese caravels took to tracing the west coast of Africa in pursuit of the continent's farthest point. Smaller than the nau and with great sweeping lateen sails, the light and swift caravel was particularly suited to navigating contrary winds, making it the vessel of choice for pirates as much as explorers. Progress was steady but slow and many decades passed before navigator Bartolomeu Dias successfully sailed his caravels around South Africa's Southern Cape to reach Mossel Bay in 1488. The continent had at long last been rounded to the south, and the possibility of reaching the source of the spices was now in sight. In the wake of Dias's voyage, the Portuguese would refer to the cape as the Cape of Good Hope, a name retained to this day.

Hope was still needed of course, as India was yet to be reached. That ultimate trophy would be claimed a decade later by Vasco da Gama who, with the sponsorship of his monarch Manuel I (d. 1521), rounded the Cape and reached Calicut on the Malabar Coast on 20 May 1498. After almost a century of exploration, the sea route to India was finally established. It heralded a new age of prosperity for Portugal, ultimately shifting the spice capital from Venice to Lisbon and rendering the small Iberian nation the richest in Europe. Manuel I styled himself Lord of Conquest, Navigation, and Commerce of Ethiopia, Arabia, Persia, and India. It was an exaggeration, of course, but audaciously so at that point. Da Gama may well have opened the path east, but his first entry to India was far from promising.

The Indian Ocean was mature and well-trafficked territory; a vast cultural contact zone long navigated by the countless nations populating Asia. Indians, Arabs, Malays and Chinese traversed the waters with native knowledge and skill. The Portuguese entered this space with the inexperience of newcomers, tasked with forging a place by trial and error. Their lack of knowledge was on abundant display from the outset: it took an experienced Gujarati pilot from Kenya to lead da Gama's fleet to Calicut. Once there, the Portuguese proceeded to misidentify the Indian residents as Christians, calling their temples churches and the artwork within of Hindu deities 'with teeth protruding an inch from the mouth, and four or five arms' as saints.[1] When the Portuguese produced the gifts intended for the local monarch – a motley collection of odds and ends comprising everything from hats to washbasins – they were laughed away. Things did not improve in the marketplace, where poor-quality Iberian merchandise did not fare well and they were only able to purchase small samples of spices and jewels. After a voyage of some eleven months, da Gama and his crew remained in Calicut for just three months before leaving for Lisbon in August 1498, but not before engaging in skirmishes with local vessels. By the time they began their voyage home, however, it was the wrong season for travel, resulting in a harrowing journey.

Nonetheless, the path had been cleared and the potential for prosperity was immense. As one North African at Calicut exclaimed to the new arrivals, 'A lucky venture, a lucky venture! Plenty of rubies, plenty of emeralds! You owe great thanks to God, for having brought you to a country holding such riches!'[2] A new age had dawned, and Portugal zealously espoused their mission, which they put succinctly: 'Christians and spices'.[3] As the Estado slowly expanded across the Indian Ocean so the Portuguese realised these objectives with a violent commitment.

Although establishing the seat of the overseas Portuguese government first at Cochin in 1503, in 1530 the capital was moved to Goa where it remained for the next four centuries. At its height the Estado da Índia extended from the Cape of Good Hope to Nanjing Bay in the East China Sea. This was far from uninterrupted territory, however. Rather, it was a disjointed scattering of trading posts in key locations functioning largely autonomously, with ultimate authority vested in the viceroy at Goa. Trade and territorial control combined with proselytising in these outposts, both backed by the Portuguese state. Spices were imported to the Casa da Índia (House of India) at Lisbon and Jesuits exported to the missions at Goa where a regional diocese was established by papal bull in 1533. Among the many missionaries exported was Father Thomas Stephens.

From their capital at Goa and numerous Asian trading posts, the Portuguese had policed the Indian Ocean and gained mastery over the spice trade, a position they sought to aggressively retain. The decades-long perilous campaign to secure the direct route had been hard fought, and they were in no mood to share the proceeds. The paradox of securing a direct path, however, was that it inevitably created competition. Other Europeans soon followed the new route by sea, no less intent on securing a share in the spices of the East.

Like most things in history, the rise and fall of the Estado da Índia was the result of a complex range of factors. What is true, however, is that its fall was brought about largely by external rather than internal factors. Although thriving for over a century in the Indies, in the seventeenth century a combination of European rivals and regional competitors brought an end to the Lusitanian dream. Regional challengers included Safavid Shah Abbas I (d. 1629), a steady line of Mughal emperors from Akbar to Alamgir I and the sultanates across the Spice Islands. Of European rivals, the Dutch were key in displacing the Portuguese from the spice trade, capturing Ambon in 1605 and over the years claiming Malacca, Macassar and the Moluccas. The Dutch success was perhaps especially galling, as these rivals hailed from a marginal northern European nation only recently born and so overrun with wetlands as to be referred to as 'the great bog of Europe'.[4] The fall of western Europe's greatest empire in Asia to these upstarts must have smarted more than a little.

The English too played their part in undermining Portugal's presence in India, not to mention benefiting immensely from their rival's fall. If Dutch competitors spelt humiliation, the English conflict bore a distinct whiff of betrayal. Henry the Navigator's mother was none other than Philippa of Lancaster (d. 1415), daughter of John of Gaunt (d. 1399). Her marriage to the Portuguese king had confirmed the 1386 Treaty of Windsor that forged a historic alliance between the two nations. It further gave birth to an Anglo-Portuguese line, hailed as Portugal's Ínclita Geração or Illustrious Generation, that oversaw the exploratory efforts leading to the discovery of the Cape route. But all this would be forgotten in the fevered race to secure the Indian Ocean and win the courts and markets of the Great Mughal. This is perhaps illustrated most resoundingly by the capture of the Portuguese-held port of Hormuz by combined Persian and English forces in 1622.

On 23 January 1622 famed Arctic explorer William Baffin was to be found stealthily making his way across the rugged terrain of Qeshm

Island towards an imposing red stone fort. Located off the Iranian coast at the mouth of the Persian Gulf, the island occupied a prime position on the regional maritime trade and travel route. The striking fortress was located at its easternmost tip, overlooking an even more strategic landmass nearby: the teardrop-shaped, multi-hued island of Hormuz. Baffin knew the gulf well, having traversed its waters five years previously. An accomplished navigator, he had been appointed master of the East India Company ship the *Anne Royal* in 1617, tasked with plotting the coastline of the Red Sea and Persian Gulf. This he delivered meticulously, earning much praise for his 'pains and good art in drawing out certain plots of the coast of Persia and the Red Sea, which are judged to have been very well and artificially performed'.[5]

As he cautiously approached the castle he was once again armed with his mathematical tools, this time ready to take an altogether different measurement. The building that rose before him was owned by the Estado da Índia and had for some years been under repeated siege by Persian forces. In recent months the East India Company had entered a pact with the powerful Abbas I to overthrow the Portuguese strongholds in the Persian Gulf and thus end the Lusitanian control of maritime trade there. The 2,000-square-metre fort at Qeshm was the first target, and an East India Company fleet had arrived intent on levelling it. As guns were landed and positioned, Baffin had been dispatched to measure the height and distance of the castle walls. Unfortunately for him, as he assessed the walls for English range, he overlooked his own range from the Portuguese stationed there. As fellow Company men looked on from the coast, a resounding crack shattered the stillness and a plume of smoke erupted from the fort. Baffin was thrown into the air, his instruments scattering about him, then fell crumpled on the ground, blood pooling about his lifeless body. The navigator had been shot, the bullet piercing his belly and killing him instantly. Although remembered for the North American island bearing his name, it would be in the Persian Gulf at the age of thirty-eight that he met his end. There was no time to mourn the loss of a skilled colleague, however, and the Company pushed on in their relentless siege upon an already weakened Portuguese defence. By 1 February the fort had surrendered. Not long after, Hormuz would also fall.

At first glance, there would seem little to recommend Hormuz beyond the aesthetic. The volcanic island is mineral rich, rendering it a stunning multicoloured landscape in shades of terracotta and ochre set against the encircling azure sea. However, its iron-rich soil is too saline and acidic for vegetation while fresh water is wholly absent. The weather is an unforgiving mix of intense heat and minimal rainfall. What marks this seemingly beautiful yet infertile plot of land for distinction, however, is its location. Positioned at the narrow entrance of the gulf not far from the coast of Bandar Abbas, Hormuz stands at the crossroads of maritime trade between Arabia, Persia and India. All vessels have of necessity to pass by it. This prime position made for the otherwise unassuming island's emergence as one of the most prosperous ports of the early modern world.

Merchandise of every description passed through Hormuz all year round, enriching the local rulers via the customs collected. The island was a hub for the region's most sought-after commodities: lengths of Persian silks and expertly bred steeds, intricate central Asian handicrafts, flawless East African ivory and those most treasured of Indian commodities, spices and finely woven textiles. All transited through Hormuz to be directed on south to the Indian Ocean, north over the Persian plateau and west towards the Levant. The island's population was as diverse as the vessels passing through its ports; the fifty thousand residents there in 1500 included ethnic Arabs, Persians and Indians. When the Portuguese entered the Indian Ocean they soon realised the centrality of Hormuz. In 1515 they claimed the island for their own, and for near a century retained control of it. Such was its prosperity that the Estado's customs revenues here were second only to those from Goa.

The success of the Estado in the Persian Gulf was owed at least in part to the instability of the Safavid Empire in its earlier years. Founded in 1501 by Shah Ismail, its first ruler, at the time of the Portuguese conquest of Hormuz the Persian kingdom was a mere fourteen years old. Furthermore, it had recently suffered a crippling defeat at the hands of the Ottomans in the Battle of Chaldiran that had shaken its very foundations. Already nursing deep wounds, the Safavids were ill-equipped to prevent a Portuguese advance in the Persian Gulf. Things were soon to change, however, with the rise to power of Shah Abbas I in 1588. The most prominent of the Safavid rulers, his was a transformative reign. Under his leadership the Persian military was strengthened, borders were secured, patronage of art was expanded and the capital moved from Qazvin to Isfahan, where extensive construction projects transformed it into a flourishing imperial centre. Perhaps most significantly, Abbas I sought to expand trade revenues for his nation. Among his first manoeuvres to that end was to turn Persia's lucrative trade in silk into a state monopoly. Securing free trade for the luxury textile was not a simple undertaking, however. Two Silk Roads served the enterprise, one north-west overland where the Ottomans stood in the way and another south-east via the Persia Gulf where the Portuguese at Hormuz blocked the path. A solution was therefore required to enable Safavid silks to pass freely.

Abbas I turned first to the overland routes. In 1598 he conceived of a plan to partner with European nations against the Ottomans and dispatched an embassy bearing letters to several European monarchs, including Queen Elizabeth I. There had already been dealings between Persia and England, albeit in limited form, by this point – the English Muscovy Company had travelled to Persia six times during the 1560s and 1570s. With the establishment of the Anglo-Ottoman trade treaty of 1580, however, English mercantile attentions were decisively shifted to the Levant. Since the Safavids were sworn enemies of the Ottomans, trade with Persia had the potential to harm the Levant trade, a risk Elizabeth I was not keen to take. Abbas I may well have saved himself a degree of trouble in Europe were it not for the arrival at his court of a singularly troublesome English privateer.

It was quite a roundabout route that had brought Anthony Sherley (d. 1635) to the Safavid court. Originally sent on a mission to Italy that proved fruitless, Sherley had travelled on through Venice and Constantinople, plunging himself into substantial debt along the way. Yet another Englishman to seek the solution to his troubles in incognito dashes across a continent, he disguised himself as a Turk and travelled overland to try his luck in Persia. With him was his younger brother, Robert Sherley. But although Robert eventually came to thrive on his Safavid connections, not least in securing an impressive partner in Teresa Sampsonia and engaging in extensive diplomatic travels with her, Anthony enjoyed a far less distinguished Persian career. Gaining an audience with the shah at Isfahan, he declared himself a cousin of James I sent as an official ambassador to the Safavid court. This grand claim was untrue, of course, but truth was rarely a matter to trouble the ambitious man.

Abbas I had by then already resolved to form an alliance with Christendom against the Ottomans. Sherley immediately latched on to the plan, recommending eight monarchs to approach. These suggestions the shah accepted, with the invitation that Sherley accompany the Persian ambassador, Hussain Ali Beg, on his mission. Although Sherley enthusiastically accepted the offer, during the mission he would steal the gifts sent for the rulers, including the Pope himself, murder a Portuguese friar accompanying the embassy to whom he owed a considerable sum, and desert the embassy mid enterprise.

Regardless of Sherley's misadventures, the shah's embassy continued its efforts in Europe, but only succeeded in securing a lukewarm response. Efforts to ease overland trade at the Ottoman frontier unsuccessful, the shah now turned to free the other route necessary for his nation's trade: the Persian Gulf. Initially the Safavids attempted to take on the Portuguese themselves. Abbas I laid repeated siege to the island, attacking in 1602, 1608 and 1616. In 1615 he successfully laid siege to the port city of Gombroon, displacing the Portuguese who had captured it a century previously, and renaming it Bandar Abbas (Port of Abbas).

Hormuz remained a problem, however. Displacing the Portuguese required superior naval power which the Persians lacked. A solution soon presented itself. As Abbas I's imperial biography, *Tārīk-e 'ālamārā-ye 'abbāsī* (*The History of Shah Abbas the Great*), records: 'a group of English foreigners . . . express[ed] their friendliness, sincerity and willingness to serve, in accordance with their dispute with the Portuguese nation, just as they differ from that race in general'.[6] Thus, a tactical alliance was forged between the forces of the shah and the fleets of the East India Company against a shared Portuguese enemy. In June 1621 the agreement was finalised with Edward Moxon, chief EIC merchant in Persia. The Company would provide naval power and the Persians would provide troops on the ground for a joint attack.

The arrival at Jask of an EIC fleet jointly commanded by John Weddell and Robert Blythe a few months later made it possible to deliver the newly signed agreement, and on January 1622 the Company dispatched four vessels to first lay siege to the fort at Qeshm and then Hormuz. On the Persian side, Imam Qoli Bey, governor of Shiraz, led a ground assault with ten thousand troops. The dated and limited artillery of the Portuguese garrisons was no match for the joint Anglo-Persian forces, and by February Qeshm had surrendered. By May Hormuz was also won, subsequently sinking the erstwhile leading port of the Persian Gulf into obscurity. In its wake Bandar Abbas, the fort favoured by Abbas I, rose to prominence. Meanwhile, the Anglo-Safavid pact founded a long-lasting relationship. Shah Abbas I went on to grant the East India Company its first *farman* for trading privileges in Persia, a permit which heralded over a century of commerce between the nations.

For the Portuguese, the loss of Hormuz, one of four key posses- sions of the Estado in Asia, was a resounding defeat and a marker in the terminal decline of their supremacy in Asia. After over a century of control, Portugal was finally on its way out, to the benefit of its English rivals. Yet even as the Estado licked its wounds, things were only set to get worse in the decade that followed. A new Mughal emperor was rising, and the Estado would feel the full force of his authority.

The Portuguese were early entrants to Asia, not only in European but also in Asian terms. The arrival of da Gama ran parallel to or even preceded regional players who would come to dominate in subse- quent years. While the Portuguese conquest of Hormuz was only a few years into the founding of the Safavid Empire, da Gama's arrival at Calicut entirely preceded the Mughal arrival in India. It would be nearly two decades later that Mughal founder Babur claimed his then landlocked Indian empire in 1526 at the Battle of Panipat. Another three decades would pass before the reign of Babur's grandson Akbar, who oversaw an expansion that extended the domain from the west- ern Indian Ocean to the Bay of Bengal in the east.

While Mughal power blossomed, the Estado maintained a wary eye on its increasingly powerful neighbours. The Portuguese foothold in Goa was far from secure but attempting a military challenge of so considerable a force was foolhardy. While the Estado pursued settlements scattered across the Indian Ocean, its efforts to influence the Mughals did not extend beyond futile Jesuit attempts at converting the emperor. Instead, it focused its energies on controlling the Indian Ocean trade with the might of its towering nau. The threat of Mughal expansionism on land, however, remained. To buffer themselves against this, the Estado sought accords with the neighbouring Deccani sultanates, who were active in resisting the Mughals. Their petitions extended to Chand Bibi (d. 1600), warrior queen of Ahmednagar, whose repeated repulsion of Akbar's forces in the 1590s became legendary. Following the passing of the queen, they sought an accord with the indomitable Malik Ambar (d. 1626), military commander and de facto ruler of Ahmednagar. Robed in austere white, a curved dagger at his hip and a long Deccan *dhup* sword in his hand, Ambar's presence was as imposing as his authority and skill. A member of the subcontinent's Habshi community of Ethiopian heritage, throughout his reign the commander remained a deep thorn in the side of the Mughals, especially that of an increasingly irate Jahangir. One can almost hear Jahangir's teeth grinding as he writes of 'the damned Ambar' in his memoirs.[7] Mughal historian, Muhammad Hadi, however, could not conceal his admiration for this indomitable Deccan ruler: 'Ambar was without equal in the arts of military command and strategy. He had consolidated the riffraff of that land as they should have been. He lived in glory until the last day of his life.'[8]

Not without reason did the Portuguese at Goa seek a strategic alliance with the man the Mughals could not subdue. The Estado was not, however, uniformly successful in protecting themselves from the Mughals. In a foolhardy move it had captured Maryam al-Zamani's ship, the *Rahimi*, for which Jahangir extracted a heavy price. Another example would be at the hands of Jahangir's successor, Shah Jahan.

In late October 1627, on his way to Lahore from Kashmir, Jahangir breathed his last. The final years of his reign had been spent in severe illness perpetuated by extreme alcoholism. Resolutely by his side, Nur Jahan had both nursed her deteriorating husband and managed the empire. As the emperor's health failed so the empress's imperial authority grew. Prince Khurram had been an ally of the queen, a key pillar of the powerful faction that had reigned over Jahangir and India itself. Eyeing Khurram for succession, Nur Jahan had even overseen the strategic marriage of her niece Arjumand Banu Begim (Mumtaz Mahal), daughter of that other factional ally Asaf Khan, to him. Yet, over the years the partnership had frayed. Nur Jahan subsequently shifted her sights to Khurram's brother, Shahryar, for the succession, and married her own daughter Ladli Begim to the young prince. But Khurram was not about to give up his claim so easily. Soon after Jahangir's passing he made sure to gain the throne as the new emperor Shahab al-Din Muhammad Khurram Shah Jahan.

The fifth Mughal emperor is perhaps most famed for his architectural feats, including the Taj Mahal, that great shrine of love for his wife Mumtaz Mahal. However, the stunning marble construction has done well to conceal both the tomb of the beloved empress and the caprices of her emperor. The rise of Shah Jahan was an exceptionally bloody affair. Having long desired the throne, in 1622 he arranged the murder of his elder brother Khusraw. Thus, beginning as he intended to carry on, once he became emperor in January 1628 he ordered the execution of all his key rivals and within a day the bodies of his brother Shahryar along with two nephews and two cousins joined the pile. This fratricidal rampage would set a precedent for Mughal princes, a trail of blood through history leading from the throne of Shah Jahan. Although his successor Alamgir I draws much criticism for the murder of a brother and imprisonment of his father, it is not difficult to see where Alamgir I drew his example. With Shah Jahan on the throne, Nur Jahan's authority was extinguished, and the once powerful queen spent her final days in Lahore with her now widowed daughter. Although diminished in influence, she continued her architectural patronage, building the white marble tomb of her father I'timād al-Dawla at Agra. This beautiful structure is seen as a precursor and inspiration for the Taj Mahal.

Much of the 1620s had seen Prince Khurram in open revolt against his reigning father, a matter of anguish for Jahangir, who had long lavished favour upon this son. Not long after the assassination of Khusraw he had refused Jahangir's summons to a military campaign in Kandahar and jealously seized lands belonging to Shahryar, who had been gaining increasing favour with their father. Eventually the rebellion escalated into outright war, Khurram's troops battling the imperial army against whom they were ultimately no match. Finally defeated, the prince fled east to the *subah* (province) of Bengal where the Portuguese retained a port settlement at Hooghly. There he sought the assistance of the Portuguese captain, Miguel Rodrigues, against Jahangir. Predictably, Rodrigues turned the prince down; assisting a rebel against the might of an emperor was far from wise. Although in that moment the Portuguese move was a pragmatic one, when the balance of power shifted on the imperial throne so too did the fortunes of their base at Hooghly.

The Portuguese had first entered Bengal in the early sixteenth century and over time the Bay of Bengal had grown to become a hub for Portuguese traders, both private and official Carreira da Índia (Portuguese East India Company) merchants. In 1516 Estado representative João Coelho was sent to the major Bengal port of Chittagong. The following year João da Silveira reached Chittagong with a small fleet of four ships, going on to establish a customs house there. From these early arrivals in the east the Portuguese presence expanded across the region to Sripur and Bandel in the west. By the 1530s the province became a buzzing centre of Portuguese commerce with a regular trading fleet sent annually. Although arriving with characteristic disruption and violence, in 1536 the Portuguese managed to advance their cause in Bengal by assisting Ghiyas al-Din Mahmud Shah, sultan of Bengal, to resist Afghan conqueror Sher Shah Suri. The sultan's gratitude translated into Portuguese factories and permission to collect customs at Chittagong and Satgaon. Of the commodities procured in Bengal were the famed regional cotton cloth, to be sent back to Lisbon, rice and textiles for inter-Asian export to the Spice Islands, and saltpetre for Estado munitions. Yet in parallel to this a further violent trade also grew up: many of the Lusitanian settlers in Chittagong were pirates and slavers. These corsairs partnered with Arakanese raiders to prey on Bengali communities along the banks of the Ganges and Brahmaputra, capturing Bengalis to traffic into slavery. The raiding flotillas became recognisable and feared, the pirates coming to be known locally as *harmad*, a corruption of the Portuguese and Spanish term for 'armada'.

As Portuguese trade in Bengali textiles grew, it caught the attention of Akbar, who in the late 1570s summoned Estado representatives to his court. The emperor subsequently granted a *farman* to establish a Portuguese settlement at Hooghly. By the end of the century this new port city was a flourishing hub and central holding of the Portuguese trade. For regional rulers, however, its rise came at an unwelcome cost. As one official Mughal chronicler, Abdul al-Hamid Lahori (d. 1654), grimly remarked, 'the markets of Satgaon declined and lost their prosperity [as a result of Hooghly]'.[9] Akbar's grandson, Shah Jahan, had kept a close eye on Hooghly. Since his days as a prince, he had followed Portuguese activities in the settlement with concern, particularly noting the Portuguese forced conversion of local people to Christianity, and 'resolved to put an end to them if ever he ascended the throne'.[10] The Mughals were wont to ascribe aggrandising religious claims to essentially political and imperialist causes, and Shah Jahan was no different. Moreover, bitter at his rejection at Hooghly during his princely rebellion, he had determined to avenge himself should he succeed in claiming the throne. Then there was outrage at ever-increasing Portuguese piracy and slave-trading, which terrorised Mughal subjects along the Bengal waterways. The Europeans needed to be brought to heel. This the emperor delivered, just a few years into his reign, at a historic siege in 1632.

The campaign levelled at Hooghly was a major intelligence and military operation of several months, later to be immortalised in florid narrative and art in Shah Jahan's official history, the *Padshahnama*. At the direction of the emperor, the sultan of Bengal Province, Qasim Khan, had dispatched his son Inayatullah with an army commanded by Allah Yar Khan to besiege and capture the settlement. Their mission was to take it by surprise; decoys were accordingly arranged, and rumours spread that the sizeable marching Bengal army was headed for Hijli along the banks of the Rasulpur River. Meanwhile, a military flotilla commanded by Khwaja Sher silently headed towards Hooghly from Sripura, ready to conduct a waterborne assault.

The Portuguese were caught unawares. As Mughal cavalry attacked by land, their warships, armed with cannons, musketeers and archers, formed a 'bridge of boats' to blockade Iberian vessels from fleeing by sea. A platoon of Allah Yar Khan's men made their way to a Hooghly building where a contingent of Portuguese forces were stationed, planting a mine. Upon detonation, the structure erupted, its inhabitants flung into the air like ragdolls. As the Portuguese sought to fight back alongside their Bengali boatmen, Mughal forces captured the latter's families, at which the boatmen swiftly abandoned their positions. For the Portuguese, managing a defence was as critical as biding time in the hope that an Estado fleet would arrive. Their musketeers fired with abandon, stripping the trees that shielded the Mughal ground forces of their leaves and branches. The attack was combined with overtures for peace and delivery of tribute to the tune of nearly 100,000 rupees in the slight hope of appeasing their foes and winning time. Burning Portuguese vessels scorched their way through the bridge of Mughal ships, although any Portuguese attempting to flee were nonetheless captured. The final outcome of the conflict, by Mughal reckoning, was staggering:

> nearly 10,000 of the enemy were killed, being either blown up with powder, drowned in water, or burnt by fire. Nearly 1,000 brave warriors of the Imperial army obtained the glory of martyrdom. 4,400 Christians of both sexes were taken prisoners, and nearly 10,000 inhabitants of the neighbouring country who had been kept in confinement by these tyrants were set at liberty.[11]

The siege lasted from 25 June to 29 September. For the Mughals, it was an exemplary victory against the Europeans, one worthy of immortalisation in writing and art. Alongside the official account, the illustrated *Padshahnama* includes a striking miniature depicting many of the dramatic details chronicled. Shah Jahan had not only conquered Hooghly but ensured his reckoning with those who had rejected him at his most vulnerable would never be forgotten.

Viceroy Linhares was entirely unprepared when Domingos de Seixas, a Portuguese settler from Nagapattinam along the Coromandel Coast, burst in upon him in late 1632 with news of Hooghly's fall. There had been no indication whatsoever that any of this had been in the offing. At Hormuz at least the Safavid shah's repeated attacks over the years meant the Portuguese were well aware of the ongoing threat. Not that they succeeded in protecting that crucial settlement from the subsequent Anglo-Persian assault, but at least there was the opportunity to try. The capture of Hooghly, however, was quite sudden. Although Linhares put on a brave face, valiantly reassuring Madrid of his 'hopes of being able to return and open these ports', the reality was that the settlement was gone and trade between the Estado ports and Bengal would never quite recover.[12] For the shaken governor, the reason was clear: several years before, Shah Jahan as the defeated rebel Prince Khurram had 'sought the aid of the Portuguese of Goly [Hooghly] who refused it to him . . . [and] expelled him'.[13] The emperor had taken his revenge. Yet this was not the only reason. The slave trade being inflicted on Bengal by Portuguese and Arakanese piracy was getting out of hand. By Linhares's own estimate, Chittagong was home to some two hundred Portuguese whose enslaved victims numbered eight hundred. By capturing Hooghly the Mughals could put a check on these activities and open the way to wrest Chittagong, the hub of the slave traders, from Portuguese and Arakanese control. While the capture of Chittagong would not take place until the reign of Alamgir I in 1666, the capture of Hooghly contributed to greater security for Bengali communities.

Hooghly was yet another blow for the Estado in a decade of many blows. For the EIC, however, each Lusitanian setback was a potential opportunity for English advancement. Although not always an active participant in the shifting fortunes of the region, the English could be savvy opportunists. They had certainly followed the events at Hooghly closely, with an eye towards benefiting from the fallout. With the Portuguese gone, the path for an English entry was opened up, and they were keen not to miss the opportunity. As one factor would fretfully write in July 1633,

> Those Portinggalls whilome exspelled Hugly hath found greate favor with Shawgahan [Shah Jahan], and reentered that place to the number of 20 persones . . . So that our exspecttacion [of] Hugly is frusstrayt, and . . . will n[ot by] us be obtainened.[14]

He needn't have worried; some Portuguese private merchants did continue to trade from Hooghly, but Lusitanian control of the area was irreversibly diminished. In their wake, the English began concerted efforts to acquire a slice of the Bay of Bengal trade. Within a year they had secured trading rights in Odisha from the provincial governor, Aga Muhammad Zaman, and set up factories at Hariharpur and Balasore in 1633. That same year EIC representatives at Agra petitioned for a permit to trade in the Bay of Bengal, which they received in February 1634. This *farman* opened a new frontier for mercantile wealth in the Mughal Empire's most prosperous province.

Things seemed to be looking up for English trade in India. But the celebrations would be premature. Back in England, clouds were gathering, and in the eventual storm they unleashed the EIC and its traders in India would be scrambling to survive.

IO

'A Loosing Trade'

THE MEN WORKED silently. Their wages for the day depended on how much they got done, and printing was difficult and meticulous work in seventeenth-century London. From carefully arranging the type pieces to the physical exertion of working the press itself, this task required immense patience and attentiveness. Not that their silence made for a silent workshop. Each stage of the printing process synchronised into an almost mindful hum. By a large open wooden case, split like a great jewellery box into dozens of compartments, albeit holding miniature metal letters or types rather than jewels, came the tinkle and clatter of the compositors. With astonishing speed, their deft fingers selected and arranged the type pieces on a composing stick, creating the text of the book to be printed, before sliding them in a single fluid motion into a long tray ready to be inked.

In the centre of the room a soft thud–thud–thud by the large manual printing press meant the beater was hard at work inking a tray with sheepskin–covered ink balls in preparation for a fresh batch of paper. Usually, this was a tricky task involving carefully inking a tray of hundreds of unstable type pieces, which had been set together as tightly as possible. At the moment, however, his was the easier job of inking a single large etched metal plate for what was to be a simple and unembellished title page. Inking complete, he gently laid a fresh sheet of paper over the text before sliding it into the press. The puller, arms toned by his strenuous vocation, was ready. Pulling the lever firmly, the press slid down with a dull thump, squeezing plate and sheet together with enough pressure to force ink to paper. Easing the lever to release the tray, the beater slid it smoothly out and removed the paper with experienced delicacy. There, in fresh glisteningly moist ink was the title of a new English rendition of a millennia-old book: *The Alcoran of Mahomet*.

Alexander Ross had followed events in England with growing alarm. It seemed to him that much of the nation had been gripped by a heretical fever, warring with each other as it was, in a conflict that would come to be known as the English Civil War. One side battled to remove the intractable and grasping monarch and establish a republic; the other sought to defend the king and the royal house. Ross was a committed Royalist to whom Charles I had granted the living of Carisbrooke on the Isle of Wight. For this man of God, opposition to the monarch who ruled with the divine right of kings was a matter of grave sin. This is likely what drew him to translating the Qur'an into English in the first place. As half the nation had taken a heretical turn, it seemed timely to illustrate for them the ways of Europe's largest 'infidel' community, the Muslim Turks of the Ottoman Empire. Perhaps that would show the Parliamentarians that their heresy in battling an anointed monarch even exceeded the disbelief of the Ottomans. Ross certainly did not mince his words, in his preface condemning 'so many sects and heresies bandied together against the truth'.[1]

The clergyman had made swift – and flawed – work of the translation. Not knowing Arabic, he turned to a French translation of the original by Andrew du Ryer (d. 1660), erstwhile French consul in Egypt, that had been published just two years previously, in 1647. However, by the time Ross's translation was complete, in early 1649, it was too late for the king. On the afternoon of 29 January 1649 Charles I was publicly beheaded, the execution taking place outside the great Banqueting House at Whitehall before a gathered crowd. It marked the start of the English Commonwealth. For Ross, the need to expose the Parliamentarians' heresy was now all the more necessary. On 7 May his *Alcoran of Mahomet* was published.

Inevitably, the publication faced resistance from the new authorities who oversaw a campaign of censorship. Printing was monitored minutely and theatres, often a platform for social and political commentary, were shut down. In September 1649, mere months after the appearance of the *Alcoran*, the new government issued an act against 'Scandalous, Seditious and Libellous Pamphlets, Papers and Books' that heavily and forcefully regulated printed materials. Despite this, Ross's *Alcoran* gained traction. It remained the only English translation for the next eighty-five years and was the first English Qur'an to be printed in America in 1806. But its most prominent role was as a text of the English Civil War, and a symbol that continued to shape Royalist propaganda. The same year the *Alcoran* was published an anonymous pamphlet play in protest at the regicide appeared, entitled *The Famous Tragedie of Charles I*. The play condemned the 'villains upon story / For having kill'd their king' and portrayed military leader Oliver Cromwell as declaring 'we two (like Mahomet and his pliante Monke) will frame / an English Alchoran'.[2] As late as 1659 Royalist satire condemned the Parliamentarian Sir Henry Vane as 'Alcoran Vane'.[3] In a deeply unsettling and turbulent conflict that was as much about the division of authority between monarch and parliament as it was about factions of Christian faith, the Qur'an became a powerful medium of dissent, imprinted, quite literally, in English national history.

Little of this religious wrangling mattered to the English overseas, of course, and especially for those in India. In the remarkably diverse Mughal lands, trading and engaging with a multitude of religious and ethnic groups were all in a day's work for English merchants, for whom profit was paramount. The English in India admiringly remarked on the religious tolerance of local people, a fact well illustrated by the muted responses to Thomas Coryate's repeated anti-Islamic outbursts. However, the revolutionary war between parliament and monarch in England sent a political earthquake convulsing through the nation that extended far beyond its borders to its overseas trade. The English merchants in India felt the full force of the fallout, scrambling to protect their mercantile project in the face of a distant turmoil over which they had little control.

Having shed much blood in acquiring his throne, Shah Jahan was soon to encounter one of the great trials of his reign, which may well have forced him to question the wisdom of his overbearing ambition. In the early 1630s famine struck India with a staggering force. Drought in 1630, loss of crops to locusts in 1631 and torrential rain in 1632 brought on a crisis of biblical proportions that saw millions perish and survivors turning to extreme measures, including the consumption of dog flesh.⁴ Gujarat, home to the port of Surat, was especially afflicted. Although Shah Jahan introduced a number of policies to tackle the crisis, including the provision of soup kitchens, distribution of alms and remission of tax, it made little difference. 'Those lands which had been famous for their fertility and plenty now retained no trace of productiveness,' grieved court historian Abd al-Hamid Lahori.⁵

Trade inevitably shrank in the battle to survive. Shah Jahan was deeply invested in international trade, commissioning half a dozen large freight ships and taking over the greater part of the maritime trade between Surat, Mokha and Bandar Abbas for several years. In Surat, the death or migration of calico weavers was a particular challenge for the EIC, who in turn expanded their freight business catering to Mughal and Persian traders to compensate for the shortfall in the textile trade. Meanwhile, the EIC persisted in its creeping commercial growth along the Indian coastline, negotiating trading permits with local authorities. In addition to advances along the Bay of Bengal, in 1632 it secured a *farman* from the sultan of Golconda enabling trade in his kingdom, a permit that was renewed in 1634. In 1635 the EIC reopened its factories at Vadodara and Ahmedabad to support calico exports to England.

The retreat of the Estado was a boon for the Company, and was furthered by a series of treaties with the Portuguese. In 1630 the Treaty of Madrid saw an end to hostilities between England and Portugal. In 1635 the Convention of Goa ratified an Anglo–Portuguese accord guaranteeing mutual cooperation in India, thus concluding thirty years of hostilities. English ships now carried Portuguese freight safe from Dutch attack while Portuguese ports were opened to EIC ships. The accord enabled the first EIC ship to venture to China that same year with the willing support of the Portuguese. The Company had sought direct trade with China since the reign of Elizabeth I, an aspiration that peace with Goa now made a possibility. EIC ship the *London* reached the Portuguese settlement at Macao on 23 July. Yet while the Portuguese only intended for the English to engage in freighting goods to and from Macao, the English sought to establish a factory at Guangzhou. This faced resistance from both the Estado and the Chinese ultimately preventing an English trade agreement being achieved with Guangzhou until 1716. Nonetheless, early connections with China were made that would later grow.

While treaties were signed and frontiers opened, back in England troubles were brewing. Much of this was owed to the actions of a most troublesome monarch. If a reign is to have a defining feature, a dogged tendency towards bad decisions may well be that of Charles I. Not content to battle endlessly with his parliament, the king decided to take on London's merchants too, by trying his luck in India. But rather than cautious steps in trade or diplomacy, he pounced on the nuclear option: privateering. As prince, Charles I's escapade to Madrid may have failed to secure him a Hapsburg bride but it had certainly established his personal favourites. Chief among them was Buckingham. Another was Endymion Porter (d. 1649), who had acted as interpreter at the Spanish court. In playing this part Porter had secured favour with both the prince and his reigning father, James I. Once Charles I took the throne, Porter continued to enjoy privileges as a courtier, including gaining lucrative grants, offices and patents. Yet, this was not sufficient for the ambitious man, who soon set his sights on the Indies. News had reached London of the large Indian junks freighting rich cargo across the Indian Ocean and Red Sea practically unarmed. Porter leapt upon an opportunity to enrich himself, setting up a privateering enterprise. Knowing well the EIC's likely views of such a venture, the arrangements were made under a shroud of secrecy. The courtier invested in two ships, the *Samaritan* and the *Roebuck*, while Charles I quietly granted a licence authorising the ships to travel anywhere in the world to capture and seize goods from vessels belonging to any nation with which England did not have an existing peace treaty.

The king may as well have lobbed a stick of dynamite into the head offices of the EIC. As the fallout from the Portuguese capture of the *Rahimi* had established, the Mughals did not take kindly to having Indian ships targeted. This was all the more so when the attacked ships carried an agreed pass. None of this mattered to Porter nor his monarch, however, and the two privateering vessels set off for India in April 1635, although only the *Roebuck* reached its destination. Once there, it proceeded to wreak havoc, attacking Indian vessels the *Tawfiqi* and *Mahmudi* in the Red Sea in September 1635. The ships belonged to Surat merchant Mirza Mahmud and carried goods belonging to numerous Indian merchants, including the wealthiest trader of Ahmedabad, Shantidas Zaveri. Furthermore, one of the vessels possessed a pass from the EIC at Surat protecting it from attack by Company vessels.

Predictably enough, Shah Jahan was livid. The Mughals generally viewed all Englishmen as one and the same, not distinguishing between Company traders, English private merchants (or interlopers, as the EIC called them) and English pirates. The emperor duly proceeded to extract full compensation from the EIC at Surat, imprisoning the factors for months and releasing them only when payment had been made. The crisis threw the EIC's entire enterprise in Mughal lands in danger, bringing trade to a standstill. Back in London, Company governors scrambled to beg an evasive Charles I to both write to the Mughal authorities to clarify the Company's innocence of the attack and permit the Company to extract compensation and pursue legal proceedings against the *Roebuck*. Porter's privateering was, however, only one of the calamities faced by the EIC in India that year with approval of the English monarch.

Among the less flattering characteristics shared by James I and Charles I was a propensity for bankruptcy. The royal budget was subject to parliamentary approval and Parliament often resisted the extravagances of both monarchs. This was especially pronounced during the reign of Charles I, who broke from the diplomacy of his father to chase expensive and unwinnable wars. Inevitably, Charles I's relations with the Commons was especially fraught. In the absence of a willing parliament – or indeed a sitting one given that Charles I repeatedly shut it down – the king turned to wealthy private individuals for loans. Among them was one William Courteen (d. 1636), a London businessman of singular ambition. Courteen had built an Anglo-Dutch empire with extensive interests in finance, land, European trade and West Indies settlements. Among his holdings were more than twenty ships and he had up to five thousand staff in his employ. As a financier, he was involved in regularly lending sizeable sums to both James I and later Charles I, gaining favour and privileges in return. One privilege, however, proved a wild enterprise that managed to overwhelm even this magnate.

At the close of 1635 Courteen along with several business partners, including the privateering Porter, conceived of a project to challenge the EIC monopoly in Asia. On 12 December a commission from his amenable king was secured permitting the dispatch of a voyage of trade and discovery to Goa, Malabar, China and Japan, along with a licence to export gold and silver of up to the value of £40,000 (£4.1 million today). The king himself invested some £10,000 (£1 million today) in the venture, in addition to letters of introduction and gifts for the viceroy at Goa. This was all in direct opposition to the EIC's existing royal charter, which granted it a monopoly in English trade in the east. In fact, the king's commission backing Courteen's enter-prise argued that the EIC was not making sufficient advances in the Indies. By February 1636 rumours began circulating about the venture and that the fleet was to be commanded by none other than erstwhile EIC employee John Weddell.

The Company was outraged and protested vehemently. On 8 March 1636 the governor formally presented a petition against Courteen's voyage to Charles I, who paid it little heed. Meanwhile, Courteen and his partners got to work, raising a fleet of six vessels at the immense cost of some £120,000 (£4.6 million today), much of it financed by Courteen personally or raised through loans. The fleet departed a month later on 14 April, reaching Goa on 8 October that year. The strain of so vast yet uncertain a project took its toll on Courteen, however, and he fell ill not long before the departure and passed away not long after, on 27 May. 'Without all Doubt the heavy Waightt of that businesse brake his [Courteen's] heart,' remarked English factor Peter Mundy, who had joined the voyage out.[6] Courteen's passing may well have been a mercy, as that first venture was a disaster. The outward voyage experienced the loss of a ship while the return voyage in 1638 was marked by plunder, the sinking of two ships at a loss of £150,000 and the passing of Weddell. Ultimately just one vessel, the *Sunne*, returned with a decent cargo of silk, gold and sugar.

Nonetheless, the Association showed no sign of disappearing. It continued under the aegis of the deceased Courteen's son and Charles I renewed its charter in 1637, this time explicitly affirming its protec-tion from 'impeachment or denial of the East India Company or others'.[7] For the EIC the damage was immense. Raising of stock, difficult on a normal day, had become near impossible now with the existence of Courteen's competition. Between lack of capital at home and rivalry from an ever-advancing and well-funded VOC, Company trade in India dwindled and sank ever deeper in debt with factors pleading with London for more funds where there were none to give. As EIC finances drained, they appealed to Charles I in growing desperation, but the king proved evasive at best. By November 1638 the EIC was forced to move out of its grand premises at Crosby House to the governor's own home on Leadenhall Street, where it remained for a decade. The following year EIC staff salaries were reduced on account of being 'upon a loosing trade'.[8]

Things only got worse and capital more difficult to come by for the embattled Company as England slowly drifted towards civil war. Since 1629 Charles had refused to recall Parliament and governed as absolute monarch, triggering much discontent. Finally, after years of petitioning, on 10 December 1639 Charles I dropped his support for Porter's privateers, permitting the EIC to undertake legal proceedings against the *Roebuck*. The Company was also granted a fresh charter with expanded privileges. But the damage was done. Furthermore, the Courteen Association continued trading in India for several years, inflicting losses on the EIC to the tune of an estimated £100,000 (£10.3 million today). As anger and unrest boiled over in the nation against its monarch, the Company felt little need to side with a king who had so flippantly and devastatingly undermined their enterprise.

Having conducted his ill-fated pursuit of the infanta Maria, Charles subsequently married Henrietta Maria, the fifteen-year-old sister of Louis XIII of France, whom he had briefly sighted en route to Madrid. The marriage took place by proxy on 11 May 1625 at the cathedral of Notre-Dame, confirming a staunchly Catholic French queen as consort for a committedly Protestant English throne. Although the marriage got off to a bumpy start, after the death of Buckingham in 1628 Charles I and Henrietta Maria grew devoted, having nine children together and spending very little time apart. Charles I's commitment to his wife coincided with the disintegration of his relationship with Parliament, drawing unfavourable attention to the royal marriage. Being Catholic and French had made the queen doubtful at best in English eyes. Hostility towards the French, rejection of Catholicism and misogynist assumptions about the wiles of women combined to create a perfect storm of suspicion directed at Henrietta Maria.

The queen was, however, only part of the problem. Charles I proved an entitled and grasping king whose reign was characterised by the repeated dissolution of Parliament when disagreements arose, as they so often did. On 10 March 1629 he dissolved Parliament for the lengthiest period, heralding eleven years of Personal Rule as absolute monarch. 'Remember that parliaments are altogether in my power for the calling, sitting, and continuance of them,' he declared, a statement by which he certainly lived.[9] Nonetheless, in this moment too Henrietta Maria became a flashpoint of anxiety among those opposed to the royal house. The absence of parliamentary sittings combined with the increasing intimacy between the monarch and his consort to fuel fears that a heretical and treacherous queen was becoming the most powerful royal adviser in the kingdom.

Throughout Charles I's reign the king and his parliament fought to assert authority. Parliament exerted its power by controlling the Crown's access to tax income, a deep frustration for an extravagant monarchy that drowned in debt. Charles's tendency to war – not that he was any good at it – and Parliament's refusal to fund it only exacerbated the Crown's financial woes. The king responded by seeking revenue elsewhere, such as from private lenders, including Courteen, who lent up to £25,000 (£3 million), much of it remaining unpaid by the time of the businessman's death. Among the king's more controversial fundraising measures was seeking to extend the levy on ship money from coastal regions to inland English counties, with fines imposed on those who refused to pay.

What finally forced Charles I to end the period of Personal Rule and recall Parliament in 1640 was the debacle of the Bishops' Wars, a conflict with the Scottish Presbyterian Church in which Charles was roundly defeated, deeply bankrupted and forced by an occupying Scottish Covenanter army to recall Parliament. Grudgingly, Charles I did so, and Parliament convened in November 1640 only to immediately pass acts to substantially reduce the king's influence, including removing his right to dissolve Parliament. Relations continued to disintegrate as Parliament punished the king's allies while steadily stripping the monarch of his power and funds. Not one to learn from experience, however, Charles I once again turned to war. In August 1642 he raised his standard at Nottingham, formally commencing the Civil War in February 1643. It went as well as expected; after several years of battle and intrigue, Charles I was ultimately defeated. Resolute to the end, at his execution on a chill January afternoon in 1649 he insisted on wearing two shirts to prevent shivers in the event that spectators mistook cold for fear. After executing the king, the Commons abolished the monarchy and the House of Lords, declaring England a commonwealth. War was not over, however, while Royalist supporters remained. The regicide provoked further unrest when Scottish and Irish Royalists supported the heir to the throne, Charles II. However, prominent parliamentarian military leader Oliver Cromwell brutally suppressed this, concluding the English Civil War in 1651.

Throughout the war the EIC had done its best to protect its trade in India. In 1643 Shah Jahan and crown prince Dara Shikoh were successfully petitioned, complete with valuable presents, in pursuit of a permit ensuring favourable rates for exported goods. Meanwhile, ships continued to arrive and be dispatched from England. All this came at considerable cost, however, which the Company in London simply could not meet. The already difficult challenge of raising credit became a Herculean task during the unrest of war. In the absence of regular or sufficient capital from England, the factors in India turned to taking loans from local lenders, often at cripplingly high rates of interest. In 1642 a loan of 100,000 rupees from Indian magnate and frequent EIC creditor Baharji Bohra enabled the Company at Surat to dispatch the *London* laden with a decent cargo of calico, sugar, cotton and cinnamon. The many debts the Company acquired through such loans created a 'necessitous and calamitous' situation in which seizure of capital by Indian creditors combined with an inability to purchase commodities demanded in England to push English trade to the brink.[10] This was all in sharp contrast to the ease and successes of the Dutch as they 'received large supplies, insomuch that they profer monies at interest, so prosperous and flourishing are they in all parts'. Meanwhile the Portuguese were seen to have revived their trade, 'their difference with the Dutch being termined'.[11]

Where decent capital and commodities were scraped together, the divisions fomented by the Civil War crept in. As the conflict raged in England, in 1644 the Company managed to raise five ships for dispatch to India: the *Endeavour, William, Blessing, Crispiana* and *John*. The latter two were headed for Surat, a matter of considerable anticipation for the desperate factors there. However, a rivalry soon emerged aboard the *John* between the chief factor, Edward Knipe, and the Royalist sympathising master, John Mucknell. This came to a dramatic head upon arrival at Anjouan Island, east of Mozambique. Feigning a conciliatory tone, Mucknell brought Knipe and his fellow factors ashore to host a 'day of jubilee' and celebratory feast.[12] Soon after the meal, the ship's master stole away and usurped the *John* with a cry of 'I here declare myself for the king!'[13] By the time Knipe and his colleagues realised what was happening, they were left to helplessly watch from the shore as the ship sped off into the sunset towards England where Mucknell was intent on handing over the vessel to Charles I. The *John* reached Bristol just as the city was being attacked by Parliamentarian forces. Nonetheless, its cargo of coral was taken ashore and largely recovered by the Company. Meanwhile, Mucknell made away with the ship to attack Commonwealth ships until finally being shipwrecked during a pursuit.

The defection of the *John* was a huge setback for the Company, which was already in straitened circumstances. In addition to the financial setback for London that the loss of an entire new vessel represented, that too in a time of war, the factors at Surat faced considerable repercussions to their trade. The promise of fresh capital and goods from the *John* had kept their many local creditors at bay, including Bohra, with the assurance that the laden vessel would finally enable loans to be repaid. Instead, the subsequent loss of the ship threw relations with creditors into turmoil resulting not only in the demand for repayment of outstanding loans but the denial of fresh credit. It took the fortuitous arrival of two relatively well-laden English vessels from the Far East to somewhat calm creditors and save the EIC at Surat from ruin. As one Company factor darkly remarked,

Mucknell 'escaped to doe future mischief, until Gods hand or the gallows make an end of him'.[14]

The Company had continued to trade as best it could in India through the war. With the end of the conflict and founding of the English Commonwealth, the EIC may well have felt hope for better prospects in the absence of a king who had actively damaged their trade and a war that stoked divisions and loss. Commerce in India was in a desperate state, the Company was drowning in debt and the need for state support was never more dire. Profit and peace were, however, only ever fleeting in the race for trade in seventeenth-century India.

While conflict at home had wreaked havoc from a distance, war would soon come knocking directly on the Company's Surat door. Several European conflicts and conciliations had taken place during the 1640s, the greatest beneficiary of which was the United Provinces. The Cretan War (1645–69) between the Ottoman Empire and Venetian Republic allowed the Dutch to overtake the commercial power of Venice in the Levant trade. In 1648 Spain recognised Dutch independence, finally bringing an end to the Eighty Years' War between the two nations and legalising Dutch trade in Spanish territories. Backed by the state with ample funds and maritime fleets, and benefiting from these political shifts, the Dutch were fast emerging as western Europe's premier player in global commerce. In Asia, the Portuguese decline enabled a well-placed VOC to replace the Estado as the leading western European presence in the region. Meanwhile war in England and its crippling effect on both English trade in India and colonial efforts in the Americas aided VOC advancement in both regions.

Now at peace with Spain and no longer in need of English support, the Dutch rejected English overtures for a partnership in 1651, much to the chagrin of the latter. Instead, the Commonwealth Parliament passed the Navigation Act of 1651, a measure that would be renewed following the Restoration of Charles II and which continued for the next two hundred years. Designed to place a check on the Dutch mercantile ascent and protect English interests, the Act required that goods entering England must arrive exclusively on English ships or ships of the country where the goods originated. In its wake

Anglo-Dutch relations soured drastically and by 1652 the two nations were at war, the first of three maritime Anglo-Dutch conflicts over a twenty-three-year period. The 1623 massacre at Amboyna would serve as a rallying call for the English throughout – a historic grievance fuelling a present conflict. During the two-year first war a strong Commonwealth fleet inflicted heavy losses on the United Provinces in Europe, including the capture of over a thousand Dutch ships. In India, however, already crippled by the caprices of Charles I and the devastations of the civil war, the English were far from equipped to take on the might of the VOC.

Early rumblings of war had made the Company in London conscious of the impact on its trade in India. On 18 June 1652 it dispatched a letter overland to Surat with the warning that war was probable and to be on guard around the Dutch: it was November by the time it arrived. Nonetheless, the English at Surat remained unconcerned as the Dutch had shown no indications of animosity. If anything, they seemed rather preoccupied; the peace they had brokered with the Estado in 1641 had expired and the VOC at Batavia had declared the renewal of war with the Portuguese. Meanwhile the Dutch were battling renewed indigenous resistance supported by the sultan of Macassar at Amboyna in which Ambonese historian, Imam Rijali, was involved. Taking on the English seemed the last thing to concern them. This was, however, a false impression.

On 11 February 1653 the English at Surat received news that war had formally broken out between England and the United Provinces. The VOC, however, were already well informed and had been merely biding their time. Just days after Surat learnt of war, on 15 February the VOC struck in the Persian Gulf, attacking and capturing two English vessels, the *Roebuck* and *Lannaret*, and taking them away in triumph to Bandar Abbas. It was a shock, rudely awakening the English from their false sense of security while humiliating them in Persia where the partnership at Hormuz had granted them a respectable reputation. Neither vessel deserved much commendation for their defence, either, the *Roebuck* putting up a weak show while the *Lanneret* merely gave in without a fight. Furthermore, the Dutch had managed to seize letters from the vessels, which they proceeded to exploit against English interests. While the English licked their wounds, within a year the Dutch struck again: on 25 March 1654 the VOC captured a further two English vessels, the *Supply* and *Blessing*, once again taking them off to Bandar Abbas. The capture of successive EIC ships was a catastrophe for an already weakened English trade. In despair, EIC factors at Bandar Abbas wrote to London that the losses must be addressed by the Company or the state, or 'you must bid adieu to your East India trade', adding the late realisation that 'the Dutch in India had order out of Holland to beginn and commence a warr heere before any was proclamed at home'.[15]

With an already dwindling fleet disappearing under the assault, the English sought the protection of the region's rulers. Unsurprisingly, a petition to the Safavid shah yielded no result while following a similar appeal to Shah Jahan they were informed the emperor 'would not meddle with itt one way nor other'.[16] The battles between Europeans were of little concern to the monarchs of Persia and India who, if anything, preferred that the northern traders kept each other in check to spare them having to do so. By March 1653 the Company instructed that English trade be sent overland from Persia to avoid Dutch attacks. Meanwhile in India the English became painfully aware of the need for a permanent port on India's western coast to protect their maritime interests. The Company had two Indian ports, both on the Coromandel Coast, at Pulicat and Madras, while the Malabar Coast remained exposed. Bombay had caught their eye, and they wrote to London proposing it be secured from the Portuguese in exchange for the English government offering the Iberians naval aid in their war against the Dutch.

In India, the EIC president at Surat was responsible for western India extending to the Deccan as well as the Persian Gulf and Red Sea. The president at Bantam, later moved to Madras in 1652, oversaw the Coromandel Coast, the Bay of Bengal and Far East. By early 1654 the ravishes of a second war so closely following the Civil War had greatly diminished an already struggling English trade, leading Company governors to decide on the drastic measure of downsizing. Letters arrived at Surat from London with instructions that all factories under the aegis of the Surat presidency be shut down apart from Surat, Agra, Isfahan and Bandar Abbas. Meanwhile staff at Surat were to be reduced to six factors and the new president to be appointed on a salary of £200 per annum, less than half that of the previous president. The presidency of Madras was instructed to close all factories apart from Madras and Machilipatnam. Although these orders were not immediately acted upon, it illustrated well just how desperate things had become.

In Europe at least the Commonwealth fleet had brought regional Dutch commerce to its knees and the Low Countries were desperate for peace. Following negotiations, a treaty was signed on 5 April 1654 at Westminster bringing hostilities to an end. By August the English were able to end the temporary dependence on overland trade in Persia. War had, however, greatly reduced the English fleet in Asia, which had suffered severely at the hands of Dutch attacks. Ill-equipped to import sufficient regional goods, English trade depended on silver bullion and European imports, the former expensive, the latter unpopular in Asia. By contrast, the VOC was flourishing. Possessed of abundant fleets with mastery over the Far East trade, they were able to bring in goods from China, Japan and the Moluccas. These they traded in India, competing with the English at every turn. The decline of the Portuguese was accelerated by the renewal of war with the Dutch, who were intent on claiming the Ceylon trade for themselves, with only a leap and a bound to taking Goa thereafter.

Things were looking grim for the English trade and by the middle of the decade the Company teetered on the verge of collapse. Although Charles I was no friend to the EIC, the Company's charter was nonetheless a royal one. The dissolution of the monarchy lent an air of redundancy to this, precipitating an increase in private merchants, or interlopers, plying the eastern trade in disregard of an EIC monopoly now considered as dead as the monarch who had granted it. Furthermore, loss of EIC ships coupled with loss of staff meant Company traders in India increasingly took to leaving, to make their fortunes elsewhere. Many turned to serving in the Mughal armies as mercenaries, usually as gunners, where they enjoyed a steady income and respectable standing. John Lewes, an Englishman who in 1655 was serving in the army of Prince Aurangzeb, described how he 'tooke my progres and came to the Mogull Prince which at present I am servant to'.[17] The move certainly served him well at a time when the Company teetered on the edge of ruin. In Aurangzeb's service Lewes earned four rupees a day and continued to serve in the prince's army for at least a year and a half. '(I thank God) I doe live well and get mony,' Lewes wrote.[18]

The year 1654 seems to have been a busy one for English mercenaries turning to the Mughal army. A letter from Company president Blackman at Surat early that year complains of up to eight men having done so.[19] By June the figure had risen to twenty-three. The English mercenaries were accompanied by many other Europeans, among them Venetian Niccolao Manucci. This slippery traveller was yet another European who became Indian in the assimilative land of the Mughals. After having spent years serving in Mughal armies, he set up shop in Lahore as a quack doctor; portraits surviving to this day depict him in Indian attire treating locals. In military service to Shah Jahan, Crown Prince Dara Shikoh and later Alamgir I, Manucci describes two hundred European servicemen in the imperial army and another eighty in the service of Mir Jumla, a military leader of Golconda.[20] In a distant Asian trade where factors were already in short supply, losing English employees to Indian employment was yet another blow for the Company.

With the disruptions of repeated wars, redundancy of its royal charter, loss of ships and a haemorrhaging of staff, the EIC had its back against the wall. In August 1654 it petitioned the then Lord Protector Cromwell to confirm a new exclusive EIC charter that would reaffirm its monopoly and enable the raising of fresh funds. But caught between managing war with Spain and the pressure from competing London merchants eyeing the Indian trade, Cromwell hesitated. The delays further sank an already sinking Company. By 1655 matters were such that the EIC only managed to send a single ship from London with the sole purpose of gathering cargo from India and bearing nothing apart from a letter showing the pangs of a dying enterprise. Plaintively describing 'our great sufferings in the many sadd losses which, both in your partes and elsewhere, wee have undergone', it asked the Surat factors to sell off everything that can be spared to purchase commodities, only leaving themselves enough 'for a very private, civill, and frugall living'. Further still, it reduced the already reduced six factors to three, adding: 'Had wee not some hope that, before much time will runn out, that the trade to East India would be againn setled in some way of honour and proffitt to the nation, wee had at this time sent you our positive order for dissolving of all.'[21]

This hope too was fleeting, and by the beginning of 1657 it was spent. Trade had come to all but a standstill and years had been wasted chasing a new charter that had failed to materialise. In January the Company took the decision it had long fought to keep at bay: it would sell up and close shop. Plans were drawn up for all EIC property and rights to be sold to the highest bidder the following month. Less than sixty years into its trading enterprise, it seemed the fortunes of the English East India Company had run out.

II

Restoration

IT TOOK SECONDS for the conflagration to take hold. A mere whisper of Princess Jahanara Begim's delicate muslin peshwas had brushed across a single lit candle. So fine was the woven fabric of this outer robe that it was almost transparent. Yet being heavily infused with scented oils and perfumes, the gentle lick of a flame had burst into a thousand tongues, engulfing the princess. At the sight of the spread, four attendants sprang to the aid of their mistress, flinging themselves upon her in the hope of smothering the flames. Instead, they too were caught, fire enrobing them with such ferocity that at least two ultimately did not survive. Eventually, the flames threatening to consume Jahanara were overcome, yet so severe were her burns that survival was far from certain.

News of the accident plunged Shah Jahan to the brink of despair. He had lost his beloved chief consort, Mumtaz Mahal, to childbirth and he was not ready to lose their daughter too. Jahanara Begim was the eldest of the girls born to the emperor and his famed empress. At the queen's demise in 1631, Jahanara had been by her mother's side, having tended to her devotedly. So beloved was the princess that Shah Jahan then chose to elevate this daughter to the status of first lady of the empire in place of his late wife, rather than render that position to any of his surviving wives. He further overlooked Jahanara's seven siblings to bestow on her half of Mumtaz Mahal's substantial estate. The princess and her father shared an exceptional bond and Shah Jahan doted and depended on her.

That his most beloved child had suffered the calamity of such a fire was therefore all the more devastating. As doctors battled to keep her alive, Shah Jahan threw open his coffers, donating generously to charity, and freed countless prisoners. Those that benefited from these gestures may well pray for the healing of his daughter, and there was no saying whose prayer God chose to accept. Although the best physicians in the land were brought in, months passed and uncertainty around Jahanara's survival remained. Finally, a Persian doctor arrived to attempt to heal the fading princess. By some miracle his treatment succeeded, and in December 1644, eight months after the accident that almost ended her life, Jahanara Begim was able to walk unaided. Shah Jahan could barely contain his joy. He rewarded the doctor handsomely, held official celebrations and showered Jahanara with a series of spectacular gifts. These included 139 priceless unpierced pearls and a single large diamond. He further granted her all the customs revenues of the most prosperous port in his realm: Surat.

The accession of Shah Jahan had put paid to Nur Jahan's years of rule. The once powerful queen was left to retreat to the shadows in Lahore while Shah Jahan raised his beloved wife and Nur Jahan's niece, Arjumand Banu Begim, to chief consort as Padshah Begim. Mumtaz Mahal (Exalted One of the Palace) was just one of the many titles he bestowed on this queen. While holding immense influence over Shah Jahan and being entrusted with the imperial seal to read and seal all documents, Mumtaz Mahal did not quite match up to her predecessor in co-sovereignty, although one can hardly blame her. Her life after marriage was consumed with bearing Shah Jahan's many children; fourteen in total, the last of whom culminated in a postnatal haemorrhage that claimed her life. Thereafter, Jahanara inherited the favours once showered on her mother.

As Padshah Begim, Jahanara was active in both matters of state and commerce. She mediated in political matters, engaged in diplomatic correspondence and issued legal documents under her seal. Said to have 'lived in state and magnificence', Jahanara enjoyed wealth worthy of the first lady of Mughal India.[1] At her father's newly built capital of Shahjahanabad, the largest mansion in the palace complex belonged to the princess, who commissioned the residence herself. The royal stipend allotted her was to the tune of millions, and this she dispensed in trade, architecture and beyond. At Shahjahanabad she sponsored no less than five major architectural projects, among them her mansion as well as the historic market complex Chandni Chowk (Avenue of Moonlight), at the centre of the city. Built in 1650, the thriving market derived its name from the moon's reflection on the waters of its central canal. To this day Chandni Chowk remains a prominent commercial hub in what is today Old Delhi.

Jahanara's commercial activities brought her into contact with Europeans including the Dutch, with whom the princess traded through her agents. The grant of Surat customs substantially expanded her commercial activities and brought her influence directly to bear upon the English there. For the EIC factors headquartered at Surat, the princess became another in a line of Indian royal women who cast their commanding shadow over the English trade, albeit in her own distinct way. While Nur Jahan had been the primary authority during the embassy of Sir Thomas Roe and Maryam al-Zamani's famed trade required they tread with care, EIC letters record how Jahanara Begim's agents meticulously collected the customs due to the princess from the factors at Surat. In this she followed in the footsteps of her prede-cessors, but in a more visible and far-reaching way. While Nur Jahan and Maryam al-Zamani's activities impacted mostly those traders who caught the queens' attention, such as Thomas Roe and William Hawkins, the army of administrators in service to Jahanara collecting customs throughout Surat made conspicuous the princess's sweeping control of the city's finances.

Among the Englishmen to recognise the princess's influence at Surat was also one who was far from favoured by the EIC and whose singular commission enabled him to avoid entanglement with Jahanara's customs officials. The year was 1656 and, if anything, avoid-ing the Company factors at all costs was the priority of the newly arrived Bellomont.

Chehel Sotoun palace in Isfahan was an extravagant affair. Built by the ruling Shah Abbas II, the entrance pavilion featured twenty carved wooden pillars that lifted a ceiling embellished with carved geometric patterns. A cooling pool stretched out for an impressive 180 metres before the building, framing the pavilion's reflection in its waters to double the grandeur. Beyond the entrance stood a great archway, its pointed peak featuring intricate muqarnas vaulting, a traditional Islamic architectural style that resembled the decorative symmetry of honeycomb. It was a palace worthy of a kingdom as grand as Safavid

Persia, and the shah proudly employed the setting to host foreign dignitaries and embassies.

As Henry Bard, Viscount Bellomont, entered the palace complex, he considered the large Portuguese cannon positioned at the gateway. Captured at Hormuz, Shah Abbas II had undoubtedly placed it there as a matter of pride. Yet, Bellomont reasoned, Hormuz would not have been captured had the English not provided the necessary naval assistance, and it was this very point that he had spent many long months impressing upon his hosts. On that evening in 1655 he intended to remind them once again of this fact. He had been invited to join a feast in one of the halls of the palace. Abbas II had hosted him earlier in the year at Qazvin, but as abundant as that gathering had been, this one in the imperial capital was a far grander affair. Bellomont felt his boots sink into the thick Persian carpets, skilfully hand-knotted by local artisans and coveted across Europe. He eyed the extravagant jewel-encrusted gold vessels set out across the great table before him, from which the heady scent of saffron wafted. Dishes were piled high with steaming pulao rice topped with almonds and raisins, an array of stewed, roasted and fried meats generously marinaded with regional spices and a wide variety of pickles. Portions were generous and each guest was served with no less than four plates of pulao, to enjoy with their chosen meats. Once the main course was complete, the dishes were spirited away to be replaced with equally tottering platters of fruit; melons, pomegranates, apricots and figs to gently wash down the richness of the main course.

Bellomont had been treated with great regard that evening. Met at the gate by a welcoming committee, he was seated near the king, who conversed pleasantly with him throughout the meal. It should have been a gratifying experience, yet this was far from the case for the increasingly impatient Englishman. It was coming up for a year since he had arrived in Persia, and there was very little to show for it. His unconcerned Persian hosts were generous with pleasantries, gifts and dinners, but evasive about the urgent and immensely sensitive matter he had travelled the great distance from Europe to discuss. Bellomont had been sent as an ambassador by none other than the exiled King Charles II. His commission: to seek funds and support to bring about a military defeat against the English Commonwealth and reclaim the throne for the Stuarts.

Born to a vicar in Middlesex, the well-travelled Royalist ambassador had served in Charles I's army during the English Civil War, rising to the position of colonel. His services gained him the favour of his monarch who created him Viscount Bellomont in 1645. The chafing blow of defeat, however, had not only left the king dead but his heir, Charles II, exiled in Europe along with his mother and desperate to reclaim the throne he saw as his birthright. In 1651 he tasked Bellomont with a secret embassy to Morocco and Persia in pursuit of financial aid for the reclamation of England's throne. Bellomont did not ultimately travel to Morocco, but he did make his way to Safavid Persia, arriving at Tabriz in September 1654. Once there he proceeded to petition the shah to fund his monarch. His argument was that the Safavids were indebted to the English after the capture of Hormuz, and this debt should be paid in money to the exiled English king. He further urged the shah to evict the English traders who supported the Commonwealth from Safavid lands. Unsurprisingly, the shah and his court were far from amenable to these forthright demands, that too from a dethroned king. Initially leaving the ambassador without a clear answer for almost a year, they subsequently dismissed both requests, much to Bellomont's frustration.

The evening meal having drawn to a close and the now much depleted platters removed, the Safavid chief minister approached the ambassador, took him by the hand and led him before the shah. Now, Bellomont thought, perhaps a last-ditch attempt at negotiating can take place. Before a word could be uttered, however, with great flourish the minister proceeded to bring forth from his pocket a small gold brocade bag. This he raised to his forehead, bowing deeply to the monarch, before offering it to Bellomont, stating that the bag carried a letter from the shah to the English king. He then invited the ambassador to make similar reverence to the Persian king. After a year of battling and begging, here, then, was the result of the exhausted emissary's efforts: a single letter in a small pouch. The dragged-out failure of his mission and its conclusion felt like a mockery. Grabbing the bag with a scowl, Bellomont turned on his heel without so much as a glance at the shah, swung the bag to his interpreter and stormed out of the court. The minister and onlookers were left aghast. The shah, however, did not even trouble himself to look up at the now retreating figure.

Persia had clearly been a non-starter, the period spent lingering here a waste of time. As the fuming ambassador arrived at his residence, he considered his options. Returning to a disappointed and displeased Charles II held little appeal. Instead, he determined to try his luck with that other great monarch of the region, the Mughal emperor. Perhaps in India he would succeed where in Persia he had failed. Four decades previously, Sir Thomas Roe had led an embassy to secure a trade agreement with the Mughals. However, after four years spent navigating the authority of Nur Jahan, Roe had not succeeded. If anything, the prospects for an exiled English king were far less promising, given that a sitting monarch had failed. Nonetheless, Bellomont headed to India, taking passage aboard a private English ship. Like Roe, in India he found that an imperious royal Mughal woman, now the Princess Jahanara, was determining affairs for the English trade at Surat. Commerce not being a concern of his mission, however, Bellomont managed to avoid a repeat of the awkward mercantile negotiations undertaken by his predecessor. His aim was to seek political and financial support, and this he immediately set out to do.

For much of his embassy in Persia and India, Bellomont had attempted to work beneath the EIC radar. The Company did not look kindly on the Royalists and their cause, nor did the latter think much of the Company. Bellomont had maintained correspondence with the chief factor of the VOC at Isfahan, begging him to 'keep the English in ignorance'.[2] Attempts at remaining incognito had been far from successful, however. As early as 20 June 1651 the Company committee had met in London to discuss how Charles II – or the King of Scotland, as they dismissively called him – was seeking to obstruct the Persian trade by deploying an ambassador. They further directed their officials at Surat to 'seize him [Bellomont] as a prisoner and return him for England with the first opportunity'.[3] Suspicion abounded during Bellomont's stay in Persia, where EIC factors referred to him as the 'pretended Embassadore' who 'is come to the Persian Court with the purpose to disturb the Companies affairs there' and 'is not on our side, but against us'.[4] When the ambassador finally left, the factors in Persia were glad to be rid of him.

Arriving at Surat in January 1656, Bellomont came ashore under a shroud of secrecy. The Company knew well of his presence, however, having been informed by their colleagues at Bandar Abbas. For the EIC, already battered and bruised by wars and dwindling funds, the machinations of a monarch they did not recognise was far from welcome. That Charles II's late father had brought much grief by encouraging the likes of Courteen and Porter only added to the annoyance that one meddlesome monarch had given way to another. This undoubtedly fuelled the Company's desire to be rid of Bellomont by any means possible. Knowing well the Surat factory's designs against him, the ambassador continued to steer clear of them, turning instead to the local VOC for advice and aid. Even when seriously ill with a sore that left his cheekbone exposed, he reached out to the Dutch traders rather than the Company for a surgeon. War with the Dutch may well have been concluded for now, but this preference for the VOC only further painted Bellomont as untrustworthy in the eyes of the EIC. While maintaining a civil front, Company factors attempted to lure him aboard one of their vessels departing Surat for England, a ploy Bellomont managed to avoid. Still, he could not avoid the EIC forever.

Having informed the Surat governor of his presence, Bellomont set off towards Delhi to secure an audience with Shah Jahan. On the way he paused at Agra, where several EIC factors invited him to dine at their factory. Perhaps believing himself safe outside of Surat, Bellomont accepted. It was the height of June, the intense heat of an unfamiliar land undoubtedly overwhelming, and the prospect of English company and fare attractive. That evening, comforted by familiar cuisine and loosened by drink, the ambassador proceeded to complain to his compatriots of the unbearable Indian heat. His hosts swiftly offered him a solution in the form of a powder, with the assurance that consuming it mixed with drink would give him much relief from the heat.

Three days following this encounter, on 20 June 1656, as Bellomont made his way to Shah Jahan's court with his small entourage, he was struck with a sudden and severe abdominal pain. The caravan halted, and men scrambled to aid the stricken ambassador as he called for water. Yet, whatever it was that ailed him proved swift and deadly. Despite the best efforts of his companions there was little they could do. Before the sun had set the unfortunate man had passed away. Whether by suspected poisoning or a more innocuous illness, six months after his arrival in India the ambassador of the exiled English monarch was no more, his embassy cut short before it had even begun. For the EIC, the interference of Charles II in the English trade in India was at a fortuitous end – for now at least.

The state of the Company's trade was desperate. The factories in India were laden with debt while the governors in London had for years fruitlessly appealed to the Commonwealth for a renewal of their charter. Without a new charter confirming their monopoly, raising fresh funds was hopeless. When the Company in London finally declared its decision to sell in January 1657, however, both the City and Parliament reacted with shock. The prospect of the leading English trading company in India disbanding alarmed the government and London's merchant community, including those who had hitherto opposed an EIC monopoly. This pushed them to immediate action, and on 10 February 1657 Oliver Cromwell approved a motion to renew the EIC monopoly. With the promise of the long sought new charter, the Company withdrew its notice of sale.

The sound of the death knell had salvaged the East India Company from early extinction. It would still be several months before the formal approval, but on 19 October 1657 Cromwell finally granted the EIC a new unlimited charter. With it a fresh appeal for capital was made, resulting in the raising of an immense £740,000 (£78.8 million today), the first permanent stock of the Company. After years of struggle, the EIC was reborn with a new vigour, and the Company immediately got to work. On 11 January the following year a new president of Surat, Nathaniel Wyche, was appointed. In marked contrast to the recent lean years that had seen staff and salaries drastically cut, Wyche was allotted a salary of £500 and granted permission to take his wife to India. Within the first five months of 1658 no less than thirteen ships were dispatched east with several more vessels following later in the year.

With a new charter and funds, the Company undertook a bold and strategic new investment that bolstered its trade in India while addressing a key criticism it had endured for years. The export of silver bullion from England for the purchase of Indian luxuries had long been damaging to the EIC's image. '[W]hether to the good of the Common wealth, so great a masse of silver being exported out of *England*, and such a multitude of Saylers consumed every yeere, let the wise speake and posterity see,' the chronicler William Camden had written in 1625.[5] Not only was it costly, but for the EIC's critics it was a morally corrupting practice that entailed expending the nation's Christian wealth in the pursuit of frivolities manufactured by Indian infidels. The EIC sought to refute its critics, arguing that 'Money is the prize of wares, and wares are the proper use of money; so that their Coherence is unseparable.'[6] An alternative model of trade was needed. The disruptions of the preceding years had further impressed the importance of diversifying, pushing the Company to seek new methods to protect and expand the Indian trade. Lack of interest in English and European goods for the most part had forced the use of silver; however, the Company had over the years identified certain goods that were popular in India's markets. The value of ivory, particularly among Indian women, had been proven early on. This was to be found in abundance along Africa's western coast, where another even more precious commodity was available: gold. It was this West African gold, then, that became an answer to the dilemma of English silver funding Indian trade. The new charter now made tapping into this market a possibility.

Among the first actions the EIC undertook with its immense new buying power was to purchase the Guinea Company (GC) with a view to benefiting from its African networks. The intention to purchase was announced in October 1657 and in December a sale was agreed at a price of £1,300. The GC had been granted its charter by James I in 1618 with a monopoly on trade throughout West Africa. The target was primarily redwood, gold and to a lesser degree ivory. Although not set out in writing in its first charter, the Company also engaged in trading in enslaved peoples. In June 1629 a French privateering vessel captured a GC vessel paradoxically named *Benediction* off the coast of Senegal. It was a slave ship the loss of which – with human souls reduced to pounds and pence – was estimated at £20,000 (£2.4 million today), a reflection of the immense numbers of trafficked people it carried. Over the years the engagement in this devastating trade continued to grow, although during the period under EIC control the primary focus was ivory and gold.

The GC had endured much turbulence since its original charter. Its early years had seen financial losses and increasing debt as it struggled to secure gold. By 1624 the Company's monopoly had been suspended and the following year its governor, William St John, was sent to debtors' prison. The arrival of new members in 1625 offered the hope that new life would be breathed into the institution, yet financial woes continued with subscribers defaulting on promised payments meaning that ships could only be sent on an ad hoc basis. In 1631 de facto head, Nicholas Crispe, went about reorganising and raising fresh capital for the embattled and debt-ridden company. That same year Charles I was convinced to withdraw the original 1618 charter and issue fresh patents with a thirty-one-year monopoly for the ardent Royalist Crispe and his colleagues. The recruitment of a disgruntled Dutch trader, Arent de Groot, who had defected from the Dutch West India Company, proved particularly opportune at this moment. De Groot was deployed to Ghana where he dispensed his experience and knowledge to secure exclusive trading rights and permission to build factories from the Fante ruler. With this agreement the GC established a permanent fort at Kormantse (termed Kormantine by the English) as its headquarters in West Africa, a position it retained until after the Restoration.

Yet throughout the English Civil War and amid increasing competition from the Dutch, the trade struggled. The Long Parliament tried and failed to take back the GC patents and in 1643 the Parliamentarian navy attacked GC ships. In 1644 Parliament took control of Crispe's majority share, passing the struggling company on to merchants it trusted. Once again under new management, a revamp of the trade was attempted, now increasingly with the trafficking of enslaved peoples. Prospects far from improved, however, and by 1651, the same year plans were drawn up for a slave-trading voyage to Gambia, GC losses stood at £100,000 (£10.3 million today). While the Committee of Trade nonetheless confirmed the GC monopoly for another fourteen years, in 1657 the directors agreed to sell the remaining lease to the East India Company. Via this purchase the EIC gained the network of factories and trading posts cultivated by the GC along the

West African coast alongside the experienced staff and mercantile networks. Under EIC control trade was directed towards ivory and gold, yet slave trading also continued at a reduced capacity. The EIC trafficked people from West Africa to India and private trade of this kind continued among its employees. In this way human enslavement and trafficking from West Africa became directly entangled with trade in India.[7] Although in September 1660 EIC company directors made a show of forbidding staff at Ghana from engaging in the practice, such trafficking did take place.

The primary purpose of purchasing the Guinea Company was to supply the Indian trade with popular West African exports. The EIC took to re-exporting large quantities of Indian goods, particularly textiles, from London to Africa's western coast, where they were traded for ivory and gold dust. These were then directed to India where they were employed in the purchase of goods for Europe. The English thus continued to turn to the superior manufacturing industries of India to facilitate their Asian trade. Of the ships dispatched in 1658, three were directed to make port calls at what is present-day Guinea and Sierra Leone for this purpose. For years thereafter, ships were regularly dispatched each year for India via West Africa. The new system was effective; moreover, it gave rise to a valuable new frontier for the Company at a time when they really needed it.

England was far from free of the political quagmire, however, and the EIC far from immune from its effects. The charter granted by Cromwell stood on shaky ground given that despite his promise to secure parliamentary approval for it, the abrupt dissolution of Parliament in February 1658 prevented this. By September Cromwell himself was dead and objections began to arise as to the continuing validity of EIC privileges granted by a deceased Lord Protector. While its core charter was questioned, the West Africa trade was a further concern. The GC lease remained active throughout the Restoration, the Company enjoying the benefits of the new strategy, but it was due to expire in 1664. While the Company pinned its hopes on a renewal there were others eyeing the West African prize.

Peter Mundy was an old hand at travelling east. Having begun his career in the Mediterranean, including a four-year stint in Istanbul, he had later joined the East India Company, serving several years in India. China was certainly new to him, however, when he joined Captain John Weddell on a voyage to Macao, arriving on 27 June 1637 complete with letters of introduction for the Portuguese governor from the then reigning Charles I. The voyage, undertaken off the back of the Anglo-Portuguese peace treaty, was under the aegis of the Courteen Association, who decided to take advantage of the accord with the support of the English monarch. Mundy's account of the journey is captivating for the details he offers about Macao's coastline and geography. 'Macao standeth at one end of a greatt Iland built on rising hills,' he writes, 'some gardeins and trees among their houses making a pretty prospecte somwhatt resembling Goa, although not soe bigge; Their houses double tyled, and thatt plaistred over.'[8] The wonder of an inexperienced Englishman newly introduced to a thriving region of which he knows little is captured well in the traveller's records. As he arrives in Macao, he tries to make sense of this new land in terms of the more familiar India. Mundy further coupled his observations with sketches, illustrating for English readers a part of the world far distant from their island and which few had had the opportunity to experience firsthand.

The traveller was particularly taken with the food of China. He describes lychee with gusto as 'ruddy browne and Crusty, the skynne like to thatt of the Raspis [raspberry] . . . the prettiest and pleasauntest Fruit thatt ever I saw or tasted'.[9] He also describes a curious drink he encounters that was clearly very popular in the region: 'The people there gave us a certaine Drinke called Chaa, which is only water with a kind of herbe boyled in itt. It must bee Drancke warme and is accompted wholesome.'[10] Mundy was, of course, describing tea, that fragrant warming beverage now so synonymous with British culture. But, like so much of British culture today, the origins of tea could not be more removed from Britain. The tumultuous history to be born of so innocuous a refreshment could hardly have been predicted as the traveller partook of his boiled herb drink.

While the EIC would take to importing tea from China from the seventeenth century it was not until the eighteenth century that the popularity of the beverage in Britain grew, aided by the Company securing trading privileges in Guangzhou in 1716. The EIC's trade in

A portrait of Moroccan ambassador Abd al-Wahid ibn Mas'ud al-Annuri painted during his six-month embassy to Queen Elizabeth I in London in 1600.

Mughal founding father Emperor Zahir al-Din Muhammad Babur consulting his chief adviser: his grandmother, Aisan Dawlat Begim.

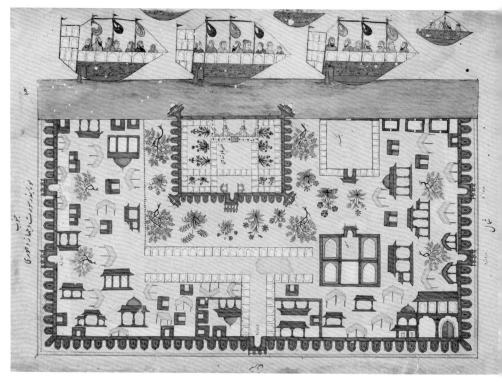

Map from a seventeenth-century Hajj pilgrimage manual showing Surat, the leading Mughal trading and pilgrim port city on India's western coast.

Mughal miniature depicting Queen Maryam al-Zamani reclining on a bed after giving birth to Crown Prince Salim (later Emperor Jahangir) in 1569. A midwife at her feet cradles the infant.

Pictures out of the Indian Copies made by the Mogols painter

Sultan Coroan &. — his woman slaue — Selim Shah the great Mogoll

An English engraving of Prince Khurram (*left*), a female slave (*centre*) and Emperor Jahangir (*right*). Taken from the travel anthology *Purchas His Pilgrimes* (1625), it drew on portraits brought back from India by English travellers to offer an accurate image of Mughal royalty.

Emperor Jahangir, seated on an hourglass throne, converses with a Sufi scholar. King James I is relegated to the margin (*below left*), illustrating the Mughals' feelings of indifference towards the English and their efforts to trade.

A mural in St Stephen's Hall, Palace of Westminster, imagining a meeting between Sir Thomas Roe, England's first ambassador to India, and Emperor Jahangir in 1616.

Sir Robert and Lady Teresa Sampsonia Sherley dressed in Persian attire, by Anthony van Dyck, c.1622. Teresa Sampsonia was an accomplished Persian noblewoman raised as a ward in the Safavid royal household, and the couple were sent as envoys to Europe by Shah Abbas I.

The defeat of the Portuguese settlers by Emperor Shah Jahan's Mughal forces at the siege of Hooghly contributed to securing Mughal control of Bengal while also easing English trade in the region.

The Torments inflicted by the Dutch on the English in Amboyna.

The Condition of the English in the Dungeon, and their Execution.

An English engraving depicting the torture of East India Company
traders by the Dutch during the 1623 Amboyna Massacre. Dutch traders at
Ambon Island had accused the English of conspiring against them,
an accusation the English strenuously denied.

Venetian traveller Niccolao Manucci feeling the pulse of an Indian patient in the early 1700s. Arriving in India in his teens, Manucci's colourful career included serving in Mughal armies, assisting Charles II's ill-fated ambassador to India and posing as a quack doctor.

A sixteenth-century Portuguese illustration showing settlers at Hormuz Island in the Persian Gulf being served by indigenous people, probably enslaved. At the top right, an individual is flooding the room with water to combat the intense heat of the island.

'Prince Aurangzeb faces a maddened elephant named Sudhakar', *c.*1635. During an elephant fight entertainment at Agra in 1633, Sudhakar broke away to charge the young prince whose bravery gained him much praise, not least from his father Emperor Shah Jahan.

In the wake of the Anglo-Mughal War, in which the East India Company attempted to strengthen its trading position by military means (with disastrous results for the English), chastened company delegates from the English fort at Bombay seek pardon from Emperor Alamgir I, December 1689.

tea leaves would come to chart connections between China, India, Europe and the Americas. In the eighteenth century the Company began trading opium cultivated in Bengal for tea in China, forging perhaps the most notorious commercial network between the two lands. The English trade in and consumption of tea became a cause for much bloodshed, giving rise to the Opium Wars, colonial annexation, the expansion of Atlantic slavery and even the American Revolution. In these early days of the seventeenth century, however, it was an edifying refreshment gaining popularity primarily for medicinal purposes among the European elite. The Portuguese had already acquired a taste for tea, having been the first to import it to Europe in the sixteenth century. Eventually, England also followed. By the late 1650s tea was on offer in London's coffee houses, including the Sultaness Head at the Royal Exchange where the proprietor advertised it in the city's weeklies as 'That Excellent, and by all Physicians approved, *China* drink'.[11] And while the colonial violence precipitated by its trade was yet to emerge, even in this early moment the 'China drink' came to play a part in English politics.

Two decades after Mundy's travels to Macao, in 1657 the *Eagle* returned to London with a letter from the factors in Surat to the Company headquarters. The factors warned of the Dutch advance as the VOC continued to gain headway over the Portuguese, and the concern that a permanent settlement in India was necessary to better protect otherwise deeply vulnerable English interests. The Portuguese and Dutch had both established key regional capitals and ports under their command. The EIC had long witnessed the Portuguese advantage from the latter's capital at Goa. The English on the other hand functioned through a network of factories at ports governed by Indian authorities over which they had little control. The Surat factors offered an interesting solution: that the English government be prevailed upon to lend aid to the Portuguese against the Dutch and in return the Portuguese cede one of their Indian ports to the EIC.

The Company in London immediately got to work, seeking an audience with Cromwell to raise the matter. Meanwhile, the newly appointed Surat president Nathaniel Wyche was instructed to attempt to secure either Danda Rajpuri or a minor Portuguese outpost some

270 kilometres south of Surat referred to by its Lusitanian governors as the island of Bombaim (Bombay or Mumbai). In August 1659 the EIC in London wrote to their factors in Persia elaborating their plan that '[in] consideration of the Dutches great successe in India, in the gaining of severall places, hath incited you to put us in mind to procure some place that wee might call our owne and be masters off'.[12] The prospect of acquiring Bombay was then raised with the Portuguese ambassador in London, Francisco de Mello, in February 1660. Although de Mello did not give much encouragement, it would seem the Portuguese authorities kept the matter in mind.

Meanwhile, England's political establishment was yet again in crisis. Following the passing of Oliver Cromwell, his son Richard Cromwell had taken up the mantle of Lord Protector, however, the son was not the father and had proved unequal to the role. On 25 May 1659 he was forced to resign. Continued instability and the threat of anarchy now culminated in the military intervention of General George Monck, who in February 1660 restored the Long Parliament MPs who had been excluded in Pride's Purge of 1648, on condition they dissolve Parliament and hold fresh elections. The subsequent dissolution saw the advent of the Convention Parliament. In the meantime, Monck and Charles II were in correspondence, and on the former's recommendation the exiled king travelled from Brussels to Breda where on 4 April he published the Declaration of Breda in which he outlined a series of commitments he would undertake if restored as king of England. The following month, on 1 May, the Lords declared that government should be by 'King, Lords, and Commons', a position with which the Convention Parliament concurred. Within a week both houses proclaimed the king, and he was invited to return to England. After a decade spent languishing on the Continent producing more illegitimate children than effective attempts at reclaiming the throne, things were looking up for Charles II. On 23 May he set sail, arriving in London in triumph on 29 May. The Restoration of England's Stuart monarch was more the product of Commonwealth failure than Royalist success, but that minor detail was not one to trouble a delighted Charles II.

The East India Company had witnessed the political proceedings with a wary eye. The return of the monarch meant the need to

re-establish themselves in royal favour. This was all the more necessary if they wished for support in their campaign to secure a
Portuguese outpost in India. The Company decided to send a celebratory gift it considered exotic and singular enough to capture the
monarch's attention: two pounds, two ounces of China tea. For a
monarch who had been careful to maintain a conciliatory tone on
his return, the luxurious gift must have been welcomed. The following year, in 1661, Charles II granted the EIC a new expanded charter which authorised it to, among other things, raise military forces
to defend its trade, arrest and deport interlopers in India, coin
money and acquire and govern its own territories.

Meanwhile, not long after returning to the throne, the discussion of
marriage arose for Charles II. The Portuguese proposed the infanta,
Catherine of Braganza. Although the match was vociferously opposed
by Spain it was backed by France who, following a year of discussions,
prevailed in the matter. Charles II signed the marriage treaty on 23 June
1661, and the ceremony took place the following year on 21 May at
Portsmouth. Among the characteristics the new English queen became
known for was her love of tea, so much so that the Royalist politician
and poet Edmund Waller (d. 1687) composed a verse about it – the first
English poem to mention the beverage:

> Venus her myrtle, Phoebus has her bays;
> Tea both excels, which she vouchsafes to praise.
> The best of Queens, and best of herbs, we owe
> To that bold nation, which the way did show
> To the fair region where the sun doth rise,
> Whose rich productions we so justly prize.
> The Muse's friend, tea does our fancy aid,
> Repress those vapors which the head invade,
> And keep the palace of the soul serene,
> Fit on her birthday to salute the Queen.

Through Restoration and marital alliance, tea wafted its subtle path
through shifts in England's political and mercantile establishments.

The marriage of Charles II and Catherine of Braganza was a
felicitous partnership for the Portuguese, who had sought the match

since an initial unsuccessful proposal in 1644. Now with the union secure, they offered a generous dowry: 2 million cruzados (approximately £300,000 or £31 million today), free trade with Brazil and the Portuguese East Indies and two strategic Portuguese bases: Tangier and Bombay. The Indian island was now on the English table and within the EIC's reach. For the viceroy at Goa, Antonio de Melo e Castro, the ceding of Bombay to the English throne was an egregious decision that not only amounted to the loss of a key outpost but further shrank and weakened an already receding Lusitanian presence in India. Efforts to resist the handover and persuade the Portuguese authorities against the decision proved futile, however, and on 14 January 1665 Bombay was formally transferred to English control.

As promising as a new Indian territory was for Charles II, in the early years the king struggled. Managing Bombay was an incredibly expensive and complicated affair made more challenging by a poorly conceived treaty with Goa that England later moved to revoke. As costs of staffing and maintaining Bombay spiralled, Charles II turned often to the Company for substantial loans. Furthermore, considerable friction soon arose between the king's forces in Bombay and the EIC factors in Surat, and this came to a head in 1667 in the shape of a crisis the Company by now knew only too well. In March 1667 EIC representatives in London sought redress from the king on account of his governor in Bombay, Humphrey Cooke, having captured a 'richly laden junk' belonging to the Mughal governor of Surat which had inadvertently wandered into Bombay's waters.[13] The vessel carried a pass from the EIC at Surat, yet Cooke had refused to release it. In a repeat of history, the governor of Surat descended on the EIC, threatening the Company president with imprisonment, demanding compensation and charging that the Company was in cahoots with fellow countryman Cooke the whole time. The Company took great pains to maintain harmonious relations with the Surat authorities. To do so was critical to their trade both at Surat, their chief factory in India, and their wider trading posts in India and the Indian Ocean which the Surat factory oversaw. The EIC complained to Charles II of how 'before this occurred they were always on good terms with the natives, especially those in command, to obtain which your petitioners have been at a considerable charge'.[14]

The callous attacks by Cooke now threatened to reverse a laboriously maintained accord. Although England's Crown did direct its staff at Bombay to avoid harming the English trade, in real terms there was little capacity to enforce things from such a distance.

By November 1667 the Treasury could bear the immense expense and challenge of Bombay no longer. Summoning the EIC, they informed them that the king would be willing to offer Bombay to them in exchange for a loan of £50,000. This the Company accepted and in December the Privy Council granted it a formal approval. On 27 March the transaction was completed and on 23 September 1668 Charles II's governor of Bombay, Henry Gary, handed over control of the island to the EIC's representative in Surat, John Goodier. The latter became the Company's first deputy governor of the island with Surat president George Oxenden as governor. With this, the erstwhile thorn in the Company's side that was Charles II's troublesome administration in Bombay gave way to a new Company settlement to serve the Indies trade. Although the charter specified that the king could terminate the agreement if the EIC failed to make profitable use of the holding, the Company kept Charles II sweet with abundant loans that by 1684 added up to a staggering £344,150 (£39.3 million today). By such payments the EIC not only secured its monopoly in India and lease of Bombay but also increasingly made itself indispensable to the English Crown and state.

The Company finally had its port in the western Indian Ocean on the holding it had long sought. Bombay was its first sovereign territory in India, but it was far from ready-made. Yielding 'nothing but a greate quantity of Coco Nuts and Rice', to raise it to an established settlement that could serve the needs of the English trade in textiles, dyes, saltpetre and spices proved another lengthy process in the ever strenuous task of gaining and retaining a commercial foothold in India.[15] It would demand decades of effort yet before the Company's new Indian territory would prove itself a worthy investment. Once established the fortified Bombay settlement would be manned by the diverse array of staff common to many of the EIC's trading posts. This included English factors, Indian agents and hired soldiers and an especially unsavoury legacy of Company trade: enslaved people.

12

Trade in Souls

I T WAS THE keenness for West African commodities that led the
EIC to purchase the Guinea Company. While the GC charter
lasted, the Company's trade in India benefited immensely from the
gold dust and ivory to be found in the African region it called Guinea.
Company factories in India grew increasingly dependent on this gold
and the EIC was far from ready to give up the enterprise. However,
the newly restored Charles II eyed both the gold leaving West African
shores for India rather than England and the profit to be made in
transporting enslaved West Africans to the Atlantic colonies, and
decided to shift the direction of the trade. In 1660 he chartered the
Company of Royal Adventurers Trading into Africa – later to be (in)
famously renamed the Royal African Company (RAC) – with a
monopoly over trade in West Africa. The leadership of the RAC he
granted to his brother James, Duke of York, who would later succeed
to the English throne as James II (r. 1685–8).

Desperate to retain their access to the gold, the EIC spent 1662
petitioning James to purchase the RAC shares and resell them to the
Company. This proved unsuccessful, and on 25 March 1663 the
Company had no choice but to relinquish all rights to the Guinea
coast. The last Company ship, the *Marigold*, was dispatched to Fort
Kormantine in December 1663. That same year Charles II reissued
the RAC's charter, now explicitly stating its aim of 'buying and selling, bartering and exchanging of ... slaves, goods, wares and
merchandizes whatsoever to be vended or found' in western Africa.[1]
In 1664 the original Guinea Company charter purchased by the EIC
finally expired. The Guinea trade was now fully in the hands of the
RAC led by the Duke of York, with transatlantic slave trading its
primary objective.

Under the aegis of the RAC English transatlantic trade in enslaved people expanded rapidly. The Company purchased thousands of enslaved men, women and children from West Africa each year to then traffic to colonial plantations and mines in the Americas, where they would be forced to labour in devastating conditions. The output of the plantations and mines, including sugar and silver, would then be shipped to England. More African men, women and children were transported by the RAC than any other institution in the entirety of the transatlantic slave trade. By this England became the most prolific trafficker in enslaved peoples to the Atlantic colonies. Within a decade of its foundation, England's 33 per cent share in the westward traffic in human souls jumped to 74 per cent. By 1720 the RAC had trafficked nearly 150,000 Africans, largely from West Africa to plantations in the Caribbean.[2] In the wake of long-standing resistance and campaigning by enslaved peoples from the inception of the triangular trade, Britain finally agreed to abolish its trade in enslaved peoples in 1834. By then well over 3 million Africans – a figure greater than that of any other European nation – had been trafficked aboard British ships.[3] The legacy of the RAC's brutality persists to this day in many forms, not least in the monuments to its members and beneficiaries dotted about Britain.

On 7 June 2020 protesters surrounded a bronze statue that for over a century had been proudly stationed on a plinth in Bristol's city centre. Casting ropes around it, the gathered crowd pulled the figure down to rapturous cheers. They then sprayed blood-red paint across its hands and face before unceremoniously shoving it into the murky waters of the harbour. The statue was that of Edward Colston (d. 1721), a man who through the late seventeenth and early eighteenth centuries had enriched himself substantially through the trade in enslaved peoples. Colston had served as a commissioner and investor in the South Sea Company, which trafficked enslaved people to the Spanish colonies in the Americas. He had profited directly from sugar plantations run with enslaved labour, including benefiting as a partner of a Bristol sugar refinery. As an MP of his city he defended what he saw as Bristol's right to engage in the slave trade. It was in 1680 that Colston rose to a prominent executive position in the Royal African Company, where he invested heavily, served on the board of directors and was deputy governor from 1689 to 1690. One estimate suggests that 84,000 Africans, including 12,000 children, were trafficked by the RAC during Colston's tenure there.[4]

The red paint was a symbol of the blood that stained his career. Since at least the 1990s campaigners had sought to have the statue removed on account of Colston's brutal legacy. However, resistance persisted from those who sought to immortalise a man they saw as a historic Bristolian philanthropist, however ill-gotten his gains and conditional his donations. The long-standing global campaign for racial equality led by the Black Lives Matter movement experienced renewed momentum in 2020 triggered by the murder of George Floyd – yet another innocent Black man killed by police – in Minneapolis. The felling of Colston's statue was an iteration of the protests sparked by this brutal murder. Today, Colston is perhaps the RAC's most widely recognised beneficiary, albeit far from its most prominent participant. That notorious status is the preserve of England's royal family, beginning with Charles II and led by James, Duke of York.

Charles II was not the first English monarch to engage the nation in the transatlantic slave trade. Elizabeth I had sponsored and lauded John Hawkins in his slaving expeditions long before Charles II arrived on the throne. But the Stuarts enabled an unprecedented expansion of the trade via direct patronage and participation in the Company that prioritised and advanced this vicious commerce. The Royal African Company bore the royal title, was established by one king, led by a prince who would become king, and its 1663 charter named both the then reigning queen, Catherine, and previous queen, Henrietta Maria, in the grant. In 1672 the charter was reissued, once again with James as key trustee, granting the RAC a monopoly for a thousand years and asserting West African trade as the 'right of the Crown of England'.[5] Many of the enslaved people traded by the RAC had DY, the initials of the Duke of York, branded on their chests. Others were branded with the company's initials, RAC. Human souls were thereby reduced to chattels, mutilated with hot irons to assert English royal ownership.

Those who survived the horrors of the Middle Passage were forced into torturous labour in the plantations and mines of the Americas, catering to Europe's ever-increasing demand for sugar, cotton and specie. Increasing consumption of eastern tea and coffee in England were among the factors that triggered increasing demand for sugar from the Atlantic plantations. Similarly, the expansion of English trade in the Indies continued to expand the demand for silver from the Americas. Through bondage the trafficked resisted and fought for emancipation, risking the inhuman retribution meted out by slave traders and plantation owners. From the inception of the triangular trade, defiance was a constant; from the struggle against capture in West Africa and rebellions aboard ship in the Atlantic to resistance in bondage in the Americas. Modes of resistance varied widely, from everyday acts of resistance such as withholding labour, damaging machinery or escaping to organised uprisings and armed rebellion. Thousands of slave-led rebellions took place, a tradition to which contemporary Black-led anti-racism movements are traced. Most successful of these was the Haitian Revolution against French colonial rule, which saw the establishment of an independent Haiti in 1804.

While the RAC superseded the EIC in West Africa, its activities were far from detached from the English trade in India. The RAC continued to acquire enslaved labour with Indian commodities re-exported from London, particularly cotton textiles and cowrie shells, alongside English commodities of woollen cloth, metalware and firearms. Meanwhile the silver mined by trafficked peoples in the Americas crossed the ocean to flow through the EIC trade in India's markets. Between England's commerce in the Indies and the Americas there were indelible connections of violence. Yet, the RAC was not alone among English companies in their engagement in human trafficking. Beyond the West African coast, in the Indian Ocean, too, trafficking was active and through the seventeenth century prolific. And here, too, its champions were the European arrivals, including the East India Company who had its hands no less steeped in the blood of bondage.

In West Africa the East India Company prioritised the trade in ivory and gold to aid its commerce in India yet was nonetheless actively involved in trafficking enslaved people across the Indian Ocean and beyond. The men, women and children trafficked were crucial to its trade and early settlement efforts in both Africa and Asia. In this the English were matched, and in the seventeenth century exceeded, by their fellow Europeans. The triangular trade essentially saw the one-way transport of West Africans, including peoples from what is today Ghana, Togo, Benin and Nigeria, across the Atlantic. However, European slave trading in the Indian Ocean was a multidirectional affair that involved the trafficking of men, women and children from West Africa, East Africa, India and south-east Asia to trading bases throughout the Indian Ocean. Like those transported to the Atlantic colonies, the enslaved across the Indian Ocean actively resisted their bondage using methods ranging from withholding labour to rebellion, including shipboard insurrection, matricide, maronage, fleeing or even the desperate act of suicide.

Europeans engaged in trading enslaved peoples on an enormous scale in the Indian Ocean basin in this period, a reality that has lacked the attention it is due. It is estimated that a thousand enslaved people were transported each year to Batavia (Jakarta) alone in the seventeenth century. By the eighteenth century European slave trading in the region had quadrupled. The Portuguese were the first to arrive and the first to engage in this violent trade, with Mozambique a primary source of enslaved labour for the Estado. Hundreds of people were trafficked each year to regional Portuguese settlements from the sixteenth to the early nineteenth centuries. The Portuguese also trafficked hundreds of Indian and south-east Asian enslaved people throughout the region each year. These included enslaved South Indian, Malayan, Javanese and Chinese peoples. Enslaved servants soon emerged in Portuguese artwork of the period. Of the many striking images contained in the Códice Casanatense, a sixteenth-century collection of seventy-six Portuguese illustrations of Africa, Asia and the Middle East, is a scene from Hormuz of a Portuguese household at dinner. Surrounding the white Portuguese diners are seven men and women serving their food and beverages. These figures are noticeably darker in complexion, dressed in regional attire and rendered diminutive in size, and thereby status. Given the scale of Portuguese engagement in slave trading – including to the Persian Gulf – it is highly probable that these seven individuals were enslaved servants.

While the Portuguese were the first Europeans to trade in enslaved peoples in the Indian Ocean, the English, Dutch and French followed swiftly once they too entered the stage. The VOC engaged in the trade on an astonishing scale, forcibly transporting up to 1.1 million people from the seventeenth to the nineteenth centuries. This was nearly twice the number of people the Dutch trafficked to the Americas in the same period. These men, women and children would be forced into labour in various Indian Ocean settlements, working on plantations and in factories and forts, and sold for profit. In the late 1670s no less than four thousand enslaved Africans were made to build the Dutch fortress in Colombo. Meanwhile, the belatedly arrived French East India Company (Compagnie des Indes, established 1664) engaged thousands of enslaved people in its colonies at Réunion Island from 1663 and Mauritius from 1721. Slavery in the region pre-existed the European entry in a smaller and fragmentary form. Malik Ambar, the undefeated general of the Deccan, had been originally trafficked from Ethiopia and enslaved before rising to become the premier general of Ahmednagar. When the Europeans arrived, however, they exploited, consolidated and substantially increased this commerce. The sharp increase in demand triggered by the Europeans forced an expansion both of the supply itself and of the structures and networks that supported it.

English engagement in Indian Ocean slave trading began very soon after their arrival. As early as 1622 – and perhaps the first instance on record of EIC active participation in this – Company officials at Batavia requested the provision of ten to fifteen males between the ages of sixteen and twenty-two from Pulicat on India's Coromandel Coast. Factors at Pulicat subsequently acquired and dispatched twenty-two enslaved individuals aboard the *Discovery* to the English factory there. In 1640 the *Francis*, a Company vessel, was dispatched from Surat to purchase enslaved people from East Africa. Thirteen of the twenty-two enslaved Africans purchased from Madagascar and Mozambique perished of smallpox on the voyage back to India.[6] The circumstances of human trafficking in these parts were clearly no less devastating than that across the Atlantic. Slaves acquired from captured Portuguese vessels were also exploited, with the enslaved then transported to EIC factories. A single captured Portuguese vessel in 1629 held a hundred people in bondage, likely originating from Mozambique. The EIC went on to traffic the individuals to Company headquarters at Surat.

Through the course of the seventeenth century the EIC continued to increase its trade and by 1654 the Company base at Madras had taken to managing a steady stream of enslaved Indian children who passed through it, on to the Dutch factory at Pulicat and elsewhere. In 1683 an EIC report recorded that 'a great number of slaves yearly' were being shipped from Madras.[7] With the acquisition of the Guinea Company, EIC human trafficking extended to West Africa, with records showing a growth in this trade in the 1660s. In a Company letter dated 31 August 1661, Guinea factors are directed to send fifteen young Black West Africans to Bantam.[8] The instructions are detailed alongside requests for trade items such as paintings, starkly illustrating how the EIC viewed the individuals it sought to acquire in bondage.

The Company in this period had no capacity to found major settlements and had little luck with minor settlements. Where some attempts were made, however, human trafficking was a cornerstone of the project. Enslaved labour became a means to manage and maintain vulnerable, short-staffed and solitary settlements many leagues from England's shores. St Helena, a volcanic island some two thousand kilometres off the coast of Angola, is perhaps most famous as the location of Napoleon Bonaparte's second exile following the 1815 Battle of Waterloo. The EIC took control of the island in 1659. Thereafter it trafficked slaves there from West and East Africa as well as India, to maintain the remote holding. A letter dated 20 February 1663 orders the purchase of a couple of 'Gentue [Indian Hindu] barbers, such as are most expert among them in letting of blood', to then be sent to St Helena and 'there to remaine for the use of our people on that island', while another letter of 11 June the same year directs that 'four men and six women of Gentues, such as are lusty, young and perfect' be sent to the island.[9]

The trafficking of people to St Helena only grew, and in 1684 Robert Knox, captain of the *Tonquin Merchant*, was instructed to purchase 250 enslaved people from Madagascar for transport to St Helena. While smaller-scale trade in the enslaved had long been practised by the Company, this was the EIC's first major slave-trading expedition. That same year Company directors expressed their willingness to purchase up to eighty enslaved West Africans from the RAC to serve at St Helena, a reflection of how English Atlantic and Indian Ocean slave trading intersected. Enslavement also became a form of judicial punishment under the Company's aegis, further serving English factories and settlements. At a Madras trial in August 1688, of 'two black criminalls', the EIC decided to brand and transport one, to be enslaved on St Helena.[10]

While St Helena was successfully acquired by the Company and remains a British Overseas Territory to this day, the EIC attempted less successfully to secure a settlement in the Spice Islands. As part of the 1654 Treaty of Westminster that concluded the First Anglo-Dutch war, the Dutch had committed to returning Pulau Run, a diminutive island of the Moluccas it had captured from the EIC some decades previously. Upon its capture the VOC, in characteristic fashion, had led a genocidal rampage to prevent any competition, in which it murdered, enslaved or banished the indigenous inhabitants and cut down all the island's lucrative nutmeg trees for good measure. With the prospect of resettling Pulau Run back on the table, the EIC got to work. Enslaved West Africans and Indians became key to the Company for this project. In 1661 'ten lusty blacks, men and women' were expected from West Africa to be sent on to Pulau Run, and on 20 February two years later the Company instructed that 'Gentues' from India be sent to work on the island.[11] In real terms, however, the Dutch were far from willing to cede even an inch of their spice trade monopoly, and certainly not the three-kilometre-long by one-kilometre-wide island. By the end of the Second Anglo-Dutch war, in the 1667 Treaty of Breda the English rescinded their claim to the island but formally secured the erstwhile Dutch settlement of New Amsterdam in America, which had been captured by the Duke of York's men in 1664. New Amsterdam was renamed New York after the duke. Although frustrating English aspirations in the Indies, the deal served English interests well in the Americas. Once again, English interests in India and America became a trade-off.

The Company's lengthy and active engagement in slave trading meant that not only were factories and settlements abroad built and operated with enslaved labour, but some of the African and Indian enslaved men, women and children were also sent to and from

England. EIC factors and other Company employees often purchased passage for enslaved servants aboard EIC ships. In 1678 at least four enslaved 'black' individuals and one enslaved Indian woman were secured passage aboard EIC vessels from England, travelling to India or Bantam.[12] Those purchasing such passage ranged from EIC traders, widows of Company employees and private merchants. This expanded the network of EIC slave-trading activities from the Indian Ocean to English shores, contributing to increasingly diverse and globalised English communities the reality of which would emerge on the nation's streets, in its houses and in its artwork. Today a portrait hangs in a celebrated gallery in New Haven, Connecticut, featuring a prominent figure for both the EIC and the gallery alongside a slave.

European slave trading in the Indian Ocean was not without its checks. In addition to slave-led resistance, regional governments tended to not look favourably upon the trafficking and enforced labour of their peoples by traders from the distant north. Such was the objection that on 14 May 1688 the EIC leadership of Fort St George in Madras gathered to discuss the tense state of affairs. There they fretted over the 'great complaints and troubles from the Country Government for the loss of their children and servants spirited and stolen from them'. Matters were all the more concerning given that Alamgir I, the reigning Mughal emperor, was 'very averse, and prohibits all Such trade in his Dominions' and had recently expressed displeasure at the Dutch for their profiteering role in the trade at Machilipatnam.[13] Those gathered agreed that a ban be placed on trading in enslaved people from Madras and adjacent ports, with fines meted out to those who defied it. Whether the ban was enforced, let alone effective, is unclear, but the impact and regional grievance against European slave trading was evident. The English had little aversion to the trade itself. Slave trading at Madras had clearly been lucrative for the Company, but at that same meeting, in observing that 'the Custome by the exportation of Slaves here, being now of little advantage to the Rt Hon Company by scarcity', they made it clear that profits were now scarce while opposition from local authorities was growing. The decision to put the ban in place was little more than an effort to cut losses and nip conflict in the bud.

Presiding at this meeting was the governor of Fort St George, thirty-nine-year-old Elihu Yale. Yale's rise to power had been swift and interesting. Born in 1649 in the colony of Boston, Massachusetts, this merchant's later rise and residence in India forged yet another connection between England's activities east and west. Yale did not remain in America long, however; his family moved to England in 1652 and he never returned to the land of his birth. Following a brief education in London, he joined the East India Company as a clerk in 1670. Two years later he was posted to Madras, where in 1678 he was promoted to factor. In 1680 Yale wedded Catherine Hynmers at St Mary's, Fort St George, the first marriage to take place at the newly consecrated Anglican church. In attendance was the then Company governor of Madras, Streynsham Master. The following year Yale attained the position of mint master, the fifth rank on the council. A series of deaths and dismissals over the next few years then saw him swiftly rise through the ranks until on 25 July 1687 he succeeded William Gyfford as governor of Fort St George.

Yale maintained his governorship until 1692 when he was dismissed, accused of profiteering and corruption. Profiting he certainly had done; with the dowry gained from his marriage he engaged in private trade, most notably in diamonds and other precious stones from Golconda, enriching himself enormously. He returned to England in 1699 a wealthy man, living out his days in great style and making a hobby of collecting luxuries. By the time of his death, in 1721, among his private collections were five thousand paintings including a Rembrandt, hundreds of snuffboxes, 116 pairs of cufflinks, and an impressive array of jewels, watches and books. Such was the mass of his belongings that thirty auctions were required to clear them. Yet objects alone were not the sole property of this dubiously enriched EIC governor. Nor were his connections to his roots in North America quite severed.

In 2020 an arresting new artwork was put on temporary display at a gallery in New Haven, Connecticut. Created by African-American painter and sculptor Titus Kaphar, and entitled *Enough About You*, it comprised a large crumpled painting at one corner of which a golden frame encircles the portrait of a ten-year-old Black child. Dressed in a pale blue coat with red buttons and with a soft white shirt beneath, the child stares defiantly and directly out from his frame at the viewer. While the rest of the artwork is crumpled out of view, the boy is magnified and centrally placed, his palette bright, as if bearing a spot-light. Kaphar had created the piece in response to another work that usually occupied that same spot in the gallery. The older portrait, dated 1719, features four wealthy white men seated around a table smoking and drinking at leisure. Behind them in the shadows is the Black child carrying a bottle of wine while looking at the men. Most disturbingly, in this portrait the child bears about his young neck a metal collar with a padlock. By this it is made clear he is enslaved. The implied slave master is the older man at the centre of the vast portrait: Elihu Yale, erstwhile governor of Fort St George.[14] The university gallery which owns the artwork bears the name of the man: Yale Center for British Art.

Eighteenth-century artwork featuring Black enslaved people wear-ing collars is far from uncommon. Such figures represented owners' status and wealth, attributes the young child in this portrait was clearly intended to symbolise. Among the enslaved individuals trafficked to England from the Indian Ocean and Atlantic slave trades were boys aged ten and under who were made to serve in domestic capacities, often as pages, in wealthy households. Like the rich velvet coat he wears and the ruby ring upon his finger, Yale in this painting objectifies this child as yet another material symbol of his personal wealth and property. He both presided over slave trading at Fort St George and brought the brutal commerce to his English home, immortalising it in art. Even as the portrait draws attention to the symbol of the Black child, simultan-eously the boy is shrunk and silenced into shadowy servitude, an aspect Kaphar challenges headlong in his reimagined portrait.

While conspicuously indulging in his riches, Yale also engaged in colonial philanthropy to further English efforts in American settle-ments. His most notable donation was to the famed university that bears his name and which now owns this portrait. In 1713 Yale, along with 180 fellow donors, contributed over eight hundred books to the then struggling Collegiate School in Connecticut. In 1718 he dispatched several trunks of textile goods to further support the insti-tution. Over time his collective donations totalled over £800 (£93,000 today), the largest donation in Yale University's first century.

So gratified were the college trustees that they offered to immortalise their most generous donor in a manner that 'your munificence might easily obtain for you such a commemoration and perpetuation of your valuable name, as would indeed be much better than an Egyptian pyramid'.[15] In September 1718, they formally renamed the college in honour of Elihu Yale, and Yale College was born. In 1887 it once again restyled itself, this time in its modern iteration, Yale University.

Elihu Yale is just one of several links to slavery in Yale University's chequered history. Other connections include the ownership of enslaved peoples by early members of the university staff and graduates, most prominently John C. Calhoun (d. 1850), who served as the seventh vice president of the United States. Calhoun was a proud slave owner who virulently campaigned in favour of slavery with his 'positive good' thesis that argued for the great benefits of slavery to white American society.[16] In 1933 the university named a residential college in Calhoun's honour. Following years of student protests, the college was finally renamed in 2017. Another building all the more deeply connected to historic slavery is Connecticut Hall, the oldest building on campus, which was constructed by enslaved Africans. Today Yale University has begun to take steps to reckon with its violent past, acknowledging that 'slavery and the slave trade are part of Yale's history – our history'.[17]

Seventeenth-century networks of slave trading, commerce and colonialism are interconnected and complex, and their continuing impact is no less so. In Elihu Yale, that entanglement of violence and profit finds a curious kind of embodiment. Perhaps this is encapsulated best in Yale's own epitaph upon his death:

> Born in America, in Europe bred,
> In Afric travell'd, and in Asia wed,
> Where long he liv'd, and thriv'd; at London dead.
> Much good, some ill, he did; so hope all's even,
> And that his soul, through mercy's gone to heaven.
> You that survive, and read, take care
> For this most certain exit to prepare:
> For only the actions of the just
> Smell sweet and blossom in the dust.[18]

What began as an American colonial birth proceeded to Indian Ocean slave trading and profiteering, then went on to fund one of the modern world's leading institutions of learning. Elihu Yale illustrates well how English-led global networks of violence were forged in his time and how they persist to this day. His story reveals the many layers of the prolific trade in human souls through the seventeenth century, not least that its reaches were far more extensive than is often appreciated. The East India Company's traffic in enslaved peoples in the Indian Ocean is a lesser-known yet no less devastating example of this most infamous commerce.

PART III

Conqueror of the World

13

Child's War

ON 7 JUNE 1633 a pair of enormous male elephants, Sudhakar and Surat Sundhar, were led to an open field by the banks of the Yamuna River. They were preparing for a bout, a favourite and regularly held entertainment of the Emperor Shah Jahan. This occasion should have been no different: it was set up at the usual spot, in good view of the palace balcony at Agra from where Shah Jahan and his family watched. Fighting commenced and the great animals battled ferociously, charging each other amid billowing dust and enraged trumpeting. It was not long, however, before Sudhakar and Surat Sundhar moved out of clear view of the royal balcony. Shah Jahan promptly decided to descend to get nearer the action. He took with him his eldest three sons, Dara Shikoh, Shuja and the then fourteen-year-old Aurangzeb. Together, the four followed the elephants from a distance on horseback.

It was not the wisest of decisions. The newcomers caught Sudhakar's attention, and the animal spun around trumpeting furiously before charging directly at Aurangzeb. Without missing a beat, the teenage prince sprang into action; grabbing a spear, he galloped headlong towards the oncoming elephant. As he neared, Aurangzeb rose upon his stirrups and took aim, flinging the weapon with all his might at the animal's head. Sudhakar stumbled from the impact, the spear piercing a wound but far from felling him. Now further enraged, the animal struck Aurangzeb's steed in the flanks, driving his tusk into the horse and flinging the prince to the ground. Undeterred, Aurangzeb leapt to his feet, swiftly drawing his sword ready to defend himself. By then Prince Shuja and Raja Jai Singh, a prominent Rajput, had joined the fray, attempting to draw Sudhakar away with weapons and fireworks. Fortuitously, Surat Sundhar took advantage of Sudhakar's distraction to charge, forcing the two beasts back into battle and sparing the prince.

Not only had Aurangzeb survived against the odds; for the first time he had achieved something that was crucial: distinguishing himself in the sight of the emperor and his court. While in Europe a crown tended to pass to the firstborn son in a system of primogeniture, this was not the practice in Mughal India where any male child was eligible to succeed. This often made for bloody rivalry among the princes. Shah Jahan himself had gained the throne having determinedly eliminated all other contenders. Distinguishing yourself at court and garnering the favour of the emperor was valuable to gaining support as a possible successor to the throne. The elephant battle was the first instance in which Aurangzeb marked himself out for notice. As the prince finally retreated, Shah Jahan embraced his brave son in relief and pride. The event of the 'lion-hearted youth' would be immortalised not only by royal chroniclers but also in art. At least two miniatures memorialising Aurangzeb's youthful bravery would be created, one of which was included in Shah Jahan's official chronicle, the *Padshahnama*.

Within a year the prince was granted his first mansab by his father, giving him command of ten thousand cavalry. A year or so on, in 1635 he was sent on his first campaign, aged just sixteen. For the next twenty-two years Aurangzeb was posted across the Mughal Empire, sharpening his skills in military campaigning and governance. It was experience that would serve him well, as although he had caught the attention of Shah Jahan at the elephant battle, the emperor openly preferred his eldest son, Dara Shikoh, as successor. Throughout Shah Jahan's reign Dara Shikoh remained by his father's side at Agra, poisoning the royal court against his brothers, and particularly Aurangzeb. The rivalry between the brothers emerged even in moments of tragedy. When their sister Jahanara endured her near fatal burning, all the brothers rushed from across the empire to her bedside with loving concern. During this visit Dara invited his father and brothers to view his new Agra mansion. While touring a riverside room, Aurangzeb had seated himself near the single exit and refused to move, before soon departing for his own palace. When later questioned on this odd behaviour the prince replied, '[I feared that] he might shut the door, and then all would be over [with us].'¹ In such a confined setting, Dara may well have dispatched his brothers to clear his own way to the throne.

Eventually the bitter contest descended into outright and unprecedentedly lengthy succession wars in which Dara Shikoh's indulgent courtly life and inexperience was no match for Aurangzeb's decades of political and military experience. Unlike Jahangir, who did not live to see his successor's bloodletting, Shah Jahan was in the unusual position of witnessing the battles between his sons. When a severe illness overcame the emperor in September 1657 it triggered the wars of succession, yet while Shah Jahan unexpectedly survived the sons nonetheless continued to battle. Throughout these wars the influential daughters of Shah Jahan took up their positions behind their chosen brothers: Jahanara behind Dara, Gauharara behind Murad and Roshanara behind Aurangzeb.

When the dust finally settled, in 1659, Aurangzeb had successfully claimed the throne. On Roshanara's advice, Dara Shikoh was executed, having first been paraded in humiliation through the streets of Delhi clapped in chains, dressed in coarse cloth and mounted on a muddied elephant. Jahanara, the sister who had backed him, was relieved of her title of Padshah Begim, which was then passed to Aurangzeb ally, Roshanara. The latter, described by Manucci as 'very clever, capable of dissimulation, bright, mirthful', continued to influence her brother as emperor from this new position for a time.² Shah Jahan himself was imprisoned at Agra Fort, having actively colluded with Dara against Aurangzeb. From there he lived out the remainder of his days with his favourite daughter Jahanara. Meanwhile, Shuja fled to Arakan, never to return, and Murad was imprisoned and later executed. The successor had learnt well from his father's fratricidal example.

On 13 May 1659 Muhi al-Din Muhammad Aurangzeb hosted a grand coronation ceremony in Delhi. He took for himself the title Alamgir (World Conqueror), inspired by an inscription on a sword given by Shah Jahan following the Battle of Samugarh the previous year. The title was apt, for Alamgir I would go on to become Mughal India's most formidable emperor. His reign spanned half a century during which he oversaw the expansion of the empire to its greatest extent, bringing most of the Indian subcontinent under single rule for the first time in history. He ruled a kingdom covering 3.2 million square kilometres and governed a population of an astonishing 150 million, around twice that of western Europe. With a treasury bursting with gold, silver and priceless gems, including the famed Koh-i-Noor diamond, he was most probably the single wealthiest man of his time.

Both Roshanara and Jahanara played prominent roles in the rise and reign of their brother. During the succession wars, reprising the role of their forebears, the princesses engaged in mediation between the warring princes as well as political intrigue. Jahanara acted as intermediary between Aurangzeb and their father, unsuccessfully attempting to persuade her brother to split the Mughal territories between their brothers rather than go to war in pursuit of the throne for himself. Roshanara had acted as Aurangzeb's eyes and ears at their father's court, feeding her brother information. When Shah Jahan fell ill in the run-up to the succession wars, she reportedly ensured Aurangzeb's seal was on all imperial decrees to pave the way for his succession. During their brother's reign, both princesses served as Padshah Begim. While at the conclusion of the succession wars Alamgir I elevated Roshanara, seven years later, following the death of Shah Jahan in 1666, Jahanara was returned as first lady, unseating her sister. If Venetian traveller Manucci's claims are to be believed, much of this had to do with Roshanara's licentious lifestyle, although given his obvious lack of access to the haram and halls of power, it is difficult to see this as much more than a fantasy. In their successive roles as first lady, the princesses issued legislative documents, *nishan*, with their seals, guided their ruling brother on matters of state, oversaw the management of the haram and dispensed their abundant wealth in commerce and architecture. In addition to Jahanara's building works in Shahjahanabad, Roshanara counted the Roshanara Bagh garden in Delhi as among her commissions.

With his sisters successively by his side, Alamgir I brought about sweeping changes to the empire. Perhaps chief among these was the streamlining and centralising of a previously chaotic and fragmentary judiciary by sponsoring the codification of law into a single compendium, the *Fatawa-i Alamgiri*. Furthermore, in a break from his predecessors he publicly subjected himself to the law. In 1675 he appointed a team of judicial officials to every city, province and neighbouring territory of the empire, to hear legal claims against him from the citizenry. As a monarch he was meticulous to the point of micro-management, sleeping no more than three hours at night and engaging directly in everything from courtly audiences twice a day to administrative minutiae. For Manucci, he was a deeply serious and indefatigable monarch:

> The third son of King Shahjahan was the prince Aurangzeb, the present King of Hindustan. This prince was very different from the others, being in character very secretive and serious, carrying on his affairs in a hidden way, but most energetically. He was of a melancholy temperament, always busy at something or another, wishing to execute justice and arrive at appropriate decisions. He was extremely anxious to be recognised by the world as a man of wisdom, clever, and a lover of the truth.[3]

With his accession to the throne, a new Mughal era had begun. And the English in India would certainly feel the force of it.

The empire Alamgir I claimed was thriving and prosperous. To this he added an expansionist zeal that saw the kingdom's frontiers extended beyond those of any of his predecessors. Through a combination of diplomacy and force he annexed territories, crushed rebellions and made vassals of regional rulers. Under his aegis, rebellions in the north-western frontier were neutralised and control of Bihar, Odisha and Bengal in the north-east was consolidated. Among his successes was the capture of the key Bengal port of Chittagong, since 1459 controlled by the Arakanese Kingdom of Mrauk U. Overrun with Arakanese and Portuguese pirates and slave traders, Bengal's coastline and waterways had long been terrorised, with many Bengalis captured and sold into slavery. In late 1665 Alamgir I's governor, Shaista Khan, deployed an armada of three hundred warships coupled with an overland expedition of thousands of troops to attack the port, wresting Chittagong from Arakanese control. Khan further oversaw the release of thousands of enslaved people, writing to Alamgir I: 'In truth, its [Chittagong's] revenue is the composure of the minds of the Muslims [with regard to pirates and slave traders]. We can easily imagine how fast cultivation will increase in Bengal, now that Magh [Arakanese] violence has been put down.'[4]

In the defiant Deccan Plateau, Alamgir I advanced further than any other Mughal. Nonetheless, it was this region that proved his greatest challenge. Having begun campaigns in the Deccan in his princely days, much of his reign as emperor was spent battling to bring the entire region under Mughal control. So bold were his adversaries that on the night of 5 April 1663, a modest contingent of men succeeded in infiltrating the residence of Shaista Khan, then governor of the Deccan, making it as far as the governor's bedchamber. In the bloodied attack, Khan lost a finger but survived. However, several of his wives, his son and many soldiers and servants were killed. Hearing of this humiliating defeat within the governor's own compound, Alamgir I dismissed Khan from the Deccan post and redeployed him to Bengal, then considered the backwater of the empire. There the governor went on to distinguish himself with the capture of Chittagong and consolidation of Mughal rule, particularly in eastern Bengal.

Less than a year later, in January 1664, Alagmir I's opponents – including a cavalry of four thousand – undertook the even bolder move of attacking Surat. They relentlessly plundered the port city for six days as the governor, Mahabat Khan, cowered in the city's fort. In the words of one European observer, Khan was simply unable to contain 'the fury of this robber'.[5] Buildings were razed, merchants' mansions looted and countless inhabitants captured, including EIC merchant Anthony Smith and a recently arrived ambassador from Ethiopia en route for Alamgir I's court. Of those captured, many had their hands hacked off. Others were summarily decapitated, a fate Smith narrowly escaped. As they rampaged, the Maratha forces set countless houses alight, reducing the city to a smouldering inferno. It was 'a fier soe great as turnd the night into day; as before the smoke in the day tyme had almost turnd day into night; rising soe thicke as it darkened the sun like a great cloud,' related one appalled EIC witness.[6] From the roof of the Company factory the merchants watched the horror unfold while at the gates they defended themselves as best they could with muskets and cannons brought in from a docked Company ship.

Surat's traders suffered devastating losses. Baharji Bohra, reputed to be the wealthiest trader in the world and from whom the EIC frequently took loans and engaged in trade, saw his mansion sacked. The loot the raiders extracted from Bohra's home was staggering. Kilos of pearls, diamonds, rubies and emeralds were swept clean, masses of gold and cash seized, before the mansion was set alight.[7] Another wealthy Indian trader, Haji Said Beg, saw his mansion similarly razed. By the time it was over, the Marathas had made off with an estimated 10 million rupees' worth of cash and valuables.[8] Yet, the siege was far from done; in the aftermath an armed fleet was deployed to capture Mughal pilgrim ships departing from Surat, and extracted substantial ransoms from the pilgrims.

Once again outdone by the relentless rebel warrior, Alamgir I decided to dispatch his most trusted veteran commander, Mirza Raja Jai Singh, the Kachwaha raja of Amber. Jai Singh went about amassing a sizeable army that included a regiment of European soldiers, among whom was the chameleon-like Manucci. Others in the regiment included French surgeon Luis Beicao, Portuguese soldier Dominigo de Saa and an English soldier recorded only as William.[9] Among several systematic retaliatory measures, Jai Singh dispatched agents to the European coastal settlements instructing them to obstruct Maratha fleets. Meanwhile, he began aggressive overland military operations. Before long, the rebels were overcome and finally submitted to negotiations. The ensuing treaty saw the Maratha fighter cede twenty-three forts and become a nominal Mughal vassal. Predictably, however, this was short-lived.[10]

The rebels should have appeared at Alamgir I's court on 12 May 1666. Understandably, Jai Singh had little trust in their commitment to the treaty he had signed, so had negotiated the courtly audience with the emperor. The meeting was the only recorded face-to-face encounter between the Mughal and his Deccan adversaries. Alamgir I accommodated the audience generously,[11] advancing the Deccans 100,000 rupees from the treasury for the journey. At Agra, they were hosted by Kumar Ram Singh, Jai Singh's son and agent at the imperial *darbar*.

The emperor's court was a dazzling affair. The vast rectangular hall was lined with marble pillars embellished with floral motifs above which rose countless decorative archways. Overhead the great ceiling too was intricately inlaid with silver and gold. Beneath this glimmering canopy nobles stood to attention rank by rank, dressed in their finest and bedecked in jewels. The emperor himself was an adorned display, his turban pinned with jewels and numerous strings of pearls and precious stones laced about his neck. Yet the most arresting feature of the scene was the Peacock Throne upon which he was seated, an exceptional indulgence originally commissioned by Shah Jahan. While the Taj Mahal has gained the most fame as the showpiece of Shah Jahan's reign, this grand royal seat alone cost twice as much to create. An astonishing feat of craftsmanship and extravagance, it was a large raised and covered platform measuring 2 by 2.4 metres (7 x 8 ft) and 4.3 metres (14 ft) from the base to the crest of its glittering domed roof. Created by a team of craftsmen over seven years, in excess of 2,600 pounds of solid beaten gold went into its construction along with 9 million rupees' worth of gems. Every single inch of the throne glittered with jewels, from the canopy held aloft by twelve emerald-encrusted pillars to the two bejewelled peacock figures on its roof from which it took its name. For those entering the imperial *darbar*, such lavish display must have been both arresting and intimidating.

The Mughal imperial court was governed by a strictly maintained code of etiquette and protocol. Disruptions were an egregious matter and dealt with accordingly. All seemed well as the rebel leader approached Alamgir I, presenting his gifts of submission and bowing at the feet of the Peacock Throne.[12] The emperor acknowledged the man who had been creating so much trouble for him, but delayed responding with customary gifts in return. To the shock of the court, the Maratha chose to deviate from the formalities of the *darbar*, and so, the rebel leader was promptly marched off and placed under house arrest. Yet this too was short-lived. Within a matter of weeks he had escaped, sneaking past his guards hidden in a basket of confectionery. He then made his way back to Raigarh via a circuitous route, all the while evading capture disguised as a Hindu monk.

By October 1670, the rebels were back at Surat conducting yet another devastating raid with an army of fifteen thousand; this despite protective city walls having been erected at Alamgir I's command. There seemed to be no stopping the rebellion. On this occasion a no less hefty 6.5 million rupees' worth of loot was seized. The attacks were devastating for the port city's residents, not least the EIC traders, who would go on to demand and secure compensation from the Company. The Surat president along with his council and factors earned gold medals and cash from the Company in London 'for their care of the Company's concerns in the time of [the] insurrection'.[13] One James Adam petitioned and secured ten pounds for his services in defending the Surat factory.[14] Another, Philip Gifford, secured twenty pounds 'in respect of his great sufferings and imprisonment'.[15] Meanwhile, Surat Company governors Gerald Aungier and Streynsham Master were both given gold medals for their services against the Maratha attacks.[16] The gratuities were well earned; the Maratha warrior they repeatedly endured was both relentless and merciless. After two major raids inflicted upon the Mughals' most prominent commercial port, trade in the region went into decline for several years as it became clear Surat could not be adequately defended.

For many years Alamgir I oversaw Mughal expansion, including the battles against the rebels and their descendants, primarily from his court at Delhi. However, by the early 1680s the struggle to conquer the Deccan proved far too frustrating to witness from afar. In 1681 the emperor packed up his entire court and moved to the Deccan front to oversee the expansionist efforts himself, there to remain for the rest of his life and reign. His sprawling imperial army included a section encamped by Danda Rajpuri, some forty miles from the English settlement at Bombay. In the ensuing twenty-five years he secured the diamond-rich kingdom of Golconda, Bijapur and parts of Tamil Nadu, all the while running a fully functioning court and governing an empire from his military encampment.

Born of nomadic traditions, the Mughals retained their heritage in their peripatetic court, which travelled in great luxury, bearing the full grandeur of a metropolitan court, with all its paraphernalia. The emperors often travelled, whether for politics or pleasure, continuing their governance from their roving court. Sir Thomas Roe knew this well, having followed Jahangir to Ajmer and travelled with the emperor on a trip to Kashmir. If the seventeenth-century travelling caravan was a scene of wonder, the grand travelling court of the

Mughal monarch was a sight of majesty. Slowly and solemnly it weaved its way across the Indian landscape, its sweeping green flags borne on the backs of countless elephants visible from a distance, before blossoming into great crimson tent cities. The court 'move[d] with the gorgeous magnificence peculiar to the kings of Hindoustan', wrote François Bernier, a French traveller who joined Alamgir I's court on a trip to Lahore.[17] The security detail alone of Alamgir I's travelling court on a normal day included cavalry and infantry to the tune of tens of thousands. Everything from heavy artillery to tents and kitchenware were carried or drawn by an army of horses, camels, oxen and elephants. Alamgir I's commitment to the nomadic court was perhaps second only to that of Mughal founder Babur. The latter, fully immersed in central Asian nomadic traditions, spent his reign in India preferring to reside and hold court in gardens. Even in death Alamgir I would break with the tradition of grand Mughal mausoleums, to be laid to rest in an open-air grave, just as Babur had been.

Each Mughal royal campsite was a four-cornered metropolis of marquees enclosed by a wall some 2.4 metres (8 ft) in height. The camp walls were constructed of foldable wooden screens covered in sturdy crimson cloth and lined with rich calicos decorated with floral motifs. The spacious royal entrance to the tent city was especially magnificent in its floral embellishments. The many marquees were constructed of richly woven silk velvet, also in deep crimson, and often adorned with gold embroidery. The travelling court included marquees to accommodate the every requirement of a fully functioning state, from halls of public audience to ministerial quarters. These were interconnected by a network of pathways lit on both sides by the burning glow of tall brass torches. The *zenana* was a particularly protected section of the campsite, surrounded by its own eight-foot enclosure and managed by its own female army of staff and security. While barely any remnants of these roving courts have survived, in 1658 Rajput prince Jaswant Singh managed to capture an imperial tent from the Mughal encampment during battle with Alamgir I. Safely retained at the palace of Jodhpur to this day, the crimson silk velvet tent gives a glimpse of the splendour of the Mughal roving court. The tradition of constructing grand tents for thousands continues to this day in south Asia, catering to everything from weddings to religious gatherings, with skill and technical knowledge passed down through centuries.

The logistics of such an immense and regal moving city was minutely managed to ensure seamless royal travel, and it is perhaps this aspect that is most impressive. Not one but two fully functioning moving courts travelled at once, each led by its own formidable camp master, such that while one encampment was erected and in use, another travelled a day ahead to the next designated campsite, where it would be set up ready to receive the emperor. On Alamgir I's journey to Lahore in 1665, the advance camp alone consisted of over 60 elephants, 200 camels and 100 mules each bearing luggage commensurate with their strength.[18] In this way the emperor travelled from one functioning encampment to the next with minimal disruption.

For Alamgir I, now permanently stationed in the Deccan, seamless travel was essential. The task of combining minutely attentive governance of one of the largest empires on earth with concerted military expansion across perhaps the most politically challenging region of the Indian subcontinent was mammoth. It was a wise man who avoided crossing the emperor and disrupting his campaign against the Marathas. Unfortunately for the East India Company, neither its governor in Bombay, John Child, nor its sometime governor and largest shareholder in London, Josiah Child (no relation to John Child), counted wisdom among their talents.

To call Josiah Child grasping would be an understatement. Described by the English diarist John Evelyn as 'most sordidly avaricious', he was a merchant who coupled greed with immense corruption and a total absence of moral principles.[19] He married three times, twice to wealthy widows, enriching himself by their assets to a point where his estate swelled to some £200,000 (£22.8 million today). With this he purchased Wanstead Abbey in Epping Forest and landscaped it at immense expense. He further went about seizing the estates of his under-age stepchildren, all of whom disliked him intensely. His stepson Francis subsequently took him to court, alleging that Child had appropriated £60,000 from the estate belonging to the stepchildren. As he was detested in family life so he made few friends in professional life. He was committed to the trade in enslaved people and was a founding member of the re-established Royal

African Company in 1672, serving as a director from 1675 to 1676. Even among that class who viewed people as chattels, Child was disliked for being too grasping. In 1672 he entered into a partnership to establish a 1,330-acre sugar works in Jamaica for which he would provide servants and enslaved workers. He also had partnerships with slave-trading shipowners.

While he pursued profit in transatlantic slavery, his primary passion was the East Indies trade. In 1671 he became a shareholder of the EIC, and by 1679 was its largest shareholder with £23,000 in shares. By 1691 this figure had risen to £51,150. From 1674 until his death in 1699 he served on the EIC Court of Directors, during which time he held the positions of deputy governor twice (1684–6 and 1688–90) and governor twice (1681–3 and 1686–8). Among his more notorious distinctions was spending the 1680s actively engaging in bribery to secure royal support for the Company, to the extent that from 1681 to 1688 an annual bribe of 10,000 guineas to the king became expected as standard from the EIC.

His unrelated namesake at the EIC in India, John Child, was in many ways no better. Sent to India at a young age, he was employed by the Company from 1659, over time rising in the ranks. In 1677 Child joined the council at Surat and two years later was appointed deputy governor of Bombay. His activities in Bombay, not least his economising, earned him praise in London, particularly from Josiah Child. Yet, his behaviour did little to endear him. Gerald Aungier, president of Surat and governor of Bombay (1669–77), complained of 'the pride and turbulence of his [John Child's] spirit, for which he hath now rendered himself notorious in all the factories wherever he hath served'.[20] By 1682, during Josiah Child's first tenure as EIC governor, John Child gained the appointment of president at Surat. A further two years and he had secured the role of 'Captain Generall of all our forces by sea and land' in India, under instructions to move the Company headquarters to Bombay, which he undertook on 2 May 1687. There he engaged in private trade, in contravention of Company charter and rules, while continuing to conduct himself in such a manner as to be universally disliked.

Between them the two Childs triggered an unprecedented storm on the EIC in India. This would come to be known as Child's War.

It was the first and, for good reason, last time the EIC attempted militarily to take on the Mughals in the seventeenth century. Begun in 1686, this unnecessary and deeply reckless conflict stretched from the EIC's eastern ports to its western trading posts in India. The Company had until then favoured a diplomatic approach to the Mughals in their pursuit of Indian trade. It certainly made sense: war was an enormous expense, a challenging undertaking at such distances and an immense risk faced with so powerful an adversary as the Mughals. However, in the 1680s Child and his faction of shareholders in London sought to pursue a militarised approach to reinforce EIC efforts in India. By this he imagined that the Mughals could be forced into a more advantageous trade deal while also challenging the many English interlopers who were then breaking the Company's monopoly by trading in Mughal territories. In early 1686 the EIC Court of Directors secured a charter from James II permitting the deployment of troops and fleets against English interlopers as well as Indian rulers. That year an EIC fleet of nineteen warships was dispatched from London.

It was on the eastern coast that the war began. The EIC, increasingly unhappy with its dealings with local governors, took advantage of the new combative approach to go on the rampage in Bengal. In November 1686 Hooghly was attacked. The town was fired on by the ships, and raids conducted ashore. Some sixty Indian soldiers died and up to five hundred houses and numerous boats and barges burnt. Bengal governor Shaista Khan, no friend of the English to begin with, having described them as 'a company of base, quarrelling people and foul dealers', was enraged.[21] He seized EIC factories and dispatched vast detachments of cavalry to Hooghly to expel the English, who soon withdrew on 20 December 1686. Yet within a matter of months Company men were back on the attack, occupying the small island of Hijli on the banks of the Rasulpur River, a tributary of the Hooghly River. They also rained violence on the town of Balasore in Odisha. The following March a hundred and seventy English soldiers and sailors raided the town, looting and burning as they went and seizing Mughal vessels. This time Shaista Khan responded by sending some twelve thousand troops against the English, who found themselves cornered for months at Hijli. Caught between a Mughal siege and the ravages of an inclement and disease-infested island, two-thirds perished before the survivors evacuated on 11 June.

The EIC governor in Bengal, Job Charnock, subsequently came to an uneasy peace with Shaista Khan's general and retreated to Sutanuti, the village where he would subsequently encourage the Company to establish its Bengal headquarters. But the peace with Shaista Khan was soon shattered by Charnock's newly arrived replacement, Captain William Heath. Although Heath withdrew the EIC trade from Bengal in early November 1688, later that month he led yet another raid on Balasore with three hundred soldiers, storming the Mughal fort and attacking the town. In January 1689 Heath sailed to the coast of Chittagong, possessed of the notion of annexing it for the English. Luckily, he was dissuaded from the suicidal project and returned to Madras, the EIC now fully ousted from Bengal. The conflict had effectively ended the Company trade there, its factories seized and razed, its traders expelled by the Mughals. And this would have remained the case had it not been for the newly appointed governor of Bengal, Ibrahim Khan, who in late 1690 permitted the Company to return.

Much as the Bengal conflicts were damaging, it was the rash actions of John Child on the western coast that really brought matters to a head. Company military activity in this region had largely been limited to attacking Indian ships, in itself sufficient to seriously damage relations with the Mughals given that such acts were viewed as piracy. Then on 18 January 1689 John Child seized a fleet of Mughal ships freighting provisions to Alamgir I's army. This disruption to the emperor's Deccan project – which by this point he was leading himself – saw all hell break loose. The emperor immediately ordered the arrest of all EIC staff at Surat, the occupation of their factories all over his dominions, and the prohibition of all trade with the audacious merchants. Within a month the latent English settlement at Bombay had been descended upon by Alamgir I's ally, Sidi Yakut Khan, of the fort of Janjira.

With up to fourteen thousand fighters, Yakut lay siege to Bombay, catching Child entirely unawares. Residents fled to the mainland as the settlement was razed and set alight. Within a week Khan's forces had overtaken the archipelago with Company soldiers and remaining civilians left to resist and seek refuge at the English fort. There over the next fifteen miserable months they became increasingly overtaken by disease, including the bubonic plague, dwindling supplies and desertion. Over the course of the siege a hundred and fifteen Company soldiers and sailors deserted the fort, defecting to the Mughal side. Dozens of these men converted to Islam for good measure. Meanwhile, Mughal officials in Surat added insult to injury by taking to parading the imprisoned EIC Surat factors in chains through the streets. Up to 90 per cent of England's flagship settlement at Bombay had either fled or perished in the assault, and as the survivors cowered in the fort, Company officials gave serious consideration to abandoning the settlement altogether, blowing up the fort and fleeing back to England. As Manucci would recall, Bombay 'was so closely pressed that it very nearly fell into the hands of the Mughal'.[22]

With matters having reached a desperate pass, John Child was forced to sue for peace, sending a mission led by G. Weldon and Abraham Navarro to Alamgir I's mobile military court in December 1689. One can only imagine how the wearied and ragged Englishmen felt as they arrived at that imposing crimson tent city surrounded by the armoured masses of Alamgir I's army. The petitioners were made to approach the emperor on their knees with hands bound, bowing penitently at the foot of his throne. It was a grovelling apology and humiliation extracted for the tomfoolery of going to war and interfering with the Mughal Deccan campaigns to boot. Alamgir I agreed to the cessation of hostilities, issuing a *farman* for the resumption of English trade. But the terms of the decree could not have been more embarrassing. The document treated the Company as if it were a wayward child, reprimanding it for behaving 'in such a shameful manner' and highlighting its 'most humble, submissive petition' such that 'His Majesty hath pardoned their faults'.[23] The decree exacted a sizeable fine of 150,000 rupees, apology before the emperor and demanded the expulsion of John Child from India. The orders were fulfilled apart for the third: John Child died on 4 February 1690 at Bombay before the Mughals or the EIC could hold him accountable for the chaos. In some ways, he had made his escape, given that the conflict he triggered had done little to endear him to either side.

So humiliating was the war and its outcome that the EIC attempted to keep the details secret in London, particularly regarding the catastrophic Bombay siege. Armed conflict in India had coincided with the Glorious Revolution in England, the latter also bruising for the EIC. James II had been deposed to be replaced by his daughter and son-in-law, Mary II and William III, and the Company's close links to the overthrown king meant it had a growing base of enemies. The colossal mess in India would only add fuel to that domestic fire. Unfortunately for the EIC, a disgruntled employee soon leaked a translation of Alamgir I's *farman* in London. The EIC's detractors leapt upon the document as proof of incompetence and excesses – as indeed it was – pressing the newly installed queen and king to not renew the charter. In 1691 a petition circulated demanding the EIC's abolition, securing no less than 420 signatures from London's merchant community. Although the Company managed to somehow survive this particular storm too, it far from quelled the critics.

In an aggressive pursuit of greater agency and trade in India, the EIC had instead almost brought about its ruin. Going to war with the most militarised emperor of the world's wealthiest empire had been a singular and near fatal folly. It was a mercy that Alamgir I had permitted the resumption of trade rather than allow his wrath to end the Company's project in India – as well he could have. Had he done so, history may well have been very different.

14

Exceeding Treasure

IN AUTUMN 1663 Captain George Pattison and his mate Thomas Lurting wearily sailed their modest trading vessel up the Thames. The sights and sounds of home were an immense relief. Neither the typical stench of the river nor the bothersome ferrymen who crowded its waters with rowing boats could dampen their spirits as they made their way towards the capital. In London, lively crowds swarmed to the theatres dotted along the South Bank, now finally reopened and revived after the Restoration. North of the river stood the rows upon rows of black-and-white buildings, built of timber and plaster and clustered together like an awkward chequerboard amid the daily bustle and hum of the city. All was familiar and reassuring after the ordeal they had just escaped.

The men had travelled to Venice, western Europe's trading capital, a journey many undertook. The promise of lucrative commerce in the region was however shadowed by an ever-present threat that hung over the choppy waters of the Mediterranean. The basin was as much a melting pot of trade and cultural interaction as it was a flashpoint of piracy. Among the offenders were the English themselves, along with Spanish, Venetian and other mainland European corsairs. The North African side had its own thriving community of privateers, with Algiers and Tunis prominent bases from which they worked. As regencies of the Ottoman Empire, the corsairs of Algiers and Tunis were often working in cahoots with regional Ottoman governors who took a handsome cut from the raids. In this were parallels with western European privateering where monarchs commissioned pirates to attack enemy ships. For many years under Elizabeth I English ships had targeted Iberian vessels. The North African privateers worked the Mediterranean waters but also extended their activities to the Atlantic and as far as the North Sea and Irish coast.

Pattison and Lurting had fallen foul of the North African corsairs but had managed to make an escape both narrow and, by Lurting's own dramatic and likely embellished retelling, exceptionally daring and merciful. Setting off from Venice, their ship had made it as far as Majorca before being accosted by an Algerian pirate vessel. At the pirate captain's orders, his men had overrun the English ship and taken Pattison and four other men onto their own vessel, leaving several corsairs to keep an eye on Lurting and the remaining English sailors. Eventually Pattison and his fellow men were returned. Thereafter, Lurting hatched a daring plan overnight which saw the overthrow of the corsairs and the English reclaimation of their ship. The pirates were then returned to shore some fifty miles from Algiers before Lurting and Pattison made a swift escape to England, not a single drop of blood having been shed in the foray.

As they travelled up the Thames and met vessels along the way, they shared their story of capture and flight. These boats then travelled ahead, relaying the tale until it reached the ears of the English king himself. Charles II was then at Greenwich along with his brother James and a retinue of lords. The royals and their courtiers were immensely intrigued and keen to hear the story from the lips of the escaped captives themselves. They made their way to the banks of the river where they awaited Pattison's ship. Once in view, the vessel was beckoned alongside and the courtiers boarded while the king and duke remained at the ropes to hear the dramatic retelling of the captain and his mate. Charles II was especially keen to hear their tale, asking many questions. He rebuked the men for releasing their corsair captives, stating they should have been brought to him. To this Lurting explained, 'I thought it better for them to be in their own country.'[1]

Buoyed up, Lurting settled back in Liverpool to compile his captivity narrative, *The Fighting Sailor Turn'd Peaceable Christian*, which he published in May 1680. It proved popular and some years later he expanded the account, republishing it in extended form in 1709. North African piracy and captivity had become such a pressing issue in the seventeenth century that captivity narratives gained prominence and popularity, with dozens of accounts published throughout the period. Lurting joined in this growing genre, adding to it his own dose of Christian piety as a narrative of bloodless English resistance and merciful release of corsairs.

However, piracy in the Mediterranean was far from a one-sided affair. Western Europeans, including English, Spanish and Venetian raiders, were no less active, often targeting North African and Ottoman vessels. Since the Middle Ages European corsairs had been targeting North African galleys. With raids often drawn along religious lines, these attacks were framed as Christians targeting Muslims and vice versa, creating diplomatic tensions between European and North African states. The first decade of the seventeenth century saw over five and a half thousand Muslim captives from North Africa in Venice and Malta. Meanwhile, such was the extent of English piracy that in the 1620s alone dozens of North African and Turkish captives languished in English jails, many to then be sold into Spanish slavery or executed. By 1624 the ruler of Algiers felt compelled to reach out to James I to initiate a prisoner exchange, writing:

> Your Majesties subjects did take some moores, and Turkes; and now our Captaines did take certaine Englishmen, and sold them; which if your Majestie shalbe pleased to send us the Moores and the Turkes, Wee shall suddainly and out of hand putt the Christians att Liberty.[2]

Things did little to improve through the course of the seventeenth century. During the Restoration the English only furthered their enterprise of targeting North African vessels, capturing ship's crews and selling them into slavery, and undermining peace treaties in doing so. In 1662 one such treaty was signed with Algeria, yet the ruling Algerian dey soon had to insist that the treaty could not hold unless there was a cessation of English corsairs 'carrying Turks or Mussulman slaves'.[3]

The Mediterranean was a thriving space for English piracy, and its proximity to England, combined with the mass of merchant vessels that coursed its waters, made it a tempting target for privateers. But England's pirates were far from tied to a single sea. Just as English traders made their way around the Cape of Good Hope so too did corsairs, keen on profiting from the fabulous riches of Indian Ocean commerce. This began early on, as the aforementioned *Roebuck* illustrates. The targeting of indigenous vessels did little to ingratiate the English with regional rulers whose permission was necessary to trade in their lands. Rampant English piracy on Mughal ships in the Indian Ocean would therefore prove among the greatest challenges for East India Company trade.

Khafi Khan had been advised against accepting the invitation from the English.[4] Trust was at an all-time low: the actions of Captain Henry Every had made for an almost intractable conflict as Mughal authorities and citizens alike demanded justice and accountability. Granted, among those who had discouraged him was the Portuguese captain conveying his merchandise. The century-long Portuguese animosity towards the English was well known, and the captain was far from likely to encourage anyone to meet with his adversaries. But Khan was also on a commission to safely transport goods to the tune of 200,000 rupees from Surat to the town of Rahiri, and protecting his cargo from theft was another concern. His route had taken him down the west coast, eventually passing near the English holding at Bombay.

As it turned out, however, Abd al-Razzaq, the Mughal administrator at Rahiri who had commissioned Khan's cargo, was on friendly terms with an Englishman at Bombay and had written to him requesting he aid the convoy. This had precipitated Khan's invitation, which the latter had – against the advice of his companions – accepted. As he passed through the settlement he noted the English forces lined up in ranks undergoing review. For a moment he admired the 'young men with sprouting beards, handsome and well clothed with fine muskets in their hands'.[5] But now as he sat opposite his host, initial pleasantries veered to the question of the EIC factors recently imprisoned by the Mughals. Khan felt his bile rise as he snapped at the Englishman:

> Although you do not acknowledge that shameful action, worthy of the reprobation of all sensible men, which was perpetrated by your wicked men, this question you have put to me is as if a wise

man should ask where the sun is when all the world is filled with
its rays![6]

'Those who have an ill-feeling against me cast upon me the blame for
the fault of others!' his host rejoined.[7]

This was a difficult argument to sustain when numerous offenders
of the recent infamy were Englishmen bearing the scars of the Mughal
siege of Bombay from just a few years previously. Khan made swift
work of pointing this detail out. The English host did have a point,
however; Every was no man of the EIC, even though his crimes had
plunged the Company into yet another devastating crisis.

Born in Plymouth, the son of a trading captain, Henry Every's
career began as his father's had, in the Royal Navy. Among other
postings, he had served as midshipman aboard the *Rupert* and as mate
aboard the *Albemarle*. He had soon put his experience to profitable
use, participating in privateering expeditions to the West Indies.
Privateering being state-sanctioned piracy meant that the slippage to
piracy proper was tempting and easy, and Every too soon made the
transition. In 1693 he joined an expedition as first mate aboard the
Charles, one of four armed merchant vessels hired by the Spanish
government to protect Spain's South American trade against French
attacks. However, the expedition was delayed at A Coruña for several
months, which, along with Spanish failure to pay the seamen's wages,
led to mutiny. In May 1694, as the captain lay indisposed with fever,
Every along with sixty-five fellow sailors took control of the *Charles*.
A boatload of seamen sent from partner vessel the *James* to save the
situation instead joined with Every, swelling the mutineers' numbers.
The men subsequently abandoned the captain and sixteen of his men
on shore. Having renamed their captured vessel *Fancy* and with Every
at the helm, they then sped off to the Indian Ocean now dedicated to
a life of piracy. Along the way they raided several vessels for good
measure. But their boldest raid was saved for the west coast of India.

English piracy in the Indian Ocean had by this time become a
long-standing thorn in the EIC's side. In the first half of the seventeenth century it was often the act of vessels licensed by the English
monarch, particularly Charles I. Both the actions of the *Roebuck* in
1635 and those of ships dispatched as part of William Courteen's

enterprise in 1638 fell into this category of privateering, much to the grief and harm of the Company in India. However, the latter half of the seventeenth century saw a waning in state sponsorship, giving rise to a new and particularly indiscriminate breed of buccaneers. Often acting autonomously as single ships, they attacked vessels of all nationalities, plundering them while brutalising those on board. Among the most notorious English pirates, one Captain Roberts destroyed a staggering four hundred merchant ships in the space of three years. In the 1680s and 1690s a series of violent English raids on trading and pilgrim vessels brought substantial anguish to regional traders and the authorities, who duly railed against the EIC. In 1684 six men, four English and two Dutch, captured a Persian vessel bound for India in the Persian Gulf, killing the captain, his family and many passengers. A few years later, in 1688, two ships flying under English colours captured trading ships in the Red Sea worth 600,000 rupees. The predations of English piracy extended as far as south-east Asia where in 1697 a ship belonging to the king of Thailand was looted of coin and cloth, an act described as 'a great disgrace' to the English by local authorities.[8]

The region's wealthier merchants found themselves continually targeted as their fleets put out to sea. Among them Abdul al-Ghafur, the most prosperous and influential merchant of Surat, had the misfortune to suffer repeated attacks. In 1691 pirates sailing under English colours captured a vessel belonging to al-Ghafur, making away with no less than 900,000 rupees. In response, the Mughal authorities dispatched officials to the EIC offices at Surat, banning their trade in India. However, when a captured crew member of the offending vessel was revealed to be Danish rather than English, the Indian authorities lifted the embargo on EIC trade. Nonetheless, within a few years al-Ghafur's trade had been struck again, this time when Henry Every attacked one of the merchant's vessels, the *Fatih Muhammadi*.

Soon English pirates previously operating in the Americas also made their way to the Indian Ocean. A growing climate of animosity in the Americas that saw European colonial governors take to targeting pirates propelled a turn to the waters of Asia. Jean-Baptiste du Casse, governor of the French colony of Saint-Domingue (Haiti) and himself an ex-privateer and trader in enslaved people, established a new policy of hanging pirates rather than harbouring them. From 1693 a reduction in North American specie further pushed the region's pirates to seek gold from the richly laden vessels of the Indian Ocean instead. The threat to lives and livelihoods, combined with the allure of merchant vessels in the east bearing treasures of gold, silver, jewels, textiles and spices, made transferring an attractive proposition.

From the popular pirate and slave trader base of Madagascar, the new arrivals joined existing buccaneers in inflicting raids on merchant ships of all stripes and engaging in the regional trade in enslaved people. By 1699 the governor of New York was complaining of how 'the vast riches of the Red Sea and Madagascar are such a lure for Seamen that there's almost no withholding them from that vile practice of Turning pyrates'.[9] With a thriving network of onshore informants and regional officials paid to look away, English and European pirates made swift and profitable business. Of the many acts of piracy that plagued the Indian Ocean, however, one achieved the notorious distinction of being among history's most scandalous raids. And its perpetrator was none other than pirate captain Henry Every.

There was good reason for the *Ganji Saway* (*Exceeding Treasure*) to enjoy such a grandiose title. At 1,600 tonnes, the royal Mughal trading and pilgrim ship owned by the emperor was the largest vessel home-ported at Surat. Each year it transported hundreds of pilgrims and vast cargoes of merchandise to Makkah in Saudi Arabia via the Red Sea port of Jeddah. Along the way it also traded at Mocha in Yemen, another leading mercantile port. By the return journey to Surat the tonnes of silks, woven cottons, indigo, jewels and spices had been converted to countless chests of silver and gold coins, the treasure from which it took its name. In September 1695 the vessel was undertaking its return voyage from the Hajj pilgrimage carrying 800 pilgrims, 400 soldiers armed with muskets and captained by Ibrahim Khan. The riches on board were immense: 5.2 million rupees' worth of silver and gold coins, the profit from the sale of merchandise at Mocha and Jeddah. To protect this, in addition to the musketeers, Khan's ship was amply armed with eighty cannons besides other weaponry. Furthermore, the vessel was head of a fleet of twenty-four merchant ships voyaging in consort to mutually defend themselves against attack.

As the fleet approached the Indian coast it dispersed, each ship headed for its destination. The *Ganji Saway* continued on its lone journey to Surat, steadily tracing the watery path along India's western coastline. It was between Bombay and Daman that a small flotilla of vessels appeared on the horizon, speeding towards the pilgrim ship with every sign of ill-intent. The *Fancy*, manned by Henry Every, had arrived to make prey of the Indian Ocean's richest prize. With it was another pirate vessel along with two smaller boats, all surging towards the Indian ship. Every's audacity is reflected well in the diminutive nature of the *Fancy* before the great vessel it sought to claim. Much smaller in size and armed with just forty-six guns and some hundred and fifty pirates, they should have been no match for the imposing, well-armed and manned *Ganji Saway*. But ample equipment was of little use in the face of an inadequate captain and a chaotic defence.

As the *Fancy* neared, the *Ganji Saway* attempted to fire a cannon in its direction. Luck was not on its side, however; the cannon misfired, the explosion killing several men and setting the surroundings on fire. Emboldened by this, Every's ship sent a counter volley into the pilgrim vessel that shattered its mainmast. Soon the small fleet had surrounded the Mughal ship and armed corsairs stormed aboard from all sides as soldiers and pilgrims scattered. What precipitated was a rapacious bloodbath. On board officers, distracted by the conflagration they had been attempting to put out, offered a feeble defence at best as Ibrahim Khan cowered in the hold. With relative ease Every and his buccaneers took control of the *Ganji Saway*, which they then relentlessly looted of its riches over several days. The material loss was nothing compared to the violence inflicted upon the passengers. Brutalisation and murder reigned, alongside a rapacious orgy levelled at the women. By this the outrage, the crime of robbery became the far greater crime of sacrilegious assault upon pilgrims, many from Mughal noble families and at least one an elderly relative of the emperor himself. As one English agent grimly reported,

It is certain that the Pyrates, which these People affirm were all English, did so very barbarously by the People of the *Gunsway*

(*Ganji Saway*) and Abdul Gofor's ship, to make them confess where their money was, and there happened to be a great Umbraws Wife (as Wee hear) related to the King, returning from her Pilgrimage to Mecca, in her old age. She they abused very much, and forced several other Women, which caused one person of quality, his Wife and Nurse, to kill themselves to prevent the Husbands seeing them (and their being) ravished.[10]

Once the pirates had stripped the *Ganji Saway* of every last coin and jewel they abandoned the vessel, absconding with the booty and leaving the ailing survivors to voyage back to Surat, where they arrived on 12 September 1695. Eventually Every and his men reached Reunion Island, another Indian Ocean refuge of pirates, where the loot was shared, Every himself taking two shares as captain, before the pirates scattered to the seas. The EIC estimated that a staggering £325,000 (£38.9 million today) had been stolen from Alamgir's prized ship.

News of the attack had reached the port even before the *Ganji Saway* had managed to return. A small boat from the vessel had escaped early on, manned by nine crew members who fled to Surat to report the atrocities. Surat governor I'timād Khan had immediately dispatched a flotilla to aid the Mughal ship, yet the vessels had not succeeded in locating it. With the ship now returned, reports of the escaped crew were added to by accounts of the aggrieved survivors, creating a massive uproar that spread like wildfire among Surat's residents. The rapacious assault on pilgrims caused particular outrage, with accountability and punishment demanded of the attackers. Survivors identified the pirates as Englishmen, reporting that they bore the scars of the Bombay siege led by Sidi Yakut Khan. All eyes now turned to the local English: the factors of the East India Company.

Angry crowds soon gathered outside the English factory, chanting for justice. They may well have broken in and lynched the cowering factors had I'timād Khan not dispatched troops led by his lieutenant Ashur Beg to occupy the factory on 14 September 1695. 'We must confess our guard was no more than necessary to defend us from the rabble,' wrote the terrified resident EIC president, Samuel Annesley, 'for the whole mobile was raised against us, demanding satisfaction of us even to our lives . . . and say[ing] that the town is so defiled that no prayer can be offered up acceptable to God till justice is done.'[11] Khan's troops confiscated the factory's weaponry and put the English traders in irons pending orders from the emperor. Meanwhile Annesley sent desperate petitions to everyone from the governor to Alamgir I and English friends in the Mughal encampment, insisting on the Company's innocence. The EIC governor of Bombay, Sir John Gayer, matched this, writing to both Khan and the emperor in protest at the arrest of the Surat factors and insisting 'We are merchants and not pirates.'[12] As one agent fearfully wrote, 'All this will raise a black cloud at [Alamgir's] Court, which we wish may not produce a severe storm.'[13] It was a fanciful aspiration in the face of so ignoble a crime.

By 1695 Alamgir had spent fourteen years warring on the Deccan front. As his generals aged and wearied and embittered officers increasingly squabbled, the emperor only grew more resolute in his desire to claim the plateau in its entirety. He eventually took to personally overseeing many sieges. Bhimsen, an officer in the Mughal encampment, dryly remarked that 'Emperor Alamgir, who is not in want of anything, has been seized with such a longing and passion for taking forts that he personally runs about panting for some heaps of stones.'[14] The emperor, however, had an intractable work ethic that fuelled his campaigns, even as he neared eighty years of age. 'So long as a single breath of this mortal life remains, there is no release from Labour and work,' he wrote to one of his administrators.[15] The conquests of Golconda (1687) and Bijapur (1686) could have heralded an end to campaigns in the region, but Alamgir I stayed on to battle the Marathas with an eye to capturing Jinji and extending into the southern Karnataka and Tamil regions. Continuing to campaign from his sprawling tent cities, he camped first at Galgali by the banks of the Krishna River, then from 1694 transferred to the banks of the Bhima at Machnur. It was at the crimson cloth city of the latter encampment that news of the *Ganji Saway*'s attack reached him.

For Alamgir, claiming the Deccan had become his calling. Disruptions to this project would have been more than a mild irritant. The capture and looting of his largest vessel and violation of the pilgrims that Mughal India's most religiously observant emperor considered his sacred guests – and at least one his own relative – was an altogether different scale of outrage. Alamgir was incandescent; so much so that he exacted retribution not just on the English but on all Europeans trading in his realm. European commerce ground to a halt in the face of a nationwide embargo and European vessels were forbidden from bearing flags. Arms and artillery were confiscated from factories, which were further instructed to break their buildings down to a low height. All Europeans were banned from bearing arms in public and riding palanquins. In addition to Khan's occupation of the English factory at Surat, EIC factors at Bharuch were clapped in irons. Alamgir, with the weight of his unmatched sprawling military force and decades of battling on the Deccan front, prepared to send an army to march upon Fort St George at Madras and dispatched Khan for yet another assault on Bombay. A second assault on the island would surely have reduced the still recovering English settlement to rubble, a devastation Governor Gayer was desperate to prevent. Furthermore, recent shortfalls in revenue meant Bombay had been forced to cut staff substantially while the remaining workforce continued in ill health, making it all the more vulnerable.

Assaulted from all sides, the merchants scrambled to protect their trade. In a sly attempt to turn a catastrophe into an opportunity, the Dutch offered Alamgir I security for all pilgrims in exchange for exclusive trading rights in India, a petition that was turned down by the Mughal much to English relief. The Company in turn offered two ships a year either to convey pilgrims or escort their vessels in exchange for 400,000 rupees. This was the amount the Mughal paid the Siddis for this service which, as the Company pointed out, the Siddis had evidently failed to perform. The suggestion was not necessarily a new one; Annesley had written to Gayer at Bombay only the previous year advising that the Mughal's 'fear of the Pyrates' offers the opportunity for Company vessels to transport Mughal goods to 'advantage and honour . . . and a way opened to procure several grants and Privileges wee want from the Mogul'.[16] The potential for improved trade by offering this conveyance now gave way to the desperate hope of saving the English trade. However, Alamgir was in no mood to bargain, less still to fork out for a company he held personally responsible for the assault on his vessel and people. Instead, he declared that trade embargoes would remain until the elusive

Every was caught and the staggering cost of the *Ganji Saway* compensated, stating that he would far sooner lose revenue from European trade than endanger his pilgrims.

Perhaps the wisest decision the EIC made in this impossible situation was to appoint a Mughal official or *vakil*, Isa Quli, a Christian Armenian, to lobby their cause at the *darbar*. Armed with presents, Quli renewed the EIC offer of conveying pilgrims or ensuring their security for the sum of 400,000 rupees annually. Animosity at court was, however, uncommonly high. The Mughal and his courtiers had not forgotten the EIC's acts of war that had led to the siege of Bombay not too long ago. The capture of the *Ganji Saway* only poured fuel on this existing flame. Nonetheless, Quli somehow managed to prevent the far-reaching military assaults Alamgir had planned. Had these come to pass, it is difficult to see how the EIC could have survived. All other retributive measures remained, however, not least the trade embargo and arrests that threatened financial ruin. The EIC and fellow European competitors battled to secure a reprieve with the English, French and Dutch eventually making common cause to appeal to Khan at Surat. After much effort and duress over several months, an agreement was finally reached on 6 January 1696 when Annesley signed a bond at Surat for the supply of an escort for pilgrims. Administrative delays, however, meant it would not be until 27 June that the English prisoners were finally released.

It took nine months for news of the outrageous attack on the *Ganji Saway* to reach English shores, which it did in July 1696. It could not have come at a worse time: Parliament and the royal court were then determining the future of the EIC charter, a matter they had been deliberating for six years at the instigation of George White, who sought to establish a new rival company. The EIC in London got to work. It petitioned the court for naval support to capture Every and sought a royal proclamation against him. The Privy Council agreed to the proclamation so long as the Company would foot the £500 reward bill, a matter the Company readily agreed to, adding a further 4,000 rupees to the sum. By this proclamation the Company secured the legal participation of Crown officials in capturing Every. Within a matter of weeks sightings of Every and his crew started coming in. Over succeeding months and years crew members began to be captured, several detained across England, from Liverpool to Pembroke. On 19 October 1696 six of Every's crew were put on trial at the Old Bailey and sentenced. Three years later another six were tried at Newgate. In all, fifteen crew members were captured of whom six were executed over a three-year period. Yet, Every himself was never caught.

While the Company ground its teeth, among the English at home the buccaneer's exploits gained legendary status rendering him something of a national hero. His capture of the *Ganji Saway* was woven into glorifying literature even as his government undertook what is possibly the first global manhunt in Every's pursuit and conducted trials of the captured crew. Evading the authorities to the end, Every lived on in the valorised writings of his compatriots who raised the already brazen exploits of the pirate to still more giddy heights. In 1709 *The Life and Adventures of Captain John Avery* appeared, an account purporting to have been written by an escaped fellow pirate. A play by Charles Johnson, *The Successful Pyrate*, inspired by Every, opened at Drury Lane in November 1712 achieving immense popularity. Even Daniel Defoe got in on the legend: *The King of Pirates, being an Account of the Famous Enterprises of Captain Avery* (1724) is attributed to the famed writer.

Meanwhile, if the EIC thought the English Crown's campaign against Every and his crew would see the last of their buccaneer-induced grief, they were sorely mistaken. Despite the efforts of England's authorities to put the piratical world on notice by the very public trials of the *Fancy*'s crew, a new impetus for piracy in the Indian Ocean was seen, propelled by the prospects of such immense booty as the *Ganji Saway* offered. Within a few months of Every's escapade, five pirate ships were known to be active in the Red Sea, two in the Persian Gulf and one around the Malabar Coast, all flying English colours. Additionally, new buccaneering vessels were appearing, many from the Americas, including three fitted at New York arriving to wreak havoc in 1697. Once again Gayer addressed the situation by offering two Company ships to accompany Mughal pilgrim vessels as protection, a commitment which exonerated the EIC from involvement in the piracy of the American vessels and eased their relations with the Mughal authorities.

Meanwhile, Every-style mutinies were on the rise aboard EIC ships. On a voyage from Bombay to China the crew of the *Mocha* mutinied near Aceh, killing the captain and setting afloat some twenty-seven officers. Renaming the vessel the *Defence*, they then turned to piracy, inflicting immense damage in the Indian Ocean over the next three years. The crew of the *Josiah Ketch* from Bombay did likewise, although their subsequent piratical career was shorter-lived. Perhaps the most controversial of the mutineer pirates was Scottish privateer William Kidd. The EIC had petitioned William III to aid them in their campaign against piracy in the Indian Ocean, and the king had contracted Kidd, captain of the *Adventure*, to serve in this effort. Dispatched by his government to rein in Indian Ocean piracy, Kidd instead turned to piracy himself.

On arriving off the coast of Calicut in early 1697, he took to conducting raids while provocatively proclaiming his actions to be legitimate privateering sponsored by the English Crown. Furthermore he drew in the mutinied *Mocha* and *Josiah* to establish a formidable fleet based at Madagascar. One of his most disruptive raids was on 2 February 1698, when he captured the *Queda Merchant*, a 400-tonne vessel carrying cargo to the tune of 400,000 rupees belonging to Mughal nobleman and merchant Mukhlis Khan. Like the piracy of the *Ganji Saway*, this raid was made all the more outrageous by the violence inflicted upon the passengers. In its wake the EIC launched yet another global manhunt until Kidd was finally tracked down to New York, whence he was extradited to London. There he stood trial and was executed, establishing a precedent to which both the Company and the English government could point when faced with difficult questions around piracy in India. Yet, bringing a single pirate to justice was far from sufficient in the face of the many thousands that infested the seas from the American coastline to China. Mere months after Kidd's attack, notorious Dutch pirate Dirk Chivers illustrated this by violently capturing a ship belonging to Surat merchant Hussain Hamdan. This one raid saw Chivers make away with no less than 1.85 million rupees.

The rise in piracy did little to help the Company, which was caught between securing its own trade and the loyalty of its servants at sea and the wrath of the Mughals. As one record grimly relates, 'Such was the extent of this contagion, and so low was the state of the garrison, that even a boat could not be manned at Bombay, for fear the crew might desert.'[17] In the face of repeated predations at sea, the EIC and its European competitors continued to experience Mughal wrath as the emperor demanded the trading companies put a stop to Anglo-European piracy across his seas. It didn't help that Surat was by now under the authority of a new governor, Amanat Khan, who had little sympathy for the English. What made matters worse was the fact that Khan himself had had 200,000 rupees' worth of goods in the *Queda Merchant* that Kidd had captured. Matters finally came to a head on 23 December 1698 when Khan dispatched hundreds of soldiers to surround the English, French and Dutch factories with a devastating ultimatum: deliver a bond to guard the seas against piracy or leave the country within ten days.

It was a terrifying moment for the Company; their hard-fought trade built with immense difficulty over the course of the century dangled at the precipice. All was not lost, however: in April 1699 the EIC along with the Dutch and French companies agreed to collaborate in suppressing Indian Ocean piracy as well as compensate for past Mughal losses. By this agreement the English patrolled the South Indian seas and paid 50,000 rupees in compensation. The emperor thereafter lifted the embargo on trade and the Company was able to breathe freely again – for now.

Henry Every's exploits in the Indian Ocean had created a storm for both the EIC and the English Crown. While both Company and state threw their weight behind finding the outlaw, the pirate was never to be seen again, successfully escaping with the largest quantity of loot ever seized in the Indian Ocean. He became the stuff of legend, each more fanciful than the next. Some claimed he married the Mughal's daughter, rose to be king of Madagascar and lived out his life in great wealth. Others suggest a far less romantic ending; a hunted and haunted man, robbed of his wealth and left to quietly perish in poverty in the port town of Bideford in north Devon. What is certain is that the impact of the buccaneer's exploits was far-reaching – from the factory at Surat and the East India Company's struggle to survive, to the English court and its royal proclamation-led campaign for retribution. Neither has Every's shadow waned; in 2014 metal detectorist Jim Bailey stumbled across a cluster of coins in an orchard in New England. Bearing unmistakable Arabic engravings, they were later identified as dating from the late seventeenth century and having been minted at Yemen. The coins were consistent with the specie carried by Hajj vessels of the day. These innocuous pieces of silver offer a possible sign of where the seventeenth century's most notorious English pirate of the Indian Ocean may have made his final escape.

15

Atonement

IN THE WINTER of 1701/2 Sir William Norris travelled with his retinue about a mile shy of the town of Brahmapuri in India's Maharashtra state.[1] The Englishman preferred to travel in style and this was clear from the small but solemn procession in which he journeyed. At the front were the drawn carts, travelling in a row. Next rolled four field guns, each manned by a pair of armed Englishmen. This was followed by twelve mounted guards bearing kettle drums and trumpets, which led the way for the two stately palanquins. The palanquins bore Norris and his younger brother and secretary, Edward Norris, the two men reclining against rich cushions of brocade and velvet. Bringing up the rear was the remainder of Norris's men, forty in number and armed, marching on foot in ranks. By such regimental form, Norris ostensibly sought to protect the travelling procession and 'be in readynesse if any onset or attempt was made'. But he also enjoyed the spectacle and the attention it drew, proudly noting the 'multitudes of people lookinge on and followinge att some distance'. Not everyone in the audience was there simply to watch, though.

The procession had not progressed far before it found itself suddenly descended upon by a multitude of Mughal troops, both mounted cavalry and infantry. Numbering in their thousands, this armed mass was made all the more daunting by several elephants, carrying senior officers, bearing down on the diminutive English caravan. Finding themselves surrounded, Norris and his retinue ground to a shuddering halt. They soon received word that the road ahead had been blocked by a line of twenty-four large Mughal field guns pointed directly at the English procession. As the surrounding troops closed in, there was little space to manoeuvre. The carts at the head of the procession were seized and the Mughal cavalrymen took to rifling through the contents. The oxen and camels bringing up the rear bearing tents and provisions were similarly halted and searched. Completely surrounded and near overwhelmed, Norris scrambled to arrange his defences, conducting his convoy 'in a square body on foot'. The four English field guns were pointed in four directions while the seventy Englishmen gathered behind ready with arms. It was a terrifying prospect, but Norris was determined his men would stand their ground and defend their caravan as best they could.

As it turned out, they needn't have bothered. The two commanding officers of the army, Hamad Khan and Dalal Khan, both astride towering elephants, sent officers to invite Norris to meet them. At the meeting the officers, with assurances of friendship at considerable odds with the military muscle on display, informed Norris that the local Mughal governor, Ghazi al-Din Firoz Jung, required that the English return to and remain at Burhanpur until the emperor's wishes be known. In the face of the imposing army, there was little for Norris to do but 'make virtue of necessity' and agree. Turning around, the caravan marched back to Burhanpur where they set up the English tents once more to await the Mughal's word. As it turned out, Alamgir's wishes were not known within two to three days as Norris had been assured. Instead, the Englishman and his retinue were detained against their will for fully two months by Firoz Jung until Alamgir finally permitted their release. For Norris, it was a bitter conclusion to a singularly unpleasant stint in India. He furiously denounced his captors as 'the vilest, basest wretches in the whole creation', and keenly looked forward to the day he could get 'away from this detested place' and return to England. Little wonder he felt so; it had been no light matter that had brought him to Mughal shores some two years earlier, and his stay had proven eventful in all the wrong ways.

The last decades of the seventeenth century were a harrowing time for the Company in India, albeit most of the problems were of their own making. Child's War had been a grim and humbling experience. Bombay had been all but flattened and recovery would take years. Time, however, was a luxury the Company were not afforded at a time when the crisis of English piracy in the Indian Ocean was only getting worse, to the heightening disquiet of both Mughal authorities and citizens. Ever more pressure was placed on the still reeling EIC to bring the corsairs under control.

Neither were their troubles isolated to India. Back home in England battle lines were being drawn between London's merchants, with the EIC and its trading monopoly in India at the heart of the conflict. The Company's control of English East Indies trade had long been a cause for dissatisfaction among London's wider merchant community. Eyeing the steady enrichment of EIC merchants and investors, the capital's commercial community increasingly sought a share in the lucrative Indian market. These merchants actively petitioned Parliament to break the EIC monopoly and open the East Indies trade to others. The Anglo-Mughal war became a flashpoint, with the Company's detractors presenting it as a case study of EIC failings. Many traders sought to break the monopoly, travelling to India with the support of London's merchant competitors to trade independently in contravention of the Company's monopoly. These interlopers were particularly active in Bengal. For the Mughals, English traders were one and the same and they cared little about differentiating between Company factors and interlopers, despite the former's desperate petitions and protests.

The Company aggressively sought to protect its monopoly both in India and at home, targeting interlopers at every turn. In November 1681 Josiah Child as EIC governor petitioned James II to issue a royal proclamation against them. In 1683 he took interloper Thomas Sandys to court, securing a ruling in the Company's favour which he then sought to deploy as a precedent to clamp down on others. Meanwhile, against the actions of their rivals in London, the Company counter-petitioned Parliament and the Crown both through formal routes and underhand methods, not least bribery. Outside the halls of power, the conflict gave birth to pamphlet wars where the Company's opponents increasingly prevailed, swaying public opinion. The EIC, still dependent on specie over the export of English commodities for which India had no interest, was accused of impoverishing the nation and harming its manufacturing industries by the mass export of bullion and neglect of trading in English goods. Alongside the perceived siphoning away of capital was the dispatch of countless ships and Englishmen to India, who then could not serve their country in times of need, especially war. By this the EIC was framed as harming the national interest in aid of its own enrichment. In response, the Company published its own pamphlets, extolling the benefits of its trade including the revenue brought to the exchequer through customs contributions. Its efforts were far less successful, and public disquiet against the Company only grew.

The conflict subsequently precipitated one of the greatest threats to the Company's existence in a long century of troubles. The EIC's rivals looked to establish a New Company (NC) to trade in the East Indies. Setting up at Skinners' Hall, Dowgate, the NC merchants petitioned Parliament to grant them a charter. As battle lines were drawn and pamphlets flew, the NC gained increasing popularity among both politicians and the wider public. In October 1691 Parliament affirmed that the joint stock company model with exclusive rights to trade worked best for the East Indies trade. Thereafter the New Company campaigned to have the EIC's charter rescinded and secure the East Indies monopoly for itself. The year 1693 saw the feud take its most bitter turn yet, culminating in a Commons vote to dissolve the EIC and petition the king to deliver on this and 'establish another Company for the better preserving of the trade to this Kingdom'.[2] The EIC's opposition was vociferous and its backdoor dealings accelerated. In October, while Parliament was not sitting, the Company secured for itself a new charter of twenty-one years which confirmed previous charters with a few regulatory amendments. Celebrations were short, however; the NC maintained that the EIC's new charter was void without parliamentary approval, and actively lobbied Parliament against it. In a matter of months, on 19 January 1694, Parliament resolved that trade in the East Indies was temporarily open to all subjects. William III accordingly enlarged the charter he had recently bestowed on the EIC.

It was a situation of immense precariousness for the Company, its unpopularity at home now compounded by the doors having been flung open to interlopers. To make matters worse, Josiah Child's long career in bribery had finally caught up with him. Critics raised the issue of corruption within the EIC, engulfing the Company in scandal. That Josiah Child was additionally responsible for the debacle that was the Anglo-Mughal war and had built up a long list of enemies through his bullish and grasping tenure at the helm of the EIC did not help matters, and he soon became too much of a liability for the Company's interests. Child subsequently stepped down, but the man who replaced him, his brother-in-law Sir Thomas Cooke, was soon arrested and sent to the Tower pending investigations. Parliament appointed a joint committee of both houses to probe the Company's finances. The findings were damning. EIC books revealed huge sums to have been siphoned off in the name of 'special services'. In pursuit of the 1693 charter alone, over £200,000 had been distributed by Child and Cooke to senior public officials, including the speaker of the House of Commons. Other recipients included the dubious figure of Thomas Osborne, Earl of Danby, a man described by one contemporary as 'greedy of wealth and honours, corrupt himself, and a corrupter of others'.[3] The king, too, was found to have received £10,000, which was no surprise given the EIC had been delivering an annual bribe of this amount to the monarch since Charles II. As the scandal threatened to overwhelm them, the Company directors agreed to modifications to their charter rights. But the reputational damage was done.

Since 1688, England had been engaging in the Nine Years' War, a messy conflict with France that had much depleted the nation's purse. As the conflict drew to a close and the Crown counted its pennies, in 1698 the New Company once again applied to Parliament for a charter. Knowing well the NC's desperation, the government announced that it was in need of a loan of £2 million. The NC took the hint and strenuously mobilised its resources to successfully raise the staggering sum, which it offered to the government at a rate of 8 per cent interest. The action paid off: a bill was introduced in the NC's favour in Parliament and voted in by a large majority. A similar majority was then secured in the House of Lords. Finally, on 5 July royal assent was granted. After years of campaigning the New Company was finally incorporated to the delight of its merchants and the utter dismay of the EIC. Although the latter retained the right to trade in India, this was now only until 29 September 1701. On 5 September a royal charter was sealed for the NC as the English Company Trading in the East Indies. Not without reason did an anonymous poet compose verse in its wake:

Fate has prevail'd, and cross'd 'em in their labours,
And *Leaden-Hall* must lose her *Leaden Neighbours.*
Their Gums, their Silks, their Muslins, & their Spices
Cannot revoke what's owing to their Vices:
Nor the rich *Tavistock* with all her lading
Make up their Breaches, or support their Trading,
Which bends its head, and yielding to declension
Defies their *Advocates* sublime invention,
To find out *Ways* to make Grim Death forbear 'em,
Tho skill'd in matters *Legum Romanarum*:
Or from his dusky *Codes* and *Digests*, tell 'em
How to prevent the Mischiefs which befell 'em.[4]

Having spent a century battling European traders, the EIC now faced a new and all the more threatening opponent: competitors from its own country. It would be its most bitter rivalry yet.

As part of its incorporation, the New Company was required to nominate and sponsor an ambassador who would be appointed by the English king to attend the Mughal court on his behalf. The task of the ambassador would be to heal Anglo-Mughal relations in the wake of Child's War and piracy, and to negotiate a trade treaty for the NC. Although sent in the name of William III, the costs of the embassy were the responsibility of the NC. The immense loan by which the NC had secured its charter had weakened its coffers, but this did little to diminish its enthusiasm. The directors planned for the most lavish of embassies to the land of the Great Mughal. In October 1698 they appointed the man deemed best for the ambassadorial role: Sir William Norris.

Politics and diplomacy were not the obvious direction for William Norris. Born in Lancashire the second of seven sons to Thomas and Katherine Norris, he was not destined to inherit so needed to make his own way in the world. Initially William embarked on an academic career at Cambridge, entering Trinity College in 1675. There he took a BA in 1679 and went on to be elected a fellow and secure an MA in 1682. Then in 1690 his fortunes were abruptly changed upon a prosperous marriage. Elizabeth Norris was twice widowed and of substantial means as a result of her two previous marriages. With the wealth acquired through this union, William Norris left Cambridge for London and took up a career in politics. In 1695 he was elected MP for Liverpool, a port city of increasing importance which caused him to develop a keen interest in maritime trade. This served him well when four years later he was named the New Company's ambassador to India. To aid his position, on 3 December 1698 he was granted a baronetcy, and in April the following year he set sail for India, voyaging for several months until he docked at Machilipatnam on the Coromandel Coast on 20 September.

The Norris embassy had been imagined and deployed on a grand scale. It was well stocked with costly presents with which to woo Alamgir I. A staff of around a hundred and thirty English and Indian men joined the retinue in a display of grandeur, all at the NC's expense. Norris's younger brother Edward also joined as the ambassador's secretary and chief adviser. An already grandiose affair was only added to by Norris's tendency towards outright peacockery. In India he preferred to travel by stately procession, borne in a luxurious palanquin accompanied by a large retinue. At Machilipatnam he rented out a palace belonging to the local governor, Faqir Ullah Khan, from which he took pains to make a spectacle of himself. In January 1700 when the newly appointed regional governor, Mehdi Khan, arrived in state at Machilipatnam, Norris was ready. The ambassador took up position at his balcony, the better to be seen, where he pompously reclined 'on a couch with a large carpett spreade before me with my hatt on' and ordered his men to stand to attention around him.[5] At the exact moment the governor passed, mounted upon his elephant, Norris instructed them to fire a 21-gun salute. It certainly worked; gleefully, Norris recorded that the undoubtedly startled governor 'turned his head twice or thrice back on me and seemed well pleased (as he had reason) with the respect that was shewn him'.

Upon his arrival, Norris, knowing well the value of an entrance, was no less flamboyant. Coming to shore borne by a large flotilla decked in royal regalia and NC crests, he had dispatched ahead of him a procession of soldiers and staff carrying flags and marching to the beat of kettle drums and a fanfare of trumpets. Norris solemnly followed behind, his pride exuding in his subsequent account of the crowds drawn to watch: 'all the English of both Old and New Company, all the Dutch, the Governour of the place and vast crowds of people not only of the town but of the country from some miles around'.[6] At a tent erected for the occasion, the local governor welcomed the ambassador with a warm embrace. Nearly a century after the first English embassy of Sir Thomas Roe (and half a century after the abortive efforts of Henry Bard), England's second official state ambassador had arrived. Things looked most promising.

William III had set his ambassador two clear tasks. The first was damage control: to repair relations with the Mughal emperor in the wake of Child's War and the piracy scandals, not least the attack on the *Ganji Saway*. In addition to instructing his ambassador to highlight England's strenuous and successful efforts in bringing the pirate Kidd to justice, William III had added: 'acquaint the Mogul and his Ministers with the great care Wee have taken to suppress the Pyrates in the East Indies having to this End sent a Squadron of our Shipps on purpose to those parts'.[7] Perhaps the most notable expense of the Norris embassy was that it was dispatched with the first English squadron to be sent to the Indian Ocean with the military capacities necessary to deal with piracy. The fleet included four men-of-war provided by the English government. In dispatching a military squadron, the NC sought to distinguish itself and its embassy from that of the EIC, as a company serious about addressing the piracy problem. Upon reaching the Indian Ocean, Norris's squadron patrolled the Malabar Coast for corsairs, chasing several away. One of the vessels sailed to the pirate base of Madagascar where in May 1700 it destroyed the corsairs' fort at St Mary's along with a number of pirate ships. If Norris had hoped to make an impression by this, however, that impression was fleeting. In January 1701 the squadron headed back to England leaving the Indian Ocean once again unprotected and English trade prospects once again vulnerable.

The second task was to inform the emperor of the creation of the New Company to replace the old and negotiate a fresh trading agreement or *farman* for 'Privileges for our Subjects of the said Generall society and Company as may be necessary for their security and protection in the carrying on and management of their Trade'.[8] It was a heavy responsibility, not least in the face of an existing and highly combative EIC still active in India. The Company rightly viewed Norris and the NC as a threat to its very existence. Furthermore, the EIC directors in London had instructed their staff in India to treat the NC as competitors and work 'against all our opposers'.[9] The Company in India therefore expended every effort to undermine the new embassy from the outset. When the ambassador stopped at Madras en route to Machilipatnam, the governor of Fort St George, Thomas Pitt, drew Edward Norris to one side to inform him in no uncertain terms that the embassy was viewed as an enemy come to destroy the Company and that it would be treated as such. Throughout the embassy's stay in India, the EIC continued to work against it by all possible means, from dispensing hefty bribes to prevent Mughal administrators dealing favourably with the embassy to spreading rumours and briefing against Norris to Mughal officials. The NC for its part had forewarned Norris that 'they [the EIC] will stick at nothing that may lessen you, and defeat the designs of this Embassy'.[10] Amid the struggle, Norris looked round for allies and found one later in Surat in the most unlikely of quarters. In the meantime, however, Machilipatnam offered sufficient drama of its own.

From the beginning, travel between England and India meant not only English men and women arriving at India's shores but Indians arriving at English shores. Maryam Khan's marriage brought her to London, but many others arrived as independent merchants or employees of the Company. The lengthy and perilous voyage to India meant lives would be lost en route. The Company would therefore replenish its crew at India, hiring local seamen for the return journey. This contributed to England's increasingly global face, enriching and diversifying the population, particularly in London and at key port cities. A group of twelve such Indian seamen had arrived in England aboard the EIC ship the *Scarborough*. Upon arriving, however, they struggled to find passage back to India. In Norris's account, the men were granted passage on the NC's expedition, with the hope that 'whatever kindnesse was shewn by them to these poore people would be well looked on in India and soe prove an advantage' to the embassy.[11] According to the seamen, however, they had been put to work by the NC over several months and then left unpaid.

In December 1699 the twelve sailors arrived at the ambassador's palatial residence at Machilipatnam demanding payment. Norris dismissed them out of hand, but they continued to show up for several days clamouring for the wages they were due. On the third occasion Norris had the ringleader seized and beaten with a stick before threatening the men never to return or they 'should be worse used'.[12] Unsurprisingly, this only made matters worse, precipitating a conflict that Norris himself admitted 'might have put a stop to all our affaires and perhaps had proved fatall to the transaction I came about', thus ending the embassy before it had even begun.[13] The aggrieved men appealed to the Mughal governor, who referred the matter to the *qazi* (judge) and sent word to the ambassador to send representation to the *qazi* to explain himself. In Alamgir I's India, wrongs were righted by a now codified law. But the ambassador took his position seriously, not least his role as representative of the English king. He therefore took great offence at a demand he saw as demeaning in his position as a royal representative and diplomat, and repeatedly refused to comply. In an echo of Thomas Roe, Norris expected diplomatic immunity from regional Mughal officials who had little interest in offering it.

In the face of intransigence, the governor arrested the ambassador's messenger and assured Norris there would be no release unless and until Norris dispatched a representative to the *qazi* as requested. At this, the peacock was provoked. The ambassador flew into an incandescent rage and undertook an excessive response only he was capable of. He ordered all his men to gather arms and be prepared to march upon the governor's palace at a moment's notice. Such was the frenzy at his residence, with several chests of muskets, blunderbusses and ammunition brought out, that the household's Indian servants were 'frightened out of their witts' and sent word to their families to leave, terrified that the English were preparing to take control of the town. Rumours reached the governor's house and a spy was dispatched. What the official witnessed was enough to send him flying back to report that all the English had taken up arms ready for an attack. It was an extraordinary move by an ambassador with more pride than sense, content that 'from so small a sparke such incendiarys should pursue'.[14] Luckily, the governor thought better than to engage and the following morning returned Norris's messenger and dropped the matter of the *qazi*. The ambassador thereafter determined never to have any dealings with the governor, thus cutting himself off from his main intermediary with the emperor. The governor in turn made no effort to ease the way for the NC factors, delaying the issuing of licences and demanding ever larger gratuities. Norris, already cut off from the governor, also grew unpopular with the New Company at Machilipatnam. The embassy had barely begun yet Norris had clashed with friend and foe alike.

Conflict with the NC at Machilipatnam having been triggered, all that was left was for an already simmering relationship with the EIC to be stoked into a fully-fledged conflagration. This Norris delivered with ease. In January 1700 the ambassador received word that Alamgir had been informed of his arrival and an official Mughal escort would be sent to bring him to the imperial court. It took several months for the escort to finally arrive in May, bearing documentation for a safe passage. The embassy immediately began preparations for overland travel and residence at the imperial tent city, purchasing everything from tents to carts and oxen. By July, however, a combination of administrative hurdles and inclement weather meant there had been no movement from Machilipatnam. A frustrated Norris demanded that the NC instead arrange for a ship for his embassy to be transferred to Surat, where for months the NC factors had been urging him to travel, believing he would serve their purposes better there. The Machilipatnam factors were far from thrilled. Having had to bear the burden of the ambassador's extortionate presence thus far with more hindrance than help to their mercantile cause, they were now expected to foot yet another sizeable bill to transport him to Surat by sea.

Neither were the Mughal officials pleased; upon receiving word of the change of plan, Alamgir's grand vizier Asad Khan advised Norris to take the formally arranged overland route while the local governor too sought to prevent the ambassador from abandoning his Mughal escort. The obstinate Norris, however, ignored them both and set sail aboard the *Sommers* on 23 August. Quite how he thought defying the emperor's own grand vizier and snubbing his escort would aid his embassy is unclear, but Norris certainly felt it incumbent on him to assert his own will as a proxy for that of his king. Added to that, Surat had by then been the trading capital of the EIC for a century and neither the NC nor its sponsored ambassador were in any way welcome there. Nonetheless, on 10 December Norris docked at Surat, there to remain for a tumultuous six weeks.

At Machilipatnam the EIC had been actively undermining both the embassy and the New Company, informing the local governor that Norris was a false ambassador who rather than represent a king, as he claimed, was in fact the representative of a cluster of piratical merchants. This played easily into Mughal anxieties, and the Company now repeated the accusations to the Surat authorities complete with a large bribe. On 15 December the governor Diyanat Khan wrote to Norris demanding he prove himself a royal ambassador. Furthermore, the governor insisted he be paid a generous gratuity to grant reception at which Norris could present the letter he carried from William III as proof of his royal embassy. Soon after arriving at Surat, therefore, the NC had to foot yet another large bill of 41,000 rupees as gratuity. Norris also directed that his ship be stripped of all NC colours and be dressed only in royal insignia to establish himself as a royal ambassador rather than only a representative of merchants, as the EIC alleged. The NC, weighed down by the sponsorship of this burdensome embassy, would have been far from pleased.

On 26 December Norris was finally permitted to disembark. A warm reception by the governor awaited him, at which he presented William III's letter in a box of 'richest brocade brought out of England, on the top of the box the Kings Armes richly embroyderd'.[15] Upon inspecting the seal closely, Diyanat Khan was satisfied, and urged Norris to proceed to Alamgir's court. The ambassador was not satisfied, however. Faced with the accusation of being false, he was intent that not simply the governor but the entire city and especially its English traders recognise him as the official representative of England's king. In a spectacle akin to his balcony performance, on 28 December Norris organised a gathering at which he summoned all the Englishmen then posted at Surat. In a grand room 'spreade over with rich carpets' with walls 'hunge with fine scarlett cloth', Norris once again reclined upon a stately seat surrounded by velvet cushions.[16] By him stood brother Edward, who proceeded to read out the ambassador's commission to the gathered audience. Attendees included members of the NC, Mughal officers and Indian and Turkish merchants. Unsurprisingly, the EIC had opted to give the gathering a miss – apart from one lone figure: Samuel Annesley.

Piracy had proved the undoing of Annesley. For all his faults, there can be no denying the Surat president had done his best in the face of the impossible. Add to that the harsh Mughal recriminations he and his men had endured in the wake of each new piratical outrage, and Annesley felt he had paid his dues. The Company in London, however, took an altogether different view of the matter. Mere months prior to the arrival of Norris, yet another aggression against Indian vessels had sent relations with the Mughal emperor into a deadly spiral. Once again European trade in India was halted and traders imprisoned by an emperor who had simply had enough. Alamgir now presented the Europeans with an ultimatum: sign a contract committing to ensuring security at sea and take responsibility for compensating piratical acts or face expulsion from India. With his back against the wall Annesley signed, as did the Dutch and the French. When news reached London, however, the Company directors were far from pleased. They dismissed the Surat president, replacing him with Stephen Colt, a man who became Norris's nemesis. Fortunately for Norris, however, the now deeply embittered Annesley, with all his knowledge and connections, would prove useful.

At the Surat gathering the absence of the EIC was as noticeable as the presence of one of its dismissed governors. Once Edward Norris had completed his reading, merchants crowded around Annesley seeking his view on the authenticity of Norris's commission. Annesley affirmed it was indeed an authentic royal commission. Armed with William III's seal and now confirmed by Annesley, the embassy had established itself as a genuine mission from the court of the English king to Alamgir. Annesley would continue to be a source of valuable information for Norris as he battled his way through an embassy facing opposition from all sides, not least from its own fellow countrymen at the EIC. For now, however, he had prevailed and the suspicions of the Mughal authorities were stilled. Mistrust was now replaced by immense expectation.

Alamgir I was glad about the arrival of William III's representative. Now there could be proper accountability in regard to the European corsairs that plagued his empire's merchant and pilgrim communities. Abdul al-Ghafur, Mukhlis Khan and others had long petitioned him for justice and better management of maritime safety. As emperor, ensuring the delivery of justice was a pillar of his reign. It was for this reason that he had commissioned a lengthy and thorough process of consolidation of the Mughal judiciary and had publicly subjected himself to it. The matter of piracy was more than a mere nuisance, it spoke directly to how he defined his reign. And, much to his frustration, it was a lingering matter that for years had only got worse while the Europeans in his lands consistently failed in their promises to manage it.

While the Mughals lorded over their lands, they lacked the same strength of authority at sea. The navy was the weakest of their military branches, and the emperor often commissioned experienced commanders, such as Sidi Yakut of Janjira Fort, to serve his maritime interests. To address the European piracy problem, the Mughal sought to make use of the maritime strengths of European traders in his realms in the Indian Ocean. Alamgir was not the first Mughal to play off Europeans to keep them in check. His grandfather Jahangir had also noted the benefit of the EIC's naval presence in keeping Portuguese transgressions under control. Neither were the Mughals the only regional rulers to seek to use European maritime strengths to their advantage, a fact seen in the joint Safavid–English siege of Hormuz. Despite Europeans benefiting from their relative maritime strength in the region, what is notable is that the Mughal emperor was eminently capable of subjecting them to his will regardless. This he did by deploying his overwhelming authority in his lands while knowing full well the European desperation for Indian trade. Furthermore, on the rare occasions Europeans attempted to assert themselves against him by deploying their maritime strength, they had met with disaster. This was starkly revealed not only by Child's War but also by the Portuguese capture of the *Rahimi* at the beginning of the century.

By the reign of Alamgir, European traders were actively contributing to the viability of the trading ports, particularly Surat. However, justice was a far greater concern and the emperor would sooner lose his mercantile presence than see his subjects relentlessly terrorised at sea. Furthermore, the assault and violation of pilgrims was unconscionable for the devoutly religious ruler. Asserting his authority over the Europeans had had some results, but this was far from sufficient. When informed of the arrival of Norris, he now expected to secure justice by engaging more directly with the English monarch. And so he instructed that swift arrangements be made for the embassy to be brought to his encampment. The urgency of the matter was only compounded when yet another piratical assault on Indian ships resulted in Alamgir once again placing the EIC at Surat under house arrest, news of which reached Norris on 6 January 1701. Furthermore, the Surat authorities had Company president John Gayer and his wife arrested and imprisoned, demanding an astonishing 11,100,000 rupees in compensation from the EIC for the latest raids.

It was amid this fresh fallout that Norris finally arrived at the roving court of Alamgir on 10 April 1701. Along the way he had snubbed Asad Khan at Burhanpur over, among other things, the vizier's disapproval of the embassy beating drums wherever it went. At Alamgir's sprawling tent city, the English embassy pitched their tents and Norris settled in, ready to conduct the negotiations for which he had been sent. It was at this very moment that a most unwelcome piece of news arrived from England. While the embassy was under way, debates had continued to rage in London as to the future of the EIC, with the Company and NC both fervently battling to assert themselves in Parliament. In his newly pitched tent at the Mughal's roving court, Norris now received a packet informing him that the EIC would not cease trading in September of that year, as stated in the NC charter, but would continue as a corporation until 1714. Evidence for this was included in the form of the relevant Act of Parliament. Having until then assured the Mughal authorities of the EIC's imminent ceasation of operations, this revelation directly undercut Norris's credibility.

Still, on 28 April Norris was finally granted an initial audience with Alamgir. The procession he oversaw for the occasion was spectacular. Festooned in royal regalia and English flags, his extensive retinue was grandly liveried and marched in ranks. Norris himself rode by richly adorned palanquin, four pages walking beside him. The procession carried with it the many gifts brought for the emperor, including a gold cabinet carrying 201 gold mohurs, 12 brass cannons, sword blades, chests of glassware and mirrors, chests of textiles including brocades and printed fabrics, and luxuriously saddled Arabian horses. Upon arriving at the emperor's *Diwan-i-Khas* (Hall of Private Audience), Norris and a small group of his key officials were permitted to enter Alamgir I's presence. There the emperor invested Norris with a robe of honour, much to the gratification of the ambassador. Thereafter the emperor accepted the numerous gifts offered, taking care to send the gold cabinet to the haram for the amusement of the royal family. When Norris later returned to his tent he felt confident in having made a positive impression and hopeful of subsequent negotiations advancing well.

Norris's task of ameliorating tensions with the Mughal over piracy and the recent war was difficult enough. The most recent attacks, which now had the EIC president along with his wife in irons, made this aspect of the embassy's mission all the more critical and sensitive. As far as Alamgir was concerned, the only solution was to make the English liable for the piracy of their countrymen, including taking responsibility for safety at sea and compensating losses incurred by India's merchants. It was only if the English agreed to this that he was willing to consider Norris's request for a trade treaty. Accordingly, an agreement was drawn up and presented to the ambassador, with the assurance that no trading privileges would be forthcoming unless he commit to English liability for piracy on Indian vessels. Alamgir further remarked that should the ambassador not agree, he may as well return to England. To add to the pressure, news arrived from Surat that both English and Dutch trade had been brought to a standstill by the emperor as a result of the recent piratical raids.

The expectation to compensate alone was enough to make Norris baulk. Piratical raids were frequent, each attack seizing a crippling amount of wealth from the extremely lucrative Indian vessels. Abdul al-Ghafur's freight alone was worth 16 million rupees. These were impossible figures for the English to meet, never mind on a regular basis. In the ambassador's view, to concede 'would forever enslave the English to this unsufferable [Mughal] government'.[17] To make matters worse, on 22 October news arrived that the English Parliament had agreed a merger between the EIC and NC, a fact that Surat governor Diyanat Khan was also aware of. This meant the piracy for which the Mughal held the EIC accountable was now also a problem of the NC, such that Norris himself became vulnerable to arrest. Faced with this fear, on 26 October the ambassador sent word to the Mughal declining to sign the proposed agreement. That same day he made swift preparations to depart for Surat before matters came to a head. Although Mughal minister Yar Ali Beg strongly advised against leaving in such a manner, Norris took flight with his retinue on 5 November, abruptly concluding his embassy without taking leave of the emperor. Alamgir was far from pleased and instructed his governor at Burhanpur, Firoz Jung, to intercept the embassy. When Norris reached Burhanpur on 15 November, Jung accordingly requested that Norris remain there pending word from the Mughal, which the ambassador agreed to for the period of a week. On 22 November, with no communication yet received from Alamgir, once again Norris departed without taking leave.

It was amid this second effort to exit that the ambassador and his entourage found themselves surrounded by thousands of Mughal soldiers, among them Mughal officers astride immense elephants. Subsequently ushered by Firoz Jung's men back to the city, Norris and his retinue were held in veritable imprisonment for two months until finally on 3 February 1702 the emperor's response arrived. Alamgir sent a letter and gifts for William III which were delivered to the disgruntled Norris by Firoz Khan at a stately presentation ceremony. What was conspicuously absent, however, was the desperately sought *farman* for trade. Thereafter the long-wearied English embassy was finally permitted to leave Burhanpur. It was a far from satisfactory conclusion to a most troublesome embassy.

Bearing the royal tokens, Norris and his retinue arrived at Surat on 12 March. There the ambassador received a frosty reception from the New Company factors for a mission they saw as an abject failure, the responsibility for which they placed squarely on Norris's shoulders. Norris had been sent to heal relations and negotiate a trade treaty. He had succeeded in neither and had racked up an extortionate bill to boot by his grandiosity. A staggering £80,000 had been spent, which the fledgling New Company had been forced to foot. It was an enormous expense which near bankrupted them at a time when finances were limited having dispensed £2 million to gain their royal charter in the first place. And to top it all was the sobering fact that all that expenditure had come to nought: Norris had failed and Parliament had determined they were to merge with the EIC anyway.

The Norris embassy to Mughal India had done little to serve the nation. A threatened EIC had campaigned to undermine the embassy at every turn, hindering an already difficult mission. Meanwhile, Norris had often proved more of a hindrance than a help. Interested more in honour than measured diplomacy, he went about his business like a bull in a china shop, fracturing relations both Indian and English while racking up an exorbitant bill. By the time his embassy was concluded, tensions with the Mughal government were at an all-time high with piracy raging and no resolution in sight. On 5 May 1702 the ambassador finally set sail for England. If he felt relief it was undoubtedly tinged with dread, for awaiting him at home was further disquiet at his failure and excesses. However, Norris never faced this reckoning. During the voyage he was struck by a severe bout of dysentery that ultimately claimed his life on 10 October 1702. Like the first EIC representative to the Mughal court, William Hawkins, Norris's representation bore little fruit and ended in tragedy at sea.

When Sir Thomas Roe returned to England following his four-year embassy to Emperor Jahangir, the EIC made much of the matter. The embassy was hailed, its stories spread widely. Extracts from Roe's diary and letters were transcribed as early as 1625. Its legacy continued through the centuries until in modern times it came to form a prominent mural in Westminster's St Stephen's Hall. In the wake of the Norris embassy, however, the NC did everything it could to forget the mission. The ambassador's diaries were left to gather dust in scattered manuscripts, where for centuries they remained. There was little pride to be found in Norris's diplomatic mission in London, and no further embassies were ever sent from England to Mughal India.

In many ways the embassy of William Norris at the close of the seventeenth century illustrates clearly to the formative relationship between England and Mughal India throughout the century. Propelled by an aspiration for trade, as in Norris's delegation England arrived buoyed with hope of commercial enrichment in the abundant lands of the Mughals, with whom they aspired to develop an enduring and lucrative accord. Yet, in the face of an overwhelmingly powerful and prosperous India that saw little need for trade with the clutch of *firingi* islanders from the distant north, the English struggled to carve a place for themselves. Over the decades this saw little change; the English continued to stumble while the Mughals only grew in power and wealth. Like Norris at the conclusion of his embassy, by the close of the century the English had made only limited progress in India. Trading posts came and went with the shifts in the often prickly relations with the Indian authorities, while the handful of permanent factories were burdened by the constant Mughal threat of expulsion in the face of relentless Indian Ocean piracy. Throughout the seventeenth century the English had remained subject to the Indians. For all they knew, the new eighteenth century would be no different.

Afterword: Accidental Empire

THE MUGHALS CONCLUDED the seventeenth century in command of a realm at its territorial peak under Alamgir I. From Kabul in the north to Mysore in the south, Bengal in the east to Baluchistan in the west, the Mughal had stretched his borders to over 4 million square kilometres, near twice the landmass of western Europe. The Indian empire and its reigning emperor appeared indomitable. So legendary was Alamgir I that England's first Poet Laureate, John Dryden, immortalised the Indian monarch in an eponymous play: *Aureng-zebe* (1675). Yet, all reigns must come to an end, even that of Mughal India's longest-serving ruler.

By early 1707 Alamgir I was nearing ninety and ailing. His life had been long and battle-worn. Lying on his deathbed, he found little by way of comfort. A man of devoted faith, his immeasurable worldly gains meant little as he paled at the prospect of judgment before God. In letters to his sons Azam Shah and Kam Baksh, he expressed grief at his spiritual shortcomings, judging himself to have 'chosen isolation from God'.[1] Yet, faith had played a primary role in his life, and he sought to encourage it in his heirs. To his eldest grandson, Bidar Bakht, he advised the shaping of kingship around faith and charity, counselling him to begin the day with prayers and drinking water over which the Qur'an had been recited. He further advised the prince to copiously engage in the weighing ceremony, adopted since the reign of Akbar and in which the monarch weighs himself against gold, silver, copper, grain, oil and other commodities which are then distributed among the poor. Alamgir I recommended Bidar Bakht to undertake the ritual no less than fourteen times a year as 'the practice greatly benefits many needy and poor people'.[2]

Just a few months later, on 3 March, Alamgir I breathed his last, heralding the end of Mughal India's last effective ruler. The passing of the emperor brought about a decline few could have anticipated. Historians differ as to the causes, but one fact seems clear: while Alamgir I ruled with vigour and commitment, he was far less successful in securing the continuity of his hard-won realm through his heirs. As he aged and his health grew frail, he became increasingly conscious of the historic wars of succession triggered by the decline in the health of the emperor. Doubtless he recalled the turbulence of his own accession to the throne, having conducted the longest war of succession himself. Keen to prevent a repeat of history in his lifetime, in early 1707 he dispatched sons Kam Baksh and Azam Shah on fresh provincial assignments while retaining at court key military loyalists. It certainly worked, and any major war of succession was avoided. Whether this was healthy for the empire after his death, however, is a matter of debate.

As news of Alamgir I's passing spread, surviving sons Azam, Kam Baksh and Muazzam, sprang to action, gathering their allies. When the dust settled in the wake of the Battle of Jaju in June 1707, it was Muazzam who emerged the victor, ascending the Peacock Throne as Bahadur Shah I. But the new Mughal emperor was a shadow of his predecessors, not least his father. At the age of sixty-four, he was the oldest monarch to ascend the throne, with the consequence that his heirs viewed him as a stopgap and refused provincial postings away from court in anticipation of the next campaign for succession. In their desperation to maintain an eye on the prize, the princes failed to secure the regional administrative and military experience as well as the support bases their predecessors had gained. Furthermore, they failed to secure the financial benefits that regional appointments and actions afforded. Instead, they remained stagnating at court and became reliant on the emperor for handouts. Princely households shrank dramatically and within a single generation became mere shadows of their former grand selves. Bahadur Shah I's eldest son and eventual heir, Jahandar Shah, retained a household cavalry of just a hundred with no cash to spare, a steep decline from the thousands of horsemen and abundant wealth of princely households past.

Meanwhile, Bahadur Shah I's support within the imperial court had become greatly diminished and he would be forced into crippling political compromises. This would spell his ruin. At court there was a rising star, Zulfiqar Khan, son of Alamgir I's *wazir* (prime minister), Asad Khan. Promoted to paymaster general, he actively consolidated his own authority while undermining that of the emperor. It certainly didn't help Bahadur Shah I that among Zulfiqar Khan's supporters was the powerful Princess Zinat al-Nisa, a favourite daughter of Alamgir I and half-sister to the emperor who had backed her full brother Azam as successor to the throne. The daughter of Dilras Banu Begim, chief consort to Alamgir I, the princess had risen to become a force to be reckoned with, particularly in the final decade of her father's reign. Like other powerful Mughal royal women, she displayed her authority through architectural commissions, including over a dozen caravanserais and mosques, perhaps the most famous of which is the marble domed Zeenat Mosque in Delhi. It was she who was first informed of the death of Alamgir I by a eunuch, at which she immediately dispatched a messenger to Azam summoning him to court to claim the throne. Following the death of Azam at the Battle of Jaju, Zinat al-Nisa had refused to submit to Bahadur Shah I, for which she was confined at the Red Fort in Delhi. This action was more effective in limiting her movements than diminishing her influence, however.

With the backing of influential figures like the princess, Zulfiqar Khan's power grew such that by May 1710 he had achieved the unimaginable: he could block the emperor in the appointment of new Mughal nobles, requiring that Bahadur Shah I's signature be countersigned by the paymaster general's office. In this way the long-standing imperial prerogative to appoint Mughal nobility was effectively subject to Zulfiqar Khan's approval. By the time of Bahadur Shah I's death, in 1712, Zulfiqar Khan was the most powerful figure in the empire, exploiting his authority to engineer the succession of the most pliable of the princely heirs, Jahandar Shah. Thereafter, Mughal emperors would be princes with little to no experience outside the royal household and court, effectively puppets of more powerful figures within the administration. The decline from the political system of the seventeenth century consolidated by Akbar was striking. No longer was ultimate authority vested in the emperor. Neither were the princely heirs, the future monarchs of the empire, sharpened in military and political prowess by years spent in the field. Furthermore, in a break from the previous practice of integrating losing factions into the court, Zulfiqar Khan oversaw the imprisonment and/or execution of Jahandar's opponents. The toxic blend of simmering enmity and ambitious power brokerage that fueled to the manoeuvrings of Zulfiqar became a new precedent for others who similarly sought to engineer their own advance through their preferred princes. By 1719 no less than four Mughal emperors had sat upon the Peacock Throne, once a glistening symbol of imperial might and now a shiny fragment of a once golden age.

The year 1722 brought the potential for revival with the arrival of veteran Mughal noble Nizam al-Mulk, governor of the Deccan, Gujarat and Malwa, who had served under Alamgir I since 1688. Appointed as *wazir*, he immediately got to work to revive the establishment. In 1723 he presented Emperor Muhammad Shah with proposals for sweeping reforms, including the sacking of incompetent nobles and the stamping out of corruption. Fearful for their positions, the emperor's courtiers prevailed and the proposals were abandoned. At this, Nizam al-Mulk appears to have despaired of the Mughal administration ever returning to its former glory. By the end of the year he had returned to the Deccan and in 1724 effectively established the breakaway state of Hyderabad, which covered the mass of the Mughal Deccan. In 1763 the capital was moved from Aurangabad to Hyderabad and thereafter Nizam al-Mulk's descendant rulers would be known as the Nizams of Hyderabad after their founder. Although Nizam al-Mulk continued to serve the Mughals in his lifetime, his actions saw the establishment of the first of the successor states formed from erstwhile Mughal territory.

Bengal soon followed, becoming independent in the 1720s although continuing to send revenue to the imperial coffers at Agra for several more decades. This financial stream was a lifeline for a depleted central treasury that had dropped from 90 million rupees at the time of Alamgir I's death in 1707 to a mere 10 million rupees in 1720. Meanwhile, the Marathas of the Deccan, long embattled and subdued by Alamgir I, regrouped to challenge the borders Nizam al-Mulk claimed. By January 1739 Malwa and the lands between the Narmada and Chambal rivers were swept under Maratha control.

Yet, it was not only internal strife that saw the undoing of the Mughals. In 1739 Nader Shah of Persia invaded northern India with a 150,000-strong cavalry, delivering a decisive defeat on the now much weakened Mughal army at the Battle of Karnal. Having secured Delhi, the Persians then oversaw the comprehensive sacking of the historic Mughal capital. In the ensuing carnage bodies littered the streets while the shah availed himself of the Mughal treasury. Among the riches seized was that once great symbol of Mughal power and wealth, Shah Jahan's Peacock Throne, as well as the Koh-i-Noor diamond. Although the Persians did not ultimately remain in India, they nonetheless made off with some 1.5 million rupees' worth of loot, bearing it back to Persia in triumph in a vast caravan. The material loss was defeat enough, but the symbolic loss of some of Mughal India's most prized imperial possessions was a grim indication of how far the empire had fallen.

The passing of Alamgir I and subsequent Mughal decline laid much of the groundwork for the rise of other powers in India, not least the Nizam and the Maratha dynasties. Eventually, the East India Company and Britain too would emerge as beneficiaries of a Mughal downturn they had had little to do with. As India slowly fragmented, back in England unifying shifts were under way. The last Stuart monarch, Queen Anne, ascended the throne in 1702. During her reign a long-sought national unification was finally achieved. The 1707 Acts of Union passed by the English and Scottish Parliaments created for the first time a united kingdom of both nations, ushering in a new Parliament of Great Britain based in Westminster. It had been a century in the making, the first attempt having been proposed in 1606. Then in 1708 the new and old East India Companies merged, replacing bitter rivalry with joint interest.

Nonetheless it would be decades after the demise of Alamgir I before the EIC conceived any notion of territorial advance. That moment eventually arrived in 1757 at the Battle of Plassey when EIC forces headed by Robert Clive (d. 1774) defeated Siraj al-Daulah, the Nawab of Bengal, leading to EIC annexation of the region. Thus, over a century and half after their arrival in India, Britain claimed its first territory from the ashes of the Mughal realms. The British Empire that subsequently emerged was distinct from that of the

Mughals in many respects, but none more so than its capacity for plunder. While the Mughals arrived and settled in India, going on to enrich and expand the land they called home, the British in India led by a commercial corporation were singularly parasitic and calculatingly so. Over near two centuries they plundered India of its wealth and resources, dispatching it aboard East Indiamen to enrich coffers back in England. With rapine plunder was combined racially charged governance of Indian subjects under an overbearing white English elite. Gone were the days of an administration that reflected the tapestry of the land. An estimated £36 trillion was extracted during the course of British rule, impoverishing what was once one of the world's wealthiest states.[3] Among them are the looted belongings of Indian monarchs overthrown by British forces, such as that of Tipu Sultan, the famed fallen king of Mysore.

When Scottish colonial historian James Mill (d. 1836) set out to write his multi-volume *The History of British India* (1817), the fact that he had never been to India and spoke none of its many languages gave him little pause. Instead, and without a hint of irony, he asserted that the qualifications acquired in Europe for writing a history of India meant he was 'in an almost infinite degree better fitted for the task' than if he had acquired them in India itself. For Mill, India was defined by one overarching feature; it was 'that great scene of British action'.[4] It was a land of British conquest and rule, where Indian impotence gave way to British 'action' and governance. His dismissive descriptor underlines a prominent argument which for centuries justified western European colonial rule: that the lands and peoples of the East are stagnant and uncivilised and require the civilising power of superior Western governance. Intrinsic to this is an underlying presumption of inevitability; that the polities of the West were by virtue of their superior nature destined to rule over the barbaric lands of the East.

Like Mill, colonial administrators and historians did much to justify western European conquest across India and beyond. In part this was by arguing for this inevitability of empire and its civilising mission. Albert Sarraut (d. 1962), governor general of French Indochina in the early twentieth century, expressed this plainly when he set 'white

Europe', in whom he proclaimed 'nature has concentrated . . . the powers of invention, the means of progress and the dynamic of scientific advancement', against the 'backward races' of Asia and Africa. In Sarraut's view, colonisation of these lands became an 'admirable act of law' against lawlessness.[5] In this way violent occupation, rapine and plunder became sanitised as a virtuous mission for law and order. In India it required British forces – Mill's men of 'action' – wresting control of India from the so-called 'backward' Indians and running in their place civilised governance under a sound British order.

Looking back on the seventeenth century, that formative period of the arrival of the English in Mughal India, the scattered and struggling English traders who begged for trade in Mughal courts, squabbled with each other over their own monarchs' charters, fought relentlessly with fellow Europeans and had a tendency towards drunken tomfoolery in India's streets, were hardly the poster children of civilised superiority. Meanwhile, the Mughals, rulers of an advanced, expansive, efficiently administered and fabulously wealthy realm, were no case study of inactive barbarity. The reality of this early history strikingly undercuts colonial discourses. It renders the alleged justification and inevitability of Britain's imperial rise rather absurd. If anything, throughout the seventeenth century a notion of English colonial advancement in Mughal India was unthinkable on any terms.

To sustain historically suspect accounts of Western civility, Eastern barbarism and the inexorable rise of Western colonial authority requires a critical element of revisionism and erasure of history. This Britain's colonial administrators and historians of India delivered with gusto. Mill's history is an illustrative example; against Europe's 'superior knowledge and art' of which England 'had happily obtained its full share' is set the 'feeble and half-civilized people' of India.[6] As for India's rulers whom the early English arrivals struggled to entice, 'the discernment of more enlightened nations, were but little understood at the court of the Mogul'.[7] It wasn't that England was a small player on the Mughal stage with little to offer, but that India was too backward to understand them. Henry Elliot in *The History of India as Told by Its Own Historians* (1867–77) is more explicit still. The Mughals are condemned as 'sunk in sloth and debauchery', a poor substitute for 'the supremacy of the British Government' under whom India's subjects ought to be 'sensible of the immense advantages accruing to them under the mildness and equity of our rule'.[8] In this manner the rule of the Mughals was distorted and dismissed, and that of the British elevated and centred.

The legacy of this revisionism lives on to this day. The early history of England's engagement in India is near forgotten in considerations of Britain's historic relationship with India. Instead, the focus remains on the partial story of Britain's later empire and the dynamic of a powerful British authority over a disempowered Indian subject. Even as renewed critical examinations of Britain's colonial legacy are undertaken, the earliest period of England's interactions with India – that crucial foundational moment to this centuries-long association – remains neglected.

History, however, is long and complex; its ebbs and flows, multiple voices and many nuances are critical to the stories it relates. This book has sought to return the forgotten early history of England and Mughal India to the centre of the conversation. The tangled tale it tells, engaging both Indian and English actors, is an essential piece in the chequered puzzle of Britain and India's long association. Its account disrupts notions of Britain's inexorable ascendancy in the fertile land of the Ganges over which the Mughals ruled. Instead, a striking alternative story emerges: that British rule in India could never have been predicted, not least by the English themselves when those first pilgrims arrived at the princely courts of Babur's heirs. In fact, India had been an afterthought of the EIC, whose first merchants were sent to the *darbar* in search of a *farman* for trade in textiles to serve their primary commerce in Moluccan spices. The English arrival in India had thus been markedly incidental. And over a century and a half of struggling trade later, its eventual rise owed much to the circumstances of Mughal decline over which it had little control. Britain was never destined for empire in India. If anything, it stumbled across it by accident.

Acknowledgements

This book was completed in the shadow of genocide. As a historian of empire and race, to research and write about colonial violence past while witnessing it in the present has been surreal and devastating. The decimation of Gaza by Israeli forces, from the massacred and mutilated civilians to the destruction of heritage, universities and infrastructure, is a harrowing inflection of a seventy-five-year colonial occupation. Its shadow stretches back to Britain. This work is dedicated to Gaza. This book honours the strength of Palestinian faith and spirit. God-willing, your freedom will come soon.

As it takes a village to raise a child, so it takes a community to compose a book. I am grateful to the generous individuals who have offered me their support, time and expertise as I have navigated this deep dive into a most complex and fascinating history.

The exceptional scholarly community at Medieval and Early Modern Orients (MEMOs) have been a treasure trove of knowledge. My appreciation to Shazia Jagot and Peter Good for their input and comments on early chapter drafts. Cecily Jones's meticulous feedback was essential in shaping a difficult chapter on enslavement. Sjoerd Levelt graciously shared essays that proved valuable. Rachel Willie's thoughts on early chapters and encouragement has been an immense and continuing support. My thanks to Guido van Meersbergen for feedback on the Norris embassy, as well as the generosity he and his colleagues showed in giving access to drafts from their forthcoming edition of William Norris's embassy papers. Georgia O'Connor's doctoral thesis on the Norris embassy was an exceptional resource very kindly shared.

Navigating a first book can be a challenge, but I have been privileged in the support of accomplished veterans, not least Shelina

Janmohamed, who has been an elder sister and cheerleader through-out. Helen Carr's advice and feedback on my very first drafts gave me the boost I needed to keep going. Jerry Brotton offered helpful guidance particularly in the early stages. David Veevers' support has been wonderful.

This book came into being in the most curious of manners. The opportunity to publish is a privilege not easily given. This is all the more so for writers of colour who remain deeply underrepresented across publishing. To Joe Zigmond, my editor at John Murray who decided to take a punt on an obscure scholar on the internet, thank you for reaching out and picking me from the crowd. It is my hope that your decision will play a role in easing a new and representative generation of historians to write our shared pasts. To Lauren Howard, my co-editor at John Murray: your guidance and sensitive feedback brought this book into a form of which I could feel proud. It has been a pleasure to work with you both.

Finally and above all, to the beloved men in my life. Shahed, the pillar without whom this could not have been possible. You are proof of God's love and wisdom. And to our boys: this, and everything, is for you. To my soul U, my big boy and best buddy, your excitement for mama's book has been a pride. To my glorious H, your patience and unmatched cuddles have lightened this task. And to my joyous baby Z, who lay, then sat, then bounced on mama's lap as I worked. You grew alongside this book and are its author too.

And my success is only by God, to Whom is all praise.

Picture Credits

Alamy Stock Photo: 1/The Picture Art Collection, 2 below/History and Art Collection, 3 below/Granger Historical Picture Archive, 4 above/Artepics, 4 below left/Impaint, 4 below right/Artgen, 8 below/Tibbut Atchive.

Khalili Collections: 2 above/Port of Surat, from Safi ibn Vali's *Anis al-Hujjaj* ('Pilgrims' Companion') from MS-1025-2b, Persian, *c.*1677–80. Public domain, Creative Commons Attribution-Share Alike 4.0 International licence.

Public domain: 6/copper engraving *c.*1700 artist unknown; 7 above; 7 below/illustration from anonymous sixteenth-century Portuguese codex now stored in the Casanata library, Rome, Creative Common CC0 1.0; 8 above/artist Abdul al-Hamid Lahori, *c.*1635.

Samuel Purchas: 3 above/engraving from *Hakluytus Posthumus, or Purchas his Pilgrimes . . .* (J. MacLehose and Sons, Glasgow, 1625).

Royal Collection Trust/© His Majesty King Charles III, 2014: 5/ Bridgeman Images.

Note on the East India Company Trading Posts Map

The map on pp. xii–xiii offers a selection of East India Company (EIC) trading posts during the seventeenth century. Trading posts varied in their nature. Many took the form of a 'factory': a large English residence that included storerooms for commodities and residential quarters for traders. Others were smaller with just a cluster of traders at a key location. The trading post at Surat is an example of an established factory, whereas Ambon was a smaller and more short-lived venture. Less common in this period were English forts. Madras, was one such fortified settlement that went on to have a long history. A few trading stations in this map were founded by other English trading companies. The trading posts in Ghana, for example, were established first by the Guinea Company and later purchased by the EIC for a limited period. The post at Toliara, Madagascar, was a short-lived settlement venture attempted by the Courteen Association.

Notes

Introduction: Forgotten History

1. Begim, *History of Humayun*, trans. A. Beveridge, p. 94.
2. Foster (ed.), *Letters received by the East India Company*, vol. V, p. 329.

Chapter 1: Good Hope

1. Stow, 'Castle Baynard warde', in Kingsford (ed.), *Survey of London. Reprinted From the Text of 1603*, pp. 11–20.
2. *Fourth Report of the Deputy Keeper of the Public Records*, appendix 2, pp. 265–7.
3. Mandeville, *Book of Marvels and Travels*, p. 76.
4. Ibid., p. 73.
5. John Fletcher, *The Island Princess*, I.iii.29–30, ed. Clare McManus, p. 123.
6. Christopher Marlowe and George Chapman, *Hero and Leander* (London: 1598), 'The Argvment of the Third Sestyad', line 207.
7. Brotton, *This Orient Isle*, p. 6.
8. Ibid., p. 7.
9. 'East Indies: September 1599', in W. Sainsbury (ed.), *Calendar of State Papers Colonial, East Indies, China and Japan, Volume 2, 1513–1616*, pp. 99–102, British History Online.
10. Ibid.
11. Ibid., pp. 105–6.
12. Ibid., pp. 113–18.
13. Babur, *Baburnama*, trans. Thackston, p. 89.
14. Ibid., p. 29.
15. Dughlat, *History of the Moghuls*, trans. Denison Ross, ed. Elias, p. 95.
16. Babur, *Babur-nama*, trans. Thackston, p. 241.

17. Ibid., pp. 326–9.
18. Babur, *Babur-nama*, trans. A. Beveridge, p. 97.
19. Fisher, *Visions of Mughal India*, pp. 28, 45.
20. Ibid., p. 45.
21. Maddison, *World Economy*, vol. I, pp. 261–3.

Chapter 2: As Musk Among Perfumes

1. William of Malmesbury, *Chronicle of the Kings of the England*, p. 118.
2. Saldana, *Christian Purana of Father Stephens*, p. xxx.
3. Ibid., p. xxvii.
4. Ibid., p. xxix.
5. Ibid., pp. xxix–xxx, xxix, xxx and xxxiv.
6. Begim, *History of Humayun*, trans. A. Beveridge, p. 161.
7. Monserrate in Fisher, *Visions of Mughal India*, pp. 40 and 48.
8. Fazl, *Akbarnama*, ed. H. Beveridge, vol. III, p. 368.
9. Monserrate, *Commentary*, trans. Hoyland, ed. Banerjee, p. 205.
10. Saldana, *Christian Purana of Father Stephens*, p. xxxi.
11. J. Harris, *First Firangis*, p. 57.
12. Ibid.
13. Ibid.
14. Saldana, *Christian Purana of Father Stephens*, p. xxxi.
15. Ibid.
16. Ibid.
17. Translated in J. Harris, *First Firangis*, p. 62.
18. Saldana, *Christian Purana of Father Stephens*, p. xxxiv.
19. *Oxford Dictionary of National Biography*, s.v. 'Stephens, Thomas (1549–1619)'.

Chapter 3: The Grand Tour

1. Hakluyt, *Principal Navigations*, p. 245.
2. Ibid., p. 266.
3. Fitch in Foster (ed.), *Early Travels in India, 1583–1619*, p. 15.
4. Ibid.
5. Ibid.
6. Ibid., p. 18.

7. Ibid.
8. Ibid., p. 19.
9. Ibid., pp. 28, 46, 47.
10. Ibid., p. 23.
11. Ibid., p. 13.

Chapter 4: Indias of Spice and Mine

1. Mildenhall in Foster (ed.), *Early Travels in India, 1583–1619*, p. 55.
2. *Oxford Dictionary of National Biography*, s.v. 'Mildenhall [Midnall], John (d. 1614)'; Foster, 'Midnall travels through Persia to India', *England's Quest*, p. 181.
3. Lancaster, *Voyages of Sir James Lancaster*, ed. Markham, p. 57.
4. Argensola, *Conquista de las Islas Malucas*, p. 7.
5. 'East Indies, China and Japan: December 1617', in W. Sainsbury (ed.), *Calendar of State Papers Colonial, East Indies, China and Japan, Volume 3, 1617–1621*, pp. 81–100, British History Online.
6. Saris, *Voyage of Captain John Saris to Japan, 1613*, first voyage, p. 113.
7. Balabanlilar, *Emperor Jahangir*, p. 34.
8. Jahangir, *Jahangirnama*, trans. and ed. Thackston, p. 51 n. 72.
9. Ibid., p. 61.
10. Ibid., p. 292.
11. Foster (ed.), *Early Travels in India, 1583–1619*, p. 148.
12. Foster (ed.), *Letters received by the East India Company*, vol. V, pp. 80, 113.
13. Markham (ed.), *Hawkins Voyages*, p. 399.
14. Schimmel, *Empire of the Great Mughals*, p. 71.
15. Jourdain, *Journal*, p. 162.
16. Ibid., pp. 155–6.

Chapter 5: A Mughal Lady and an English Khan

1. Balabanlilar, *Emperor Jahangir*, p. 53.
2. Khan and Hayy, *Maathir-ul-Umara*, trans. H. Beveridge, ed. Prasad, vol. I, p. 328.
3. William Hawkins in Foster (ed.), *Early Travels in India, 1583–1619*, p. 81.
4. Herbert, *Some Yeares travels*, p. 203.

5. Pietro della Valle quoted in Carmen Nocentelli, 'Teresa Sampsonia Sherley: Amazon, Traveller and Consort', in Andrea and Akhimie (eds), *Travel and Travail*, p. 84.
6. William Hawkins in Foster (ed.), *Early Travels in India, 1583–1619*, p. 85.
7. 'East Indies: February 1614', in W. Sainsbury (ed.), *Calendar of State Papers Colonial, East Indies, China and Japan, Volume 2*, British History Online.
8. Andrea and Akhimie (eds), *Travel and Travail*, p. 52.
9. 'East Indies: February 1614', in W. Sainsbury (ed.), *Calendar of State Papers Colonial, East Indies, China and Japan, Volume 2*, British History Online.
10. Andrea and Akhimie (eds), *Travel and Travail*, p. 52; British Library (BL), London, India Office Records (IOR) B/5, 38–39, FEB 21, 1613/14.
11. Foster (ed.), *Letters received by the East India Company*, vol. VI, pp. 290–1.
12. Roe, *Embassy of Sir Thomas Roe to the Court of the Great Mogul*, ed. Foster, vol, II, p. 447.
13. Ibid., vol. II, p. 455.
14. Ibid., vol. II, p. 463.
15. Ibid., vol. II, p. 448.
16. Foster (ed.), *English Factories in India, 1618–21*, p. 169.
17. Roe, *Embassy of Sir Thomas Roe to the Court of the Great Mogul*, ed. Foster, vol. II, p. 455.

Chapter 6: A Queen's Ransom

1. 'Charles I – Volume 283: February 1635', in Bruce (ed.), *Calendar of State Papers Domestic: Charles I, 1634–1635*, pp. 497–531, British History Online.
2. Findly, *Nur Jahan*, pp. 130, 150.
3. Ibid., p. 151.
4. Foster (ed.), *Early Travels in India, 1583–1619*, p. 203.
5. Foster (ed.), *Letters received by the East India Company*, vol. II, p. 150.
6. Jahangir, *Jahangirnama*, trans. and ed. Thackston, p. 165.
7. Roe, *Embassy of Sir Thomas Roe to the Court of the Great Mogul*, ed. Foster, vol. I, pp. iii–iv.
8. Ibid., vol. I, p. 45.
9. Ibid.
10. Ibid., vol. I, p. 119.

11. Ibid., vol. I, p. 109.

12. Foster (ed.), *Early Travels in India, 1583–1619*, p. 94.

13. Roe, *Embassy of Sir Thomas Roe to the Court of the Great Mogul*, ed. Foster, vol. I, p. 111.

14. Jahangir, *Jahangirnama*, trans. and ed. Thackston, p. 161.

15. Ibid., p. 355.

16. Begley, 'Four Mughal Caravanserais', 170.

17. Mu'tamid Khan, 'Iqbal-Nama-I Jahangiri', in Elliot, *History of India as Told by Its Own Historians,* vol. 6, ed. Dowson, p. 405.

18. Roe, *Embassy of Sir Thomas Roe to the Court of the Great Mogul*, ed. Foster, vol. II, p. 436.

19. Ibid., vol. I, p. 118.

20. Ibid., vol. II, p. 436.

21. Ibid., vol. I, p. 97.

22. Ibid., vol. I, p. 390.

23. Ibid., vol. II, p. 427.

24. Ibid., vol. I, p. 119.

25. Foster (ed.), *Letters received by the East India Company*, vol. IV, p. 13.

26. Ibid., vol. IV, p. 207.

27. Roe, *Embassy of Sir Thomas Roe to the Court of the Great Mogul*, ed. Foster, vol. I, p. 135.

Chapter 7: The Fakir of Odcombe

1. Coryate, *Coryat's Crudities*, n.p.

2. Terry, *Voyage to East-India*, p. 70.

3. Ibid., p. 57.

4. Ibid., pp. 57, 68.

5. Coryate in Foster (ed.), *Early Travels in India, 1583–1619*, p. 247.

6. Ibid., p. 243.

7. Ibid., p. 259.

8. Ibid., p. 253.

9. Ibid., p. 260.

10. Jahangir, *Jahangirnama*, trans. and ed. Thackston, p. 149.

11. Coryate in Foster (ed.) *Early Travels in India, 1583–1619*, p. 252.

12. Terry, *Voyage to East-India*, p. 67.

13. Thomas Roe to Lord Pembroke, 14 February 1616, quoted in Roe, *Embassy of Sir Thomas Roe to the Court of the Great Mogul*, vol. I, p. 103 n. 2.

14. Coryate in Foster (ed.), *Early Travels in India, 1583–1619*, p. 244.
15. Terry, *Voyage to East-India*, p. 253.
16. Ibid.
17. Coryate in Foster (ed.), *Early Travels in India, 1583–1619*, p. 262.
18. Ibid., p. 258.
19. Fryer, *New Account of East India and Persia*, vol. I, p. 253.

Chapter 8: Amboyna

1. Amboyna ballad, English Broadside Ballad Archive, University of California at Santa Barbara, https://ebba.english.ucsb.edu/ballad/20280/xml
2. Roe, *Embassy of Sir Thomas Roe to the Court of the Great Mogul*, vol. II, p. 448.
3. William Foster (ed.), *The Voyages of Sir James Lancaster to Brazil and the East Indies*, pp. xxv.
4. *Merchant of Venice*, I.i.31–4.
5. Games, *Inventing the English Massacre*, p. 10.
6. Towerson to Fursland, 19 September 1622, BL, IOR, Java Records, III, i, fol. 351.
7. Fursland to Towerson, 17 December 1622, BL, IOR, Java Records, III, i, fol. 455.
8. Quoted Wilson, *Profit and Power*, p. 177.
9. Sacha Pfeiffer and Meg Anderson, 'Architect of CIA's Torture Program Says It Went Too Far', NPR, 22 January 2020, https://www.npr.org/2020/01/22/798561799/architect-of-cias-torture-program-says-it-went-too-far
10. Imam Rijali, *Hikayat Tanah Hitu* (*History of Hitu*) (*c.*1650), quoted in Su Fang Ng, 'The "Amboyna Massacre" Through Native Eyes', in Levelt, Raamsdonk and Rose (eds), *Anglo-Dutch Connections*, p. 73.

Chapter 9: Christians and Spices

1. Da Gama, *Journal of the First Voyage*, ed. Ravenstein, p. 55.
2. Ibid., p. 49.
3. Ibid., p. 48.
4. Owen Feltham, *Three Moneths Observations of the Low-Countries*, p. 786.

5. Baffin, *Voyages*, p. xxxix.
6. Monshi, *History of Shah Abbas*, p. 1202.
7. Jahangir, *Jahangirnama*, trans. and ed. Thackston, p. 418.
8. Ibid., appendix by Muhammad Hadi, p. 444.
9. Abdul al-Hamid Lahori, *Padshahnama*, in Elliot, *Shah Jahan*, p. 34.
10. Ibid., p. 35.
11. Ibid., p. 38
12. Translation in Subrahmanyam, *Portuguese Empire in Asia*, p. 175.
13. Ibid.
14. Foster (ed.), *English Factories in India, 1630–1633*, p. 308.

Chapter 10: 'A Loosing Trade'

1. Ross and Ryer (trans.), *Alcoran of Mahomet*, p. A2.
2. *The Famous Tragedie of Charles I* (London: 1649), p. 4; BL, Thomason Collection.
3. Matar, *Islam in Britain*, p. 105.
4. Elliot, *Shah Jahan*, p. 26.
5. Lahori, *Padshahnama*, in ibid., pp. 26–7.
6. *Oxford Dictionary of National Biography*, s.v. 'Courten, Sir William (c. 1568–1636)'.
7. E. Sainsbury (ed.), *Calendar of the Court Minutes of the East India Company, 1635–39*, p. 276.
8. Ibid., p. xxviii.
9. Bidwell and Jansson, *Proceedings in Parliament* (1626), 2.395, quoted in *Oxford Dictionary of National Biography*, s.v. 'Charles I (1600–1649)'.
10. Foster (ed.), *English Factories in India, 1642–1645*, p. 5.
11. Foster (ed.), *English Factories in India, 1646–1650*, p. 21.
12. Foster (ed.), *English Factories in India, 1642–1645*, p. 196.
13. Ibid., p. 197.
14. Ibid., p. xiv.
15. Foster (ed.), *English Factories in India, 1651–1654*, p. 166.
16. Ibid., p. 214.
17. Foster (ed.), *English Factories in India, 1655–1660*, pp. 19–20.
18. Ibid.
19. Foster (ed.), *English Factories in India, 1651–1654*, p. 252.
20. Manucci, *Storia*, trans. Irvine, p. 265.
21. Foster (ed.), *English Factories in India, 1655–1660*, p. 11.

Chapter 11: Restoration

1. Manucci, *Storia*, trans. Irwine, p. 216.
2. Ibid., p. 79.
3. Ibid., p. 75.
4. Ibid., pp. 76, 80 (3 December 1655) and 78.
5. Camden, *The Historie of the Most Renowned and Victorious Princesse Elizabeth*, p. 528.
6. Mun, *Discourse of Trade, from England unto the East-Indies*, p. 26.
7. Makepeace, 'English Traders', 239.
8. Mundy, *Travels*, vol. 3, pt 1, p. 164.
9. Ibid., vol. 3, pt 1, p. 162.
10. Ibid., vol. 3, pt 1, p. 191.
11. Tea served at the Sultaness Coffee House in London was first advertised on 2 September 1658 in the London news pamphlet, *The Gazette*. It was advertised again a fortnight later, on 23 September 1658, in *Mercurius Politicus*.
12. E. Sainsbury (ed.), *Calendar of the Court Minutes of the East India Company, 1655–1659*, p. xxv.
13. E. Sainsbury (ed.), *Calendar of the Court Minutes of the East India Company, 1664–1667*, p. 296.
14. Ibid.
15. Khan, *Anglo Portuguese Negotiations*, p. 462.

Chapter 12: Trade in Souls

1. Charter granted to the Company of Royal Adventurers of England relating to trade in Africa, 1663, The National Archives (TNA), T70/1505.8
2. Pettigrew, *Freedom's Debt*, p. 11.
3. Many historians consider 3 million to be a conservative estimate and the actual figure much higher. Figures based on written records do not necessarily account for the many who died, were killed or committed suicide during capture and transit, for example.
4. Tristan Cork, 'Row Breaks Out as Merchant Venturer Accused of "Sanitising" Edward Colston's Involvement in Slave Trade', *Bristol Post*, 23 August 2018.

5. 'America and West Indies: September 1672', in W. Sainsbury (ed.), *Calendar of State Papers Colonial, America and West Indies: Volume 7, 1669–1674*, pp. 404–17, British History Online.

6. Foster (ed.), *English Factories in India, 1637–1641* (Oxford: Clarendon Press, 1927), pp. 39, 205.

7. Allen, *European Slave Trading in the Indian Ocean*, p. 18.

8. Foster (ed.), *English Factories in India, 1661–1664*, p. 157.

9. Ibid., pp. 276 and 271.

10. *Records of Fort St George: Diary and Consultation Book*, 1688, p. 137.

11. Foster (ed.), *English Factories in India, 1661–1664*, pp. 43 and 276.

12. E. Sainsbury (ed.), *Calendar of the Court Minutes of the East India Company, 1677–1679*, pp. 215, 217, 230 and 236.

13. *Records of Fort St George: Diary and Consultation Book*, 1688, p. 78.

14. Nora McGreevy, 'Who Is the Enslaved Child in This Portrait of Yale University's Namesake?', *Smithsonian Magazine*, 15 October 2021.

15. *American National Biography*, s.v. 'Yale, Elihu (1649–1721), governor of Fort St George (Madras) for the East India Company and benefactor-namesake of Yale College'.

16. Jamiles Lartey, 'Yale University to Drop Name of Slavery Advocate From Calhoun College', *Guardian*, 11 February 2017; John C. Calhoun, Speech in the US Senate, 'The Positive Good of Slavery', 1837.

17. Kevin Dennehy and Susan Gonzalez, 'Yale Publicly Confronts Historical Involvement in Slavery, Yale News, 1 November 2021, https://news.yale.edu/2021/11/01/yale-publicly-confronts-historical-involvement-slavery

18. *American National Biography*, s.v. 'Yale, Elihu (1649–1721), governor of Fort St George (Madras) for the East India Company and benefactor-namesake of Yale College'.

Chapter 13: Child's War

1. Eaton, *India in the Persianate Age*, p. 292.

2. Manucci, *Storia*, trans. Irvine, vol. 1, p. 239.

3. Ibid., vol. 1, p. 229.

4. Quoted in Richards, *Mughal Empire*, p. 168.

5. Manucci, *Storia*, trans. Irvine, vol. 2, p. 120.

6. Browne, *Works*, p. 436.

7. Ibid., pp. 434–6.

8. Richards, *Mughal Empire*, p. 209.

9. Manucci, *Storia*, trans. Irvine, vol. 2, p. 124.

10. Eaton, *India in the Persianate Age*, p. 317.

11. Richards, *Mughal Empire*, p. 211.

12. Ibid.

13. E. Sainsbury (ed.), *Calendar of the Court Minutes of the East India Company, 1668–1670*, pp. 34, 41.

14. Ibid.

15. Ibid., p. 38.

16. E. Sainsbury (ed.), *Calendar of the Court Minutes of the East India Company, 1671–1673*, pp. xii and xxiv.

17. Bernier, *Travels in the Mogul Empire*, p. 357.

18. Ibid., p. 359.

19. Quoted in Dalrymple, *Anarchy*, p. 24; Letwin, *Origins of Scientific Experimentation*, p. 37.

20. *Oxford Dictionary of National Biography*, s.v. 'Child, Sir John, baronet (1637/8–1690)'.

21. Quoted in Wilson, *India Conquered*, p. 39.

22. Manucci, *Storia*, trans. Irvine, vol. 3, pp. 91–2.

23. Sarkar, *Aurangzib*, p. 254.

Chapter 14: Exceeding Treasure

1. Lurting, *Fighting sailor*, p. 46.

2. Quoted in Matar and Vitkus, *Piracy, Slavery and Redemption*, p. 10.

3. Ibid.

4. Khafi Khan, *Muntakhab al-Lubab*, in Elliot, *History of India*, ed. Dowson, vol. 7, pp. 350–5.

5. Ibid., p. 352.

6. Ibid.

7. Ibid.

8. *Records of the relations between Siam and foreign countries in the 17th century*, pp. 138–9.

9. Bellomont to Admiralty, 7 September 1699: TNA Co5/860, fols. 314–15; quoted in Bialuschewski, 'Pirates, Slaves', 408.

10. East India Company, letter from Bombay, 12 October 1695, TNA, PRO Privy Papers, 1/46, quoted in Burgess, 'Piracy in the Public Sphere', 888.

11. Sarkar, *Aurangzib*, p. 281.

12. Ibid.
13. East India Company, letter from Bombay, 12 October 1695, TNA, PRO Privy Papers, 1/46, quoted in Burgess, 'Piracy in the Public Sphere', 888.
14. Quoted in Eaton, *India in the Persianate Age*, p. 323.
15. Quoted in Truschke, *Aurangzeb*, p. 93
16. Samuel Annesley to Bombay, 31 May 1694, BL, IOR, Records of the East India Company, G series, vol. 36/94, fol. 2; Pettigrew, 'Itimad Khan and the Statute to Suppress Piracy', p. 163.
17. Bruce, *Annals*, p. 214.

Chapter 15: Atonement

1. First-hand accounts of and quotes from the Norris Embassy are drawn from transcripts in the forthcoming Meersbergen et al. (eds), *Norris Embassy to Mughal India* – my thanks to the editors for making the transcripts available – and from Georgia O'Connor, '"For Nation, King, and Company": William Norris, Two English East India Companies, and a Forgotten Embassy to Mughal India, 1699–1702', PhD thesis, Monash University, Melbourne, 2021 – with thanks to Dr O'Connor for making her thesis available.
2. Das, *Norris Embassy to Aurangzib*, p. 25.
3. Ibid., p. 27.
4. *An Elegy on the Death of the Old East-India Company who Died of a Wound she Receiv'd from a Patent, Value Two Millions* (1699).
5. Meersbergen et al. (eds), *Norris Embassy to Mughal India*.
6. William Norris, The Norris Diaries, 1699–1702, Volume I: September 1699–April 1700, Bodleian Library, Oxford, Rawlinson Collection, C.912, fol. 14.
7. William III, 'Instructions for our Trusty and well beloved Sr William Norris Bart: whom wee have appointed R. ambassador to the great Mogull & other Princes in India. Given at our Court at Kensington the 31st day of December 1698, in the tenth year of our Raigne', 31 December 1698, BL, MS 31302, fols. 3–4.
8. Ibid.
9. Letter from Old Company directors in London to their agents at Fort St. George, London, 26 August 1698, BL, IOR/E/3/93, fols. 99–100.
10. The New Company, 'Directions & Instructions given by the English Company Trading to the East Indies', 3 January 1699, BL, MS 31302.

11. Meersbergen et al. (eds), *Norris Embassy to Mughal India*, 18 January 1700.
12. Ibid.
13. Ibid.
14. Ibid.
15. Meersbergen et al. (eds), *Norris Embassy to Mughal India*, 26 December 1700.
16. Ibid., 28 December 1700.
17. Quoted in O'Connor, 'For Nation, King, and Company', p. 16.

Afterword: Accidental Empire

1. Truschke, *Aurangzeb*, p. 2.
2. Ibid., p. 98.
3. Chakrabarti and Patnaik (eds), *Agrarian and Other Histories*.
4. Mill and Wilson, *History of British India*, pp. xi and xx.
5. Quoted in Spurr, *Rhetoric of Empire*, p. 29.
6. Mill and Wilson, *History of British India*, pp. 3–4.
7. Ibid., p. 33.
8. Elliot, *History of India*, ed. Dowson, pp. xx–xxiii.

Bibliography

Acharya, Pradipta, 'The Early Expansion of English Trade in Suba Bengal', *IOSR Journal of Humanities and Social Science* 19:7, version VI (July 2014), 30–1

Akbari, Susan Conklin, *Idols in the East: European Representations of Islam and the Orient, 1100–1450* (Ithaca, NY: Cornell University Press, 2009)

Ali, M., 'The Use of Sources in Mughal Historiography', *Journal of the Royal Asiatic Society* 5:3 (1995), 361–73

Alington, Gabriel, *The Hereford Mappa Mundi* (Leominster: Gracewing, 1996)

Allen, Richard B., 'Satisfying the "Want for Labouring People": European Slave Trading in the Indian Ocean, 1500–1850', *Journal of World History* 21:1 (2010), 45–73

——, *European Slave Trading in the Indian Ocean, 1500–1850* (Ohio: Ohio University Press, 2015)

——, 'Exporting the Unfortunate: The European Slave Trade from India, 1500–1800', *Slavery & Abolition* 43:3 (2022), 533–52

Alvi, Sajida Sultana, *Perspectives on Mughal India: Rulers, Historians, 'Ulamā', and Sufis* (Oxford: Oxford University Press, 2012)

Andrea, Bernadette, *Women and Islam in Early Modern English Literature* (Cambridge: Cambridge University Press, 2009)

——, and Patricia Akhimie (eds), *Travel and Travail: Early Modern Women, English Drama, and the Wider World* (Lincoln, NE: University of Nebraska Press, 2019)

Argensola, Bartolemë Leonardo de, *Conquista de las Islas Malucas* (Madrid: 1609)

Asher, Catherine B., and Cynthia Talbot, *India Before Europe* (Cambridge: Cambridge University Press, 2006)

Athar, M. Ali, *Mughal India: Studies in Polity, Ideas, Society and Culture* (New Delhi: Oxford University Press, 2007)

Babur, Zahir al-Din Muhammad (trans. Annette Beveridge), *Babur-nama: Memoirs of Babur* (New Delhi: M. M. Publishers, 1979)

—— (trans. Wheeler M. Thackston), *The Baburnama* (New York: Modern Library, 2002)

Baffin, William (ed. Clements R. Markham), *The Voyages of William Baffin, 1612–1622* (London: Hakluyt Society, 1881)

Balabanlilar, Lisa, 'The Begims of the Mystic Feast: Turco-Mongol Tradition in the Mughal Harem', *Journal of Asian Studies* 69:1 (2010), 123–47

——, *Imperial Identity in the Mughal Empire* (London: Bloomsbury, 2015)

——, *The Emperor Jahangir: Power and Kingship in Mughal India* (London: I. B. Tauris, 2020)

Barbot, John, *A Description of the Coasts of North and South-Guinea*, 6 vols (London: 1732)

Bassett, D. K., 'The "Amboyna Massacre" of 1623', *Journal of Southeast Asian History* 1:2 (1960), 1–19

Begim, Gulbadan Banu (trans. Annette S. Beveridge), *The History of Humayun* (Delhi: LPP, 2011)

Begley, Wayne E., 'Four Mughal Caravanserais Built during the Reigns of Jahāngīr and Shāh Jahān', *Muqarnas* 1 (1983), 167–79

Bernier, François (ed. Archibald Constable), *Travels in the Mogul Empire* (London: Edinburgh University Press, 1891)

Bialuschewski, Arne, 'Pirates, Slaves, and the Indigenous Population in Madagascar, c. 1690–1715', *International Journal of African Historical Studies* 38:3 (2005), 401–25

Biddulph, John, *Pirates of Malabar* (London: 1907)

Bidwell, William B., and Maija Jansson (eds), *Proceedings in Parliament 1626: Volume II: House of Commons* (New Haven: Yale University Press, 1992)

Blow, David, *Shah Abbas: The Ruthless King Who Became an Iranian Legend* (London: I. B. Tauris, 2014)

Bowen, H. V., Margarette Lincoln and Nigel Rigby (eds), *The Worlds of the East India Company* (Rochester, NY: Woodbridge, 2002)

Braddick, Michael J., *State Formation in Early Modern England* (Cambridge: Cambridge University Press, 2009)

Broeck, Adrian van, *The Life and Adventures of Capt. John Avery* (London: 1709)

Brotton, Jerry, *History of the World in Twelve Maps* (London: Penguin, 2013)

——, *This Orient Isle: Elizabethan England and the Islamic World* (London: Penguin, 2017)

Browne, Thomas (ed. Simon Wilkin), *Sir Thomas Browne's Works* (London: William Pickering, 1836)

Bruce, John, *Annals of the East India Company from their Establishment by the Charter of Queen Elizabeth, 1600, to the Union of the London and English East India Company, 1707–8*, 3 vols (London: Black, Parry & Kingsbury, 1810)

—— (ed.), *Calendar of State Papers Domestic: Charles I, 1634–1635* (London: Her Majesty's Stationery Office, 1864)

Bührer, Tanja et al. (eds), *Cooperation and Empire: Local Realities of Global Processes* (New York: Berghahn, 2017)

Burgess, Douglas R., 'Piracy in the Public Sphere: The Henry Every Trials and the Battle for Meaning in Seventeenth-Century Print Culture', *Journal of British Studies* 48:4 (2009), 887–913

Camden, William, *The Historie of the Most Renowned and Victorious Princesse Elizabeth, Late Queen of England* (London: 1635)

Canny, Nicholas (ed.), *The Oxford History of the British Empire*, vol. I, *The Origins of Empire: British Overseas Enterprise to the Close of the Seventeenth Century* (Oxford: Oxford University Press, 1998)

Cartwright, John, *The Preacher's Travels* (London: 1611)

Chakrabarti, Shubhra, and Utsa Patnaik (eds), *Agrarian and Other Histories* (New York: Columbia University Press, 2019)

Chancey, Karen, 'The Amboyna Massacre in English Politics, 1624–1632', *Albion: A Quarterly Journal Concerned with British Studies* 30:4 (1998), 583–98

Chaudhuri, K. N., *The Trading World of Asia and the English East India Company 1660–1760* (Cambridge: Cambridge University Press, 1978)

——, *The English East India Company: A Study of an Early Joint Stock Company 1600–1640* (London: Routledge, 1999)

Clulow, Adam, *Amboina 1623: Fear and Conspiracy on the Edge of Empire* (New York: Columbia University Press, 2019)

Coates, Ben, *The Impact of the English Civil War on the Economy of London, 1642–50* (Farnham: Ashgate, 2004)

'Coins Found in New England Help Solve Mystery of Murderous 1600s Pirate: "One of the Greatest Crimes of the 17th Century"', CBS News, 8 December 2022, https://www.cbsnews.com/news/coins-new-england-help-solve-mystery-of-murderous-1600s-pirate-henry-every

Cork, Tristan, 'Row Breaks Out as Merchant Venturer Accused of "Sanitising" Edward Colston's Involvement in Slave Trade', *Bristol Post*, 23 August 2018, https://www.bristolpost.co.uk/news/bristol-news/row-breaks-out-merchant-venturer-1925896

Correia-Afonso, John, *Jesuit Letters and Indian History, 1542–1773* (Oxford: Oxford University Press, 1969)

Coryate, Thomas, *Coryat's Crudities* (London: 1611)

Curtin, Philip D., *Cross Cultural Trade in World History* (Cambridge: Cambridge University Press, 1984)

Da Gama, Vasco (ed. E. G. Ravenstein), *A Journal of the First Voyage of Vasco da Gama, 1497–1499* (Cambridge: Cambridge University Press, 2010)

Dale, Stephen F., *Indian Merchants and Eurasian Trade, 1600–1750* (Cambridge: Cambridge University Press, 1994)

——, *The Garden of the Eight Paradises: Babur and the Culture of Empire in Central Asia, Afghanistan and India (1483–1530)* (Leiden: Brill, 2004)

——, *Babur: Timurid Prince and Mughal Emperor* (Cambridge: Cambridge University Press, 2018)

Dalrymple, William, *The Anarchy* (London: Bloomsbury, 2019)

Das, Harihar, *The Norris Embassy to Aurangzib, 1699–1702* (Calcutta: R. Chatterjee, 1959)

Das, Nandini, *Courting India* (London: Bloomsbury, 2023)

Defoe, Daniel, *The King of the Pirates, being an Account of the Famous Enterprises of Captain Avery* (London: 1720)

Dennehy, Kevin, and Susan Gonzalez, 'Yale Publicly Confronts Historical Involvement in Slavery', Yale News, 1 November 2021, https://news.yale.edu/2021/11/01/yale-publicly-confronts-historical-involvement-slavery

Donkin, R. A., *Between East and West: The Moluccas and the Traffic in Spices up to the Arrival of Europeans* (Philadelphia: American Philosophical Society, 2003)

Dughlat, Mirza Muhammad Haidar (trans. E. Denison Ross, ed. N. Elias), *A History of the Moghuls of Central Asia Being the Tarikh-i-Rashidi of Mirza Muhammad Haidar Dughlat*, 2nd edn (London: Curzon Press, 1898)

Dunn-Hensley, Susan, *Anne of Denmark and Henrietta Maria: Virgins, Witches, and Catholic Queens* (New York: Palgrave Macmillan, 2017)

Dunthorne, Hugh, *Britain and the Dutch Revolt, 1560–1700* (New York: Cambridge University Press, 2013)

Dutta, Deepashree, 'Portuguese in Bengal: A History Beyond Slave Trade', Sahapedia, 9 August 2019, https://www.sahapedia.org/portuguese-bengal-history-beyond-slave-trade

Eacott, Jonathan, *Selling Empire* (Chapel Hill, NC: University of North Carolina Press, 2016)

East India Company, *A true relation of the unjust, cruell, and barbarous proceedings against the English at Amboyna in the East-Indies by the Netherlandish Gouernour and Councell there* (London: 1624)

Eaton, Richard, *India in the Persianate Age: 1000–1765* (London: Penguin, 2020)

An Elegy on the Death of the Old East-India Company who Died of a Wound she Receiv'd from a Patent, Value Two Millions (London: 1699)

Elliot, H. M., *Shah Jahan* (Lahore: Sh. Mubarak Ali, 1875)

—— (ed. John Dowson), *The History of India as Told by Its Own Historians*, 8 vols (London: Trubner & Co., 1867–77)

Erikson, Amy Louise, *Women and Property in Early Modern England* (London: Routledge, 1993)

Evelyn, John (ed. Austin Dobson), *The Diary of John Evelyn*, 3 vols (London: Macmillan, 1906)

The Famous Tragedie of Charles I (London: 1649)

Faruqui, Munis D., *The Princes of the Mughal Empire* (Cambridge: Cambridge University Press, 2012)

Fazl, Abu'l (ed. Henry Beveridge), *Akbarnama*, 3 vols (Calcutta: Asiatic Society, 1939)

Feltham, Owen, *Three Moneths Observations of the Low-Countries, Especially Holland* (London: 1652)

F. E. P., *Marriages at Fort St. George, Madras* (Exeter: William Pollard, 1907)

Findly, Ellison Banks, 'The Capture of Maryam-Uz-Zamānī's Ship: Mughal Women and European Traders', *Journal of the American Oriental Society* 108:2 (1988), 227–38

——, *Nur Jahan: Empress of Mughal India* (New York: Oxford University Press, 1993)

Fisher, Michael H., *Visions of Mughal India: An Anthology of European Travel Writing* (London: I. B. Tauris, 2007)

Fletcher, John (ed. Clare McManus), *The Island Princess* (London: Arden, 2013)

Foster, William (ed.), *Letters received by the East India Company from its Servants in the East*, 6 vols (London: Sampson Low, Marston & Co., 1896–1902)

——, *Early Travels in India, 1583–1619* (London: Oxford University Press, 1921)

——, *The English Factories in India, 1618–1669*, 13 vols (Oxford: Clarendon Press, 1927)

——, *The English Factories in India, 1670–1684*, 4 vols (Second Series) (Oxford: Clarendon Press, 1927)

——, *England's Quest of Eastern Trade* (London: A & C Black, 1933)

Fourth Report of the Deputy Keeper of the Public Records (London: William Clowes & Sons, 1843)

Fryer, John (ed. William Crooke), *New Account of East India and Persia*, 3 vols (London: 1672; Hakluyt Society, 1915)

Fury, C., 'The First English East India Company Voyage, 1601–1603: The Human Dimension', *International Journal of Maritime History* 24:2 (2012), 69–96

Games, Alison, 'Anglo-Dutch Connections and Overseas Enterprises: A Global Perspective on Lion Gardiner's World', *Early American Studies* 9:2 (2011), 435–61

——, 'Violence on the Fringes: The Virginia (1622) and Amboyna (1623) Massacres', *History* 99:3 (336) (2014), 505–29

——, *Inventing the English Massacre: Amboyna in History and Memory* (Oxford: Oxford University Press, 2020)

Gaughan, Joan Mickelson, *The 'Incumberances': British Women in India, 1615–1856* (Delhi: Oxford University Press, 2013)

George, Annie Rachel, and Arnapurna Rath, '"Musk among Perfumes": Creative Christianity in Thomas Stephens's "Kristapurana"', *Church History and Religious Culture* 96:3 (2016), 304–24

Gokhale, Balkrishna Govind, *Surat in the Seventeenth Century* (Bombay: Popular Prakashan, 1978)

Good, Peter, 'Hormuz and Memory', *Renaissance Studies* (forthcoming 2024)

Grogan, Jane, *The Persian Empire in English Renaissance Writing, 1549–1622* (New York: Palgrave Macmillan, 2014)

Habib, Irfan, and Tapan Raychaudhuri (eds), *The Cambridge Economic History of India*, vol. I, *c.1200–c.1750* (Cambridge: Cambridge University Press, 1982)

Hakluyt, Richard, *The Principal Navigations, Voyages, Traffiques and Discoveries of the English Nation*, 2 vols (London: 1599)

Hambly, Gavin R. (ed.), *Women in the Medieval Islamic World* (New York: St Martin's Press, 1999)

Harris, Carolyn, *Queenship and Revolution in Early Modern Europe: Henrietta Maria and Marie Antoinette* (New York: Palgrave Macmillan, 2017)

Harris, Jonathan Gil, *The First Firangis: Remarkable Stories of Heroes, Healers, Charlatans, Courtesans and Other Foreigners Who Became Indian* (New Delhi: Aleph, 2016)

——, 'Hi Mho Ji Kudd: The Transformation of Thomas Stephens in Goa', in Mary Floyd-Wilson and Garrett A. Sullivan (eds), *Geographies of Embodiment in Early Modern England* (Oxford: Oxford University Press, 2020), ch. 3, 39–59

Hasan, Farhat, 'Conflict and Cooperation in Anglo-Mughal Trade Relations during the Reign of Aurangzeb', *Journal of the Economic and Social History of the Orient* 34:4 (1991), 351–60

Headrick, Daniel R., *Power Over Peoples: Technology, Environments, and Western Imperialism, 1400 to the Present* (Princeton, NJ: Princeton University Press, 2010)

Hedges, William (ed. Henry Yule), *The Diary of William Hedges (1681–1687)*, vol. I (London: Hakluyt Society, 1887)

Herbert, Thomas, *Some Yeares travels into divers parts of Asia and Afrique* (London: 1638)

Hibbard, Caroline, 'Translating Royalty: Henrietta Maria and the Transition from Princess to Queen', *Court Historian* 5:1 (2000), 15–28

Hofmeester, Karin, and Bernd-Stefan Grewe (eds), *Luxury in Global Perspective: Objects and Practices, 1600–2000* (Cambridge: Cambridge University Press, 2016)

Howarth, David, *Adventurers: The Improbable Rise of the East India Company: 1550–1650* (New Haven, CT: Yale University Press, 2023)

Hunt, Margaret R., 'The 1689 Mughal Siege of East India Company Bombay', *History Workshop Journal* 84 (Autumn 2017), 149–69

Ingrams, R. A., 'Rubens and Persia', *Burlington Magazine* 116:853 (April 1974), 190–7

Irvine, William, and Jadunath Sarkar, *Later Mughals*, 2 vols (Calcutta: M. C. Sarkar & Sons, 1922)

Jackson, Nicholas D., *The First British Trade Expedition to China: Captain Weddell and the Courteen Fleet in Asia and Late Ming Canton* (Hong Kong: Hong Kong University Press, 2022)

Jadhav, Kiran Sampatrao, 'Nature of Factionalism in the Adil Shahi Sultanate of Bijapur', *Proceedings of the Indian History Congress* 78 (2017), 333–9

Jahangir, Nur al-Din Muhammad Salim (trans. and ed. Wheeler M. Thackston), *Jahangirnama: Memoirs of Jahangir, Emperor of India*, with appendix by Muhammad Hadi (Oxford: Oxford University Press, 1999)

Jayasuriya, Shihan de Silva, *The Portuguese in the East* (London: I. B. Tauris, 2017)

Jourdain, John, *The Journal of John Jourdain, 1608–1617* (London: Hakluyt Society, 1905)

Juan, Don, *Relaciones de Don Juan de Persia* (Valladolid: Juan de Bostillo, 1604)

Kaicker, Abhishek, *The King and the People: Sovereignty and Popular Politics in Mughal Delhi* (New York: Oxford University Press, 2020)

Khan, Eradut (trans. Jonathan Scott), *A Translation of the Memoirs of Eradut Khan, a Nobleman of Hindostan, containing interesting anecdotes of the Emperor Alumgeer Aurungzebe and of his successors Shaw Aulum and Jehaundar Shaw* (London: John Stockdale, 1786)

Khan, Samsam-ud-Daula Shah Nawaz, and Abdul Hayy (trans. Henry Beveridge, ed. Baini Prasad), *Maathir-ul-Umara*, 2 vols (Patna: Janaki Prakashan, 1952–79)

Khan, Shafaat Ahmad, *Anglo Portuguese Negotiations Relating to Bombay, 1660–1677* (London: Oxford University Press, 1922)

Khan, Sumbul Halim, and Masrat Ahmad Mir, 'Commanding Mandates of Royal Line: A Case Study of Mughal Nishans', *International Journal of Social Science and Economic Research* 5:6 (June 2020), 1578–621

Knights, Mark, 'Corrupt Life? 2: Elihu Yale', Corruption, Now and Then, Warwick Blogs, 11 February 2023, https://blogs.warwick.ac.uk/history-ofcorruption/entry/corrupt_life_2/

Lach, Donald F., *Asia in the Making of Europe*, vol. I, *The Century of Discovery* (Chicago: University of Chicago Press, 2008)

Lal, Ruby, 'Rethinking Mughal India: Challenge of a Princess' Memoir', *Economic and Political Weekly* 38:1 (2003), 53–65

——, *Domesticity and Power in the Early Mughal World* (Cambridge: Cambridge University Press, 2005)

——, *Empress: The Astonishing Reign of Nur Jahan* (New York: W. W. Norton, 2018)

Lancaster, James (ed. Clements R. Markham), *Voyages of Sir James Lancaster to the East Indies* (London: Hakluyt Society, 1877)

Letwin, John, *The Origins of Scientific Experimentation* (London: Methuen, 1963)

Levelt, S., E. van Raamsdonk and M. D. Rose (eds), *Anglo-Dutch Connections in the Early Modern World* (London: Routledge, 2023)

Lim, Walter S. H., and Debra Johanyak (eds), *The English Renaissance, Orientalism, and the Idea of Asia* (New York: Palgrave Macmillan, 2010)

Linschoten, John Huyghen van (ed. Arthur C. Burnell and P. A. Tiele), *The Voyage of John Huyghen van Linschoten to the East Indies*, 2 vols (London: Hakluyt Society, 1885)

Lurting, Thomas, *The fighting sailor turn'd peaceable Christian* (London, 1710)

Luttrell, N., *A Brief Historical Relation of State Affairs*, 6 vols (Oxford: Oxford University Press, 1857)

Maddison, Angus, *The World Economy*, vol. I, *A Millennial Perspective* (Paris: OECD, 2006)

Makepeace, Margaret, 'English Traders on the Guinea Coast, 1657–1668: An Analysis of the East India Company Archive', *History in Africa* 16 (1989), 237–84

Malekandathil, Pius, *Maritime India: Trade, Religion and Polity in the Indian Ocean* (Delhi: Primus, 2014)

Malieckal, Bindu, 'Maryam Khan and the Legacy of Women in Early Modern Literature of India', in Bernadette Andrea and Linda McJannet (eds), *Early Modern England and Islamic Worlds* (New York: Palgrave Macmillan, 2011), pp. 97–121

Mandeville, John (trans. Anthony Bale), *The Book of Marvels and Travels* (Oxford: Oxford University Press, 2012)

Manucci, Niccolao (trans. William Irvine), *Storia do Mogor*, 4 vols (London: John Murray, 1907–8)

Markham, Clements R. (ed.), *The Hawkins Voyages* (London: Hakluyt Society, 1878)

Marlowe, Christopher, and George Chapman, *Hero and Leander* (London: 1598)

Matar, Nabil, *Islam in Britain, 1558–1685* (Cambridge: Cambridge University Press, 1998)

——, 'A Note on Alexander Ross and the English Translation of the Qur'ān', *Journal of Islamic Studies* 23:1 (2012), 76–84

——, and Daniel Vitkus, *Piracy, Slavery and Redemption* (New York: Columbia University Press, 2001)

Mathee, Rudi, *The Politics of Trade in Safavid Iran: Silk for Silver, 1600–1730* (Cambridge: Cambridge University Press, 1999)

——, 'Between Arabs, Turks and Iranians: The Town of Basra, 1600–1700', *Bulletin of the School of Oriental and African Studies* 69:1 (2006), 53–78

—— (ed.), *The Safavid World* (London: Routledge, 2021)

Meersbergen, Guido van et al. (eds), *The Norris Embassy to Mughal India, 1699–1702*, unpublished transcripts (London: Hakluyt Society, forthcoming)

Mehta, Makrand, *Indian Merchants and Entrepreneurs in Historical Perspective* (Delhi: Academic Foundation, 1991)

Melo, João Vicente, 'Thomas Stephens (c. 1549–1619)', in Nandini Das (ed.), *Lives in Transit in Early Modern England: Identity and Belonging* (Amsterdam: Amsterdam University Press, 2022), pp. 122–7

Middleton, Thomas, *Sir Robert Sherley his Entertainment in Cracovia* (London: 1609)

Mill, James, and Horace Wilson, *The History of British India*, vol. I (London: James Madden & Co., 1840)

Monserrate, Antonio (trans. J. S. Hoyland), *The Commentary of Father Monserrate*, ed. S. N. Banerjee (London: Oxford University Press, 1922)

Monshi, Eskandar Beg, *Tarikh-i Alam-ara-yi Abbasi*, 3 vols (Tehran: 1896)

——, (trans. Roger M. Savory), *History of Shah Abbas the Great*, 2 vols (Boulder, CO: Westview Press, 1930)

Morga, Antonio de, *History of the Philippine Islands, From Their Discovery by Magellan in 1521 to the Beginning of the XVII Century; With Descriptions of Japan, China and Adjacent Countries* (Cleveland, OH: Arthur H. Clark, 1907)

Mukherjee, Soma, *Royal Mughal Ladies and their Contributions* (New Delhi: Gyan, 2001)

Mukhia, Harbans, *The Mughals of India* (Oxford: Blackwell, 2004)

Muller, Aislinn, *The Excommunication of Elizabeth I* (Leiden: Brill, 2020)

Mun, Thomas, *A Discourse of Trade, from England unto the East-Indies: Answering to Diverse Obiections Which Are Usually Made against the Same* (London: 1621)

Mundy, Peter (ed. Richard Carnac Temple), *The Travels of Peter Mundy*, 3 vols (London: Hakluyt Society, 1919)

Nocentelli, Carmen, *Empires of Love: Europe, Asia, and the Making of Early Modern Identity* (Philadelphia: University of Pennsylvania Press, 2013)

O'Connor, Georgia, ' "For Nation, King, and Company": William Norris, Two English East India Companies, and a Forgotten Embassy to Mughal India, 1699–1702', PhD thesis, Monash University, Melbourne, 2021

Palsaert, Francisco (trans. W. H. Moreland and P. Geyl), *Jahangir's India: The Remonstratie of Francisco Palsaert* (Cambridge: W. Heffer & Sons, 1925)

Panzani, Gregorio, *The Memoirs of Gregorio Panzani: Giving an account of his agency in England in the years 1634, 1635, 1636* (Birmingham: Swinney & Walker, 1793)

Parliament of England and Wales, *The diurnall occurrences of every day's proceeding in Parliament since the beginning thereof, being Tuesday the twentieth of January, which ended the tenth of March Anno Dom. 1628. With the arguments of the members of the House then assembled* (London: William Cooke, 1641)

Parry, H., *Trade and Dominion: The European Overseas Empires in the Eighteenth Century* (London: Weidenfeld & Nicolson, 1971)

Parthesius, Robert, *Dutch Ships in Tropical Waters: The Development of the Dutch East India Company (VOC) Shipping Network in Asia 1595–1660* (Amsterdam: Amsterdam University Press, 2014)

Peirce, Leslie P., *The Imperial Harem* (Oxford: Oxford University Press, 1993)

Pettigrew, William A., *Freedom's Debt: The Royal African Company and the Politics of the Atlantic Slave Trade, 1672–1752* (Chapel Hill: University of North Carolina Press, 2013)

——, 'Itimad Khan and the Statute to Suppress Piracy, 1694–1700', *Global Trade and the Shaping of English Freedom* (Oxford: Oxford University Press, 2024)

———, and M. Gopalan, *The East India Company, 1600–1857: Essays on Anglo-Indian Connection* (New Delhi: Routledge India, 2017)

Pinkston, Bonnie, 'Documenting the British East India Company and Their Involvement in the East Indian Slave Trade', *SLIS Connecting* 7:1 (2018), article 10, https://doi.org/10.18785/slis.0701.10

Platt, Virginia Bever, 'The East India Company and the Madagascar Slave Trade', *William and Mary Quarterly* 26:4 (October 1969), 548–77

Porter, R., 'The Crispe Family and the African Trade in the Seventeenth Century', *Journal of African History* 9:1 (1968), 57–77

Potter, Lawrence G. (ed.), *The Persian Gulf in History* (New York: Palgrave Macmillan, 2010)

Prasad, Ram Chandra, *Early English Travellers in India* (Delhi: Motilal Banarsidass, 1965)

Puga, Rogério Miguel, *The British Presence in Macau, 1635–1793* (Hong Kong: Hong Kong University Press, 2013)

Purchas, Samuel, *Purchas his Pilgrimes* (London: 1625)

Raman, Shanka 'Imaginary Islands: Staging the East', *Renaissance Drama* 26 (1995), 131–61

Rawat, Sugandha, *The Women of the Mughal Haram* (Chhattisgarh: Evince, 2019)

Raynal, Guillaume-Thomas, *Histoire philosophique et politique des établissemens et du commerce des Européens dans les deux Indes* (Geneva: 1782)

Records of Fort St George: Diary and Consultation Book, Volumes 1–26 (Madras: Printed by the Superintendent, Govt. Press, 1678)

Records of the relations between Siam and foreign countries in the 17th century, 1688–1700, vol. V (Bangkok: Council of the Vajiranana National Library, 1921)

Richards, John F., *The Mughal Empire* (Cambridge: Cambridge University Press, 1993)

Rijali, Imam, *Hikayat Tanah Hitu* (*c.*1650), quoted in Su Fang Ng, 'The "Amboyna Massacre" Through Native Eyes', in Sjoerd Levelt, Esther van Raamsdonk and Michael Rose (eds), *Anglo-Dutch Connections in the Early Modern World* (London: Routledge, 2023), ch. 5

Roe, Thomas (ed. William Foster), *The Embassy of Sir Thomas Roe to the Court of the Great Mogul, 1615–1619*, 2 vols (London: Hakluyt Society, 1899)

Ross, Alexander, and André du Ryer (trans.), *The Alcoran of Mahomet: Translated Out of Arabique into French* (London: 1649)

Roy, Atul Chandra, *A History of Mughal Navy and Naval Warfare* (Calcutta: World Press, 1972)

Said, Edward, *Orientalism* (London: Penguin, 2003)

Sainsbury, Ethel (ed.), *A Calendar of the Court Minutes of the East India Company, 1635–1679*, 11 vols (Oxford: Clarendon Press, 1938)

Sainsbury, W. Noel (ed.), *Calendar of State Papers Colonial, East Indies, China and Japan, Volume 2, 1513–1616* (London: Her Majesty's Stationery Office, 1864)

——, *Calendar of State Papers Colonial, East Indies, China and Japan, Volume 3, 1617–1621* (London: Her Majesty's Stationery Office, 1870)

——, *Calendar of State Papers Colonial, America and West Indies, Volume 7, 1669–1674* (London: Her Majesty's Stationery Office, 1889)

Saldana, Joseph, *The Christian Purana of Father Thomas Stephens of the Society of Jesus* (Mangalore: Simon Alvares, 1907)

Saris, John (ed. Ernest M. Satow), *The Voyage of Captain John Saris to Japan, 1613* (London: Hakluyt Society, 1900)

Sarkar, Jadunath, *Anecdotes of Arangzib* (Calcutta: M. C. Sarkar & Sons, 1917)

——, *History of Aurangzib: Based on Original Sources, Volume 5, The Closing Years 1698–1707* (Calcutta: M. C. Sarkar, 1952)

Schimmel, Annemarie, *The Empire of the Great Mughals: History, Art and Culture* (London: Reaktion, 2004)

Screech, Timon, *The Shogun's Silver Telescope* (Oxford: Oxford University Press, 2020)

Selwood, Jacob, *Diversity and Difference in Early Modern London* (Burlington, VT: Ashgate, 2010)

Seth, Mesrovb Jacob, *Armenians in India from the Earliest Times to the Present Day* (London: Luzac & Co, 1897)

Seth, Vijay, *The Story of Indian Manufacturing: Encounters with the Mughal and British Empires, 1498–1947* (Singapore: Palgrave Macmillan, 2018)

Sherley, Antony, *Sir Antony Sherley his relation of his travels into Persia* (London: 1613)

Singh, Brijraj, 'The First Englishman in India: Thomas Stephens (1547–1619)', *Journal of South Asian Literature*, 30:1/2 (1995), 146–61

Singh, Jyotsna G., 'Boundary Crossings in the Islamic World: Princess Gulbadan as Traveler, Biographer, and Witness to History, 1523–1603', *Early Modern Women* 7 (2012), 231–40

Smith, Edmond, 'The Global Interests of London's Commercial Community, 1599–1625: Investment in the East India Company', *Economic History Review* 71:4 (2018), 1118–46

——, *Merchants: The Community That Shaped England's Trade and Empire, 1550–1650* (New Haven, CT: Yale University Press, 2021)

——, 'The Social Networks of Investment in Early Modern England', *Historical Journal* 64:4 (2021), 912–39

Southwood, James, 'Thomas Stephens, S.J., the First Englishman in India', *Bulletin of the School of Oriental Studies, University of London* 3:2 (1924), 231–40

Spurr, David, *The Rhetoric of Empire* (Durham, NC: Duke University Press, 1993)

Stow, John, 'Castle Baynard warde', in C. L. Kingsford (ed.), *A Survey of London. Reprinted from the Text of 1603* (Oxford: Clarendon Press, 1908), pp. 11–20

Subrahmanyam, Sanjay, *Explorations in Connected History From the Tagus to the Ganges* (Delhi: Oxford University Press, 2005)

——, *Courtly Encounters: Translating Courtliness and Violence in Early Modern Eurasia* (Cambridge, MA: Harvard University Press, 2012)

——, *The Portuguese Empire in Asia 1500–1700: A Political and Economic History*, 2nd edn (New York: Wiley-Blackwell, 2012)

Taagepera, Rein, 'Expansion and Contraction Patterns of Large Polities: Context for Russia', *International Studies Quarterly* 41:3 (September 1997), 475–504

Tavernier, Jean-Baptiste (ed. William Crooke), *Travels in India*, 2 vols (London: Oxford University Press, 1925)

Teltscher, Kate, *India Inscribed: European and British Writing on India, 1600–1800* (Oxford: Oxford University Press, 1995)

Terry, Edward, *A Voyage to East-India* (London, 1655)

Thackston, Wheeler M. (trans.), *Three Memoirs of Homayun* (Costa Mesa, CA: Mazda Publishers, 2009)

Thomas, James H., 'Merchants and Maritime Marauders: The East India Company and the Problem of Piracy in the Eighteenth Century', *Great Circle* 36:1 (2014), 83–107

Thornton, John, *Africa and Africans in the Making of the Atlantic World* (Cambridge: Cambridge University Press, 1998)

Truschke, Audrey, *Aurangzeb: The Life and Legacy of India's Most Controversial King* (Stanford: Stanford University Press, 2017)

Veevers, David, *The Great Defiance* (London: Ebury, 2023)

Vink, Markus, ' "The World's Oldest Trade": Dutch Slavery and Slave Trade in the Indian Ocean in the Seventeenth Century', *Journal of World History* 14:2 (2003), 131–77

White, Michelle, *Henrietta Maria and the English Civil Wars* (Farnham: Ashgate, 2006)

Wilkinson, William, *Systema Africanum: Or, A treatise, discovering the intrigues and arbitrary proceedings of the Guiney Company* (London: 1690)

William of Malmesbury (ed. J. A. Giles), *Chronicle of the Kings of England* (London: Bell & Daldy, 1866)

Wilson, Charles Henry, *Profit and Power: A Study of England and the Dutch Wars* (London: Longmans Green & Co., 1957)

Wilson, Jon, *India Conquered* (London: Simon & Schuster, 2016)

Manuscript and Archival Sources

Bellomont to Admiralty, 7 September 1699, The National Archives (TNA) Co5/860, fols. 314–15

[Court of Committees to] St Helena, 6 November 1684, British Library, London, India Office Records (IOR) E/3/90, fo. 416

Fursland to Towerson, 17 December 1622, British Library, London, India Office Records (IOR), Java Records, III, i, fol. 455

'Letter from Old Company directors in London to their agents at Fort St. George, London, 26 August 1698', British Library, London, India Office Records (IOR) E/3/93, fols. 99–100

New Company, 'Directions & Instructions given by the English Company Trading to the East Indies', 3 January 1699, British Library, London, MS 31302

Pope Pius V, *Regnans in Excelsis*, 1570, papal bull excommunicating Elizabeth I of England, British Library, London, 18.e.2.(114★)

Samuel Annesley to Bombay, 31 May 1694, British Library, London, India Office Records (IOR), Records of the East India Company, G series, vol. 36/94, fol. 2

Towerson to Fursland, 19 September 1622, India Office Records (IOR), Java Records, III, i, fol. 351.

William III, 'Instructions for our Trusty and well beloved Sr William Norris Bart: whom wee have appointed R. ambassador to the great Mogull & other Princes in India. Given at our Court at Kensington the 31st day of December 1698, in the tenth year of our Raigne', 31 December 1698, British Library, London, MS 31302, fols. 3–4

William Norris, The Norris Diaries, 1699–1702, vol. I, September 1699–April 1700, Bodleian Library, Oxford, Rawlinson Collection, C.912, fol. 14

William Norris, The Norris Diaries, 1699–1702, vol. II, December 1700–April 1701, Bodleian Library, Oxford, Rawlinson Collection, C.913, fol. 30

Reference Works

American National Biography, ed. John A. Garraty and Mark C. Carnes (New York: Oxford University Press, 1999)

Encyclopedia of Africa, ed. H. L. Gates and K. A. Appiah (Oxford: Oxford University Press, 2010)

The Grove Encyclopedia of Islamic Art and Architecture, ed. J. Bloom and S. Blair (Oxford: Oxford University Press, 2009)

The Oxford Companion to Black British History, ed. C. Jones et al. (Oxford: Oxford University Press, 2007)

The Oxford Companion to British History, ed. R. Crowcroft and J. Cannon (Oxford: Oxford University Press, 2015)

An Oxford Companion to the Romantic Age, ed. I. McCalman et al. (Oxford: Oxford University Press, 2009)

The Oxford Companion to Ships and the Sea, ed. I. C. B. Dear and P. Kemp (Oxford: Oxford University Press, 2006)

The Oxford Companion to World Exploration, ed. D. Buisseret (Oxford: Oxford University Press, 2007)

The Oxford Encyclopedia of American Political and Legal History, ed. Donald T. Critchlow and Philip R. VanderMeer (Oxford: Oxford University Press, 2013)

The Oxford Encyclopedia of Economic History, ed. J. Mokyr (Oxford: Oxford University Press, 2003; online edn 2005)

The Oxford Encyclopedia of Islam and Politics, ed. Emad El-Din Shahin (Oxford: Oxford University Press, 2014)

The Oxford Encyclopedia of Maritime History, ed. J. Hattendorf (Oxford: Oxford University Press, 2007)

The Oxford Encyclopedia of the Modern World, ed. P. Stearns (Oxford: Oxford University Press, 2008)

Trade, Travel, and Exploration in the Middle Ages: An Encyclopedia, ed. J. B. Friedman and K. Mossler (New York: Routledge, 2000)

Websites

African Studies Centre, Leiden University, 'Indian Ocean Slave Trade', https://www.ascleiden.nl/content/webdossiers/indian-ocean-slave-trade

American National Biography, www.anb.org

Atlas of Mutual Heritage, www.atlasofmutualheritage.nl

British History Online, www.british-history.ac.uk

British Library, www.bl.uk

English Broadside Ballad Archive, www.ebba.english.ucsb.edu

Gale Primary Sources, State Papers Online www.gale.com/intl/primary-sources/state-papers-online

History of Parliament, www.historyofparliamentonline.org

Map of Early Modern London, www.mapoflondon.uvic.ca

Medieval and Early Modern Orients, www.memorients.com

The National Archives, www.nationalarchives.gov.uk

Norris Embassy to Mughal India, www.norrisembassy.com

Oxford Dictionary of National Biography, www.oxforddnb.com

Princeton University Library, 'Strait Through: Magellan to Cook and the Pacific', library.princeton.edu/visual_materials/maps/websites/pacific/contents.html

Slave Voyages, Trans-Atlantic Slave Trade Database, www.slavevoyages.org

Index

Note that non-European personal names are listed in their uninverted form.